TRANSITIONS
in
LEADERSHIP

The Story of the MBV
A Unique Program for
Transitioning Veterans

ROBERT B. TURRILL, Ph.D.

pine peak press

www.pinepeakpress.com

Published in the United States by Robert B. Turrill

Copyright © 2020 by Robert B. Turrill
First Edition — 2020

ISBN
978-0-578-74449-0 (Hardcover)
978-0-578-74450-6 (Paperback)
978-0-578-74451-3 (eBook)

1. Business & Economics, Leadership
2. Biography & Autobiography, Military
3. Biography & Autobiography, Educators

Produced through FriesenPress

◆ FriesenPress

Suite 300 - 990 Fort St
Victoria, BC, V8V 3K2
Canada

www.friesenpress.com

Distributed to the trade by The Ingram Book Company

Dedicated to the men and women of
the armed forces of the United States

TABLE OF CONTENTS

PREFACE

There are many books about military units—in combat (e.g., *We Were Soldiers Once*), as identifiable units (e.g., *82nd Airborne, Delta Force*), and even about specific events (e.g., *Black Hawk Down*). These books typically focus on combat, the individuals involved, or the consequences of the combat. In almost all, the commonality is the military unit on which the story focuses and the group dynamics that bring them together and turn them into a solid unit of membership with a shared experience and shared history. One of the most common titles of such a unit is *Band of Brothers*, both a book (Stephen Ambrose, 1992) and a miniseries about a special unit of individuals identified through their special dynamics, special battles in WWII, and close interpersonal ties with each other.

Transitions in Leadership is also about a unit of people—not a military unit, but one whose members all have a military background. The common background factor for membership in this unit is that all its members have been in the military or still are—active duty, active reserve, or national guard. Membership is earned through both a common characteristic of their personal history and their common aspirations to be effective contributors to their communities and careers as they transition from military life and orientation to civilian life. The unit includes members of all five branches of the military. It is a unique unit of men and women who have a strong background in leadership within the military or elsewhere. It is the MBV, or master of business for veterans program. It is not easy to earn a spot in this unit, nor is it easy to be a successful member of this community. As such, members in this unit could be considered elite, earning the respect of other veterans for their leadership, academic background, drive, and performance in a challenging academic environment.

Currently, there are almost 400 MBV alums and 92 members in Cohort VII in this unique educational program at the Marshall School of Business at the University of Southern California. In existence since 2013, the program was developed to facilitate the transition from a military to a civilian career. Its story is one of personal change and growth; in many cases, it's a story about transformational change and new possibilities.

It is a unit in that it has all the strong social dynamics of shared membership in a common experience, based on a common background of service in an all-volunteer military. This sense of membership as a unit with dynamics experienced on active duty is one of the program's strongest attractions to recruits. I'm adding three statements from students from the most recent cohort, VI, to support this assertion about an MBV actually substituting, in many cases, for what veterans left behind as they separated from active duty. Their voices represent the majority of the MBV program members who have a sense of closeness and commitment to one another.

> "Being an MBVer has reminded me how much I've missed this type of veteran connection since separating from the military." (Corey Polopek, Cohort VI)

> "This to me is what made this cohort so special. It's been so long since I left the military that I was starting to think all the support and camaraderie I had in the military was just a figment of my imagination." (Carlos Amador, Cohort VI)

> "I feel that our cohort has really adopted the 'no man left behind' attitude and everyone is super willing to talk to each other, teach, or help in any way that they can." (Rey Clanor, Cohort VI)

In this common context of a live classroom environment, the opportunities, challenges, excitement, moments of progress, and enjoyment are often either overlooked or taken for granted on the one hand, or criticized for not doing enough on the other. The physical classroom, where they spend so much time, can even become a crucible of intense struggle and profound transformation for the students—and in a world of mutual influence, potentially the teaching faculty as well. While many students see the classroom as a holding place for getting ready for the real world, the classroom becomes their *actual* world for a fairly significant period, personal investment, and personal impact.

While my role was academic and faculty director and leadership instructor, I became a member of this unique unit as well, by virtue of being an army veteran (in the last century), but more because my students accepted me as part of a unit with specific roles to play. I think they also appreciated my willingness to fully engage with the life, challenges, and celebrations of a unit whose members were men and women aged twenty-five to sixty-one from all five branches of the military. I describe my participation and membership as embedded engagement—embedded because I felt that I had become one of the members, and engagement because of the congruence I experienced working one-on-one and with the entire group, the sense of being fully involved, and the personal meaning I took from what I was doing and what we were trying to achieve.

I will share with you my personal and professional experience over these six years as well as that of the students. The MBV program grants a unique degree. The MBV degree is designed as an executive program for military veterans with significant leadership experience to assist their transition into different careers and levels of responsibility and achievement. As Marshall has itself, the MBV has a distinctive entrepreneurial focus in addition to a general business and management focus.

The purpose of capturing and documenting this experience with an all-veteran professional program was to move away from the typical portrayal of military veterans as either heroes or broken people needing help and healing. There is a third stereotype that characterizes anyone attached to the military as an agent of the military-industrial complex that starts and engages in wars for economic profit. Probably the best example of this negative stereotyping could be seen in how returning veterans from the Vietnam war were treated as they disembarked at their separation centers. I have been told by returning veterans that they were spit upon or stoned as they left the ships return-ing them to their home base, as if somehow they were the reason we were engulfed in the Vietnam conflict. There seemed to be little knowledge of and understanding that the policy decisions and other involvement actions came from civilian leadership, several presidents and secretaries of defense, and the Congress of the United States.

During my time with the veterans, none of these three stereotypes was apparent in our classroom, discussions, or behavior. We learned of veterans suffering from PTSD (post-traumatic stress disorder), TBI (traumatic brain injury), and MST (military sexual trauma), along with other injuries. But we neither inquired into nor pursued these issues and stories; we simply supported the person.

We used a concept our program director James Bogle suggested of referring to the veterans as civic assets, with the intent of developing them further and assisting in their being deployed effectively in service of positive leadership within the civilian segment of our society and economy. It is a story of courage, service, humility, focus, and perseverance. It is also a story of family, community, a quest for personal growth, and civic contribution. In short, it is a story of positive citizenship.

All 392 of the students/alums came to us with undergraduate degrees and many with graduate degrees. Most are married and have families, and most are employed. Some may have recently separated from active duty, and as a result, may have been unemployed during the program. But we mostly have students with jobs and relatively stable home lives. Are they without troubles and problems? No. Quite a few are divorced and in second marriages. Some are single parents. A number have been through child custody struggles. Many suffered from PTSD and TBI or were recovering from other problems and injuries, including a few women who were suffering from MST. But the six cohorts presented as functioning, service-oriented, hard-working adults wishing to continue to contribute to society in a meaningful way while providing a solid, loving life for their families. As we were presenting the MBV program as an example of positive diversity and inclusion at a recent diversity and inclusion conference, one of the attendees suggested that the women veterans wanted to get finished with their deployments to be with their children, and I replied that men did, as well.

The majority of our veterans did face an uncertain future in terms of employment and career, and second careers, but that is where the program filled in many of the gaps and dealt directly with their uncertainty. We helped them become focused on growth, and active in their personal search for their own future. We used a supportive, collaborative community-based approach to their learning and their time together as members in this program.

I had often heard that veterans missed three key things upon leaving military service: 1) service to a purpose beyond self, 2) the camaraderie that comes with membership in a close-knit unit, and 3) the personal identity that comes with the uniform, rank, function, and performance. The second, camaraderie, we could design and offer to a great extent. The following comment by Ty Smith reflecting on the outdoor training day discussed in Chapter 3 is an example of this dynamic.

> "One of the personal thoughts that was the most dominant in my mind was how close we all were through this experience. I have worried that I would have a hard time finding true camaraderie, post-military, but I really understand now that this will not be the case. I gained a sense of family, and a bond that will never be broken. I really love this class, and the experience that I am living while navigating this program. Every individual is uniquely wonderful, and I promise to be there for each and every one of you from this day forward." (Ty Smith, Cohort III)

The search for continued service to a larger mission was the first missing item. Identity would probably be a long-term issue that was central to many of the struggles veterans experienced in their own transition. This search for purpose and identity was aspirational, and we supported it, as did our community and unit of membership. Later, I will discuss our veterans' involvement in volunteer and community-based organizations alongside their professional careers.

In addition to my own voice and experience, you will hear the voices of forty-four of our alums representing all six cohorts of veterans. As I did, I think you will find their stories to be rich, honest, and engaging. They include difficult challenges, but all express persistence, mission-focused endurance, and personal growth, optimism, and achievement. The collaborative nature of this effort is one of the program's most important values. We downplay individual competition in order to work together for both individual and group success. We become committed to each other's success, not just our own—you will hear more about this from the alums throughout the book. I have added pictures to the narrative. Though we don't have all we would have liked, I think these pictures provide a glimpse into the students, alums, and program activities, as well as the context in which we work.

My own career in education and in the classroom spans sixty-three years (including time in the army and graduate school), beginning in high school classrooms and the football field in 1956, in El Monte, California. I have spent a combination of classroom commitments and program administration at the university level, forty-seven years at USC, and have learned that much is accomplished through thoughtful program design and program values in addition to good faculty and motivated students. I will address some of those design principles and cultural values throughout the book, and specifically discuss the values of diversity, inclusion, and equity, which are increasingly important at not only the individual level, but the system/program level, as well.

I would also state my immense gratitude beginning with Professor Arvind Bhambri and Karla Wiseman (at the time, executive director of executive education where the program was housed), who convinced me that we're never too old to begin a new program adventure of transformational personal growth. Too, I'm grateful to the Marshall School of Business's dean at the time, Jim Ellis, and the University of Southern California for providing the context for this positive program addressed to a specific set of stakeholders, our military veterans, in their personal transitions from a military to a civilian career and mindset.

It is worth noting that USC's support for both the military and military veterans has a long history, beginning in the First World War. Many students left campus to join the military, an ROTC program opened on campus, and much of the campus was physically involved in the national military effort. The ROTC program began again in 1940 with naval ROTC, followed by army and air force units. With no limits on veterans' admissions, the student body doubled from about 12,000 to 24,000 students between 1945 and 1948, supported by the GI Bill signed in 1944. During the turbulent years of the Vietnam conflict, the university stood firm with its commitment to the ROTC programs that many other universities disbanded during that time (Krieger 2017). One of the most celebrated events on campus is the ROTC/

Veterans' Dinner event conducted every spring to recognize this relationship, our veteran alumni, and ROTC cadets.

What motivated me to begin to chronicle this experience and distill meaning from it was an event in May 2016, after the graduation of Cohort III. One of the graduates, Ty Smith, whom you will meet at the end of Chapter 3, was retiring from the Navy SEALs. The ceremony was to take place in Coronado, California, the training site for the SEALs on the West Coast, a week after graduation, after all the goodbyes had been said, and the disbanding of Cohort III as an educational community had taken place. Ty had suggested that anyone who wanted to could join him for the ceremony, so my wife and I decided to spend the weekend in San Diego and attend his retirement on Friday. We were surprised when we saw who else decided to make the trip from Los Angeles to San Diego, in addition to those in the cohort who lived in the San Diego area. Fully 40 percent of the cohort was in attendance. The ceremony was very moving as well as inspiring. The reception at the house of Ty and his wife, Alexa, afterward was very warm, and very much a reunion of the students from Cohort III. I began documenting the program that night as I felt compelled to capture this special time, these special people, this incredible community, and the sense that we all belonged to something unique. In addition, I began to realize the meaning this program was having for me, an army veteran and a veteran instructor and administrator at Marshall for forty-four years at the time of this event. It was the fairly dramatic realization of my embedded engagement with this group that led to the creation of this document.

What you will read throughout the book is my description and analysis of the context, students, outcomes, and experience. Along with my own eyes and interpretations, you will meet the forty-four alums and read their stories, and I have included numerous comments, assessments, and other material produced by the veterans addressing the leadership portion of the program, their personal goals, and their sense of achievement and growth throughout the year-long intensive experience.

I conducted a discussion board between each class meeting on every other Friday and Saturday. We had a total of twenty weekend meetings during the two-semester program. I would suggest a topic and ask the students to respond to it and to each other. I would select topics that either related to the leadership portion of the course, for which I was responsible, or to assessment of specific activities. There was even some surveying of their thoughts and experiences related to what we were doing in the program. It was an important opportunity to press them further into certain issues, to assess the program and our progress, continue to develop our learning community focus, and share thoughts and feelings.

One of my big insights is that the cohorts would become closer and often more vulnerable with sharing, which led to greater sharing and openness within the class sessions, themselves. I found this process helped develop a more caring, supportive, and sharing environment than if I had merely asked for such a dynamic in the class. This process was also powerfully instrumental in reducing the possibility of anyone's personal isolation during the short year we were together.

This dynamic, formed by a common background in the military, which was very strong and took form almost instantly within each cohort, was probably the most profound of the program's experiences. We had to be explicit about the limits of collaboration when it came to individual assignments and performance evaluation, but this combination was successful for individual and community growth.

> "The difference between this course and any other is the camaraderie between the students/veterans. Any other student in the world is more worried about finishing their homework while veterans are worried about everyone finishing their homework. I sincerely like how the course was geared to me on a personal level . . . I wasn't just a number in a seat. I was a person who added value to the course." (Robert Peña, Cohort III)

There were individuals skilled in certain subjects conducting workshops for those who could benefit from help from colleagues. There were those in each cohort who organized the class in terms of what assignments were due each class weekend. There were individuals who stepped up for special roles within the work of the community. There were constant study groups formed by the students, typically geographically, which operated autonomously and effectively. Other individuals took on roles that assisted the community of students in their holistic approach to their common mission. And always there were the reliable and constant San Diego car pools!

We developed a learning community focus and mentality with two major meanings. The first was the obvious one that our mission, through intensive learning, was to achieve success, a degree, and potentially a new career. The second was how the learning community could, through collective self-assessment and self-awareness, evaluate itself and make improvements toward greater maturity and effectiveness. I often used the discussion board activity for assessment and improvement as well as some of our time spent in an overall team meeting on the Saturday afternoon. While critical for individual growth, the technique of reflection and self-evaluation is also useful at the group level. While independence is often valued as a goal of both education and maturity, interdependence within a social context, like a team or organization, is what drives effective performance and synergistic results.

Throughout these six years, I found my own engagement with students to be exceptional. I learned some new values and the importance of others. I learned this entire group of veterans was very service-oriented. While it would be a stretch to conclude that this is their strongest value, it was the value that presented itself to me on a regular basis, and the one of which I was most aware. I've known individuals who were very service-oriented, but I have never been exposed to entire groups sharing this value. This value, along with other values like humility, integrity, community and family focus, and caring about others, was both moving and impressive to experience on a daily basis. Since they are all volunteers with the concept of service to country, this orientation carries over to their professional life, friendships, and family.

Most of our veterans have either been in combat themselves, or in a combat zone, so knowing and caring about the people with whom you serve is critical—often to one's survival but certainly to one's well-being. There will be other opportunities to witness and discuss values throughout this journey, but this value of service and connection to others in service was dramatic to me in my work with the veterans, and solidified my sense that service to others leads to both meaningful work and a meaningful life. I also learned that leadership is about service to others, not about oneself, and fundamental to our classes and discussions on the subject.

To make this story more complete, I will share some activities that demonstrate many individuals' personal growth in thinking, behavior, and commitments to possibilities in their lives.

I was not alone on this six-year journey, and the management team that shared it was also exceptional. Our sense of approaching the program as a team was notable as well, and I shall be forever grateful for their competence and commitment to it and our friendship. James Bogle is the director and face of the program. He is a retired army officer, and this role is his transition role after retirement. Jamie Saure is the associate director and our operations officer. The three of us have been consistent members of the management team for over five years. Matt Lorscheider and Joseph Chicas have served as the director of the career-development program during the last two to three years. Matt is the current director.

We've had five amazing student interns from the school of social work for three years: Neva Wallach, Alex Savage and Maude LaBelle in the second year, and Kimberly Nguyen and Gabriela Merida during the most recent year. All have contributed in excellent fashion to our team, and we regard them as team members. Being part of a high-performing team is one of the program's greatest advantages, and it has been a huge support for me, for which I am extremely grateful. I greatly appreciate the partnership I've experienced with James Bogle, which is essential in program performance and personal well-being. Jamie has been the person keeping us all on track (and fed), and is also an outstanding partner.

While I didn't know Karla Wiseman at the time, I appreciate her bringing me on board the MBV program. Arvind Bhambri and I had been colleagues since we started the Executive MBA Program in 1985, and he has been a member of the EMBA faculty for the entire thirty-five cohorts of its history. I appreciate the opportunity he provided for me, and his guidance throughout the startup of the program. The MBV is connected to the EMBA through some common curriculum and common format. Again, I'm indebted to the dean at the time, Jim Ellis, as well as to our CFO, Sunny Donenfeld, for their support throughout our startup.

I owe a debt of gratitude to my faculty team. We asked only for volunteers who wanted to teach in this special environment and program. The following are the faculty who have taught in the program, and who have added so much through their competence, professionalism, and caring: Mark DeFond, Ken Simmonds, Mark Young, and Smrity Randhawa (accounting); Gareth James and Abbass Sharif (statistics and data analytics); Scott Abrams, Julia Plotts, Ty Callahan, and Bob Bridges (finance); Violina Rindova and Kyle Mayer (strategy); Michael Coombs (negotiations); Morgan McCall (leadership); Nate Fast (power and influence); Gerry Ledford (human resources), Dennis Rook and Rex Kovacevich (marketing); Allen Weiss (mindfulness and social media marketing); Dina Mayzlin (social media marketing); Kevin Fields (contract and real estate law); Steve Byars and Daylanne Markwardt (communications); Tommy Knapp, Chris Harrer, Elissa Grossman, and Steve Mednick (entrepreneurship); Baizhu Chen (macroeconomics); Omeed Selby, Raman Randhawa, and Hiroshi Ochiumi (operations). John Bertrand provided exceptional service and education in the career service and development area in his role with the Career Services Office of the Marshall graduate division, and also as a volunteer to work with the veterans in assisting them in career change and preparation for job search.

I would also like to express my appreciation to General (and Professor) David Petraeus, who for these six years was the Widney Professor in the Price School, and an affiliated faculty member with our program, who spent two sessions each year with our veterans. He shared his wisdom, insights, and leadership point of view with our veterans, many of whom had served with him in Iraq and Afghanistan.

While we have over 100 business leaders in the community who make up our board of counselors, three stand out for their consistent and inspirational service to our veterans and to the program itself: Greg Hillgren, Chris Lord, and Clint Salee. Greg Hillgren took the leadership role in the formation and development of the Board of Counselors. Chris Lord is a tireless individual counselor to veterans (and is now the Chair of the Board of Counselors), and Clint Salee initiated, developed, and guides a full mentoring program for the veterans. Their support and commitment and that of the rest of the 100 community and business leaders has been an immense and powerful boost to us and our veterans in their mentorship and leadership.

Two others, colleagues for many years, who have been my partners in the experiential learning component of the MBV program (and many classes before), are: Dr. Gita Govahi, director of the Experiential Learning Center

(ELC) in Marshall, and Philip Folsom, founder, with his wife Tanya Folsom, of Philip Folsom Programs. These individuals have not only partnered with me but enriched my own learning and life in regards to emphasizing a mission of competence, development, and personal growth. They have been long-term partners with me in experiential learning in our quest for personal growth outside of a more traditional classroom setting. And they have always made our collaboration easy, positive, and successful. They have consistently demonstrated the value of service to others in our mutual quest for growth, insight, transition, and leadership.

An earlier assignment with the Marshall School's Leadership Institute under the direction of the founder, Professor Warren Bennis, challenged me to develop and run a university-wide graduate program for emerging leaders, the Presidential Fellows Program, from 1995 to 2001. We spent a year after-hours with the students, working on their leadership development and community service contributions. One of the graduates of the program became my partner in the last three years of the program, Cleve Stevens, whose book, *The Best of Us,* is cited and referenced later in this story. Bennis, who I had known for 50 years beginning in my own graduate program, had a profound effect on my intellectual background, and Dr. Stevens had a more immediate impact on my approach to working with others in their development and growth. I am grateful for both relationships and our experience.

I would also like to give a special acknowledgment to two other long-term community partners. First, to Bennie Davenport, founder of the Blazer Youth Organization in South Los Angeles. His incredible community values and service set him as an exemplar as a selfless contributor to community service and positive health and education. Bennie and I have collaborated over many years and helped many of my students become engaged in the community for mutual benefit and learning. Second, a special acknowledgment of another long-term collaborator, Alyson Daichendt, a managing director of human capital at Deloitte Consulting, who, for about seventeen years, has contributed both to my classroom as a speaker as well as to many of my students eager to get assistance in career thinking and job search. She has been tireless in her commitment to my students in their career searches and preparation, and in support of our educational mission.

I'm very appreciative to two of my department colleagues at Marshall for planning, developing, and engaging in collaborative programs with the MBV and their undergraduate leadership programs: Professor Carl Voigt, with the Global Leaders Program, and Professor Jody Tolan, with the Coury Leadership Program. We are engaged in annual sharing and learning across programs, asking our veterans to share their insights into military leadership with our undergraduate students in Marshall and to engage with them in an outdoor, experiential learning context. These two half-day workshops are very powerful learning experiences for both the undergraduates and the veterans.

I would also like to acknowledge the support staff of the Department of Management and Organization. Queenie Taylor, Martha Maimone, Marie Dolittle, and Ruth Joya have always supported me in my work. I am happy to count them as friends, as well.

I'm very appreciative for the excellent and professional assistance, consulting, and hard work of my team at FriesenPress, who managed the process of editing, design, and production of the manuscript throughout. Judith Hewlett, my project manager, was an outstanding partner and manager of the entire process. I'm also grateful for the other members of the team, Laura, my editor, Araba, my designer, and James, the promotions specialist for their fine work and assistance. I'm grateful for your professionalism and contribution.

And while it may be obvious, I want to give my highest appreciation to the almost 400 veterans with whom I've shared this journey these six years. They have enriched my life and experience incredibly, and have renewed my faith in what we need to do as citizens and in the ability and willingness of the good people who raise their hands and volunteer to serve all of us. And a special thank you to the forty-four veterans who have shared their personal story in the pages to come.

Finally, to my family. First, my special appreciation to my son and writing partner, Steven, who bailed me out of my technical problems on a regular basis, and who has become a calming influence on me when I feel the computer has become my enemy. I'm very grateful for his problem-solving and guidance. And to my wife, Peggy, who matches me step for step in our workouts, and without whose support and encouragement and careful reading ability this book would still be in process. I appreciate her incredible partnering ability and am grateful for her love. My appreciation and love, too, to the rest of my family for their support and encouragement throughout—sons Michael and Brendan and daughter Allison; also my brothers, Tom and Curt (a Vietnam veteran).

There is one other person I would like to mention and that is my father-in-law, US Navy Captain (Ret.) H. Dale Hilton, who passed away in 2000. He was a navy pilot, and was flying into Pearl Harbor on December 7, 1941. He was shot down over the Pacific in 1942, flying his Douglas SBD Dauntless dive bomber. He and his rear gunner were captured and spent three and a half years as POWs. Once the war was over, he continued his navy career commanding an aircraft carrier, the *USS Lexington*, in the early '60s. During his career, he served as Naval ROTC Commandant at USC in the mid-'50s. He also captained the golf team and produced an El Rodeo yearbook while an undergraduate at USC. Later, he served as associate vice-provost for university affairs while performing as executive director of the USC alumni association, from about 1968 to 1981. I've thought often over these past several years how he would have loved this program, and how proud he would have been that we were doing this at USC. I wish I could have shared the experience with him.

Now, please join me as I share my personal experience with this incredible unit of veterans in our journey discovering opportunity, growth, and transformation. And please enjoy the voices of the forty-four members of the MBV unit whose personal stories will inspire you and give you hope for the future—not just for theirs, but for ours, as well.

CHAPTER 1

INTRODUCTION TO THE PROGRAM, PURPOSE, DESIGN, AND STUDENTS

"Who's feeling victorious this morning?" John Park, MBV '19, yelled excitedly to the Global Leadership Program (GLP) students gathered around him on the Bridge Hall lawn. "Let me see that V! Let me hear you! Fight on!"

Now pursuing a master of business for veterans (MBV) degree at USC Marshall, Park was a machine gunner with the marines in Iraq, fighting for his life at the age of nineteen. As master of ceremonies, his call to action on October 12, kicked off the second annual GLP/MBV leadership event, which bridges two academic programs in a powerful experiential learning experience. Ninety-five GLP freshmen, the top tier of business administration students, joined thirty-two MBVs for a fast-paced morning of military-inspired exercises meant to sharpen their leadership skills, as well as challenge their strategic thinking and communication abilities.

"We wanted our vets interacting with our freshmen. We thought there was a lot of sharing to take place," said Professor Emeritus Robert Turrill, academic director of the MBV program. "They hear a lot about corporate leadership, and I wanted them to hear about military leadership and see where the overlaps are. This group of veterans knows leadership quite well, and they have a lot to give."

Each of five exercise stations focused on a core value shared among all branches of the US military (army, navy, air force, marine corps, and coast guard) and the British Army—all of which were represented by

MBVs. Those values, each essential to good leadership, are: honor, respect, loyalty, service, and integrity.

At the end of each exercise, a debriefing session allowed time for questions, analysis, and discussion about how things could have gone better. Every session offered lessons on multiple dimensions, with applications for students' futures in business and life in general.

"This is all about being present in the moment, interacting with and learning from each other, both us from them and them from us," said Nick Seidel, MBV '19, US Army Infantry Major (Ret.), who helped coordinate the program with Turrill. "It's about learning to come into their own, through stretching their comfort zone and giving them time for active and meaningful reflection."

Core Values

When the whistle blew, the first group of students gathered at the "honor" station. Small plastic cones were laid out on the Bridge Hall lawn to resemble a minefield. The students were tasked with selecting two leaders who would be the only eyes and voices on the field to guide the remaining fifteen safely through the mines—with their eyes closed—in under fifteen minutes. "You need to make the best decisions you can with limited information, and you can't leave anyone behind," said Juan Reyes, MBV '19 (coast guard).

For marine Andrew Hodlin, MBV '19, this exercise had a real-world parallel with his tour of duty in Afghanistan, which he shared with the students waiting their turn. He said it was always the young recruits who led the company through minefields with metal detectors and Holly sticks, while their backpacks emitted a radio frequency to block remote detonators like cell phones or garage door openers. "This is about facing an unknown environment and having the courage to go out there," he said. "You know there are threats all around you, and you need to trust the people in front to get you through."

What's the best way to face the unknown? The same way students learn in their business classes—with a team. "You always need help accomplishing your objectives. It's much more difficult and time-consuming on your own," Reyes said after the exercise.

The students got very close to beating the timer, but as one active-duty air force reserve member said, "Horseshoes and hand grenades, my friends." Still, lessons learned without the high stakes of the real world was part of the point: Try things out now, make mistakes while in school, and learn to do it right out in the real world.

"The point is that these are dots, memorable little things that the students may not connect right away, but as they develop their careers, they can see how it all fits together. That's the whole purpose of giving them so many different experiences, and opportunities to meet so many different people," said Carl Voigt, professor of clinical management and organization and academic advisor for the GLP.

Theory into Practice

With the cell phone stopwatch counting down three minutes at the "respect" station, groups of four students tried to replicate a complex ten-piece Lego build they couldn't even look at. They had to rely on a team leader to describe it and couldn't talk to that leader. While extremely precise communication was key, some of the students also figured out that communication—and respect—has to be a two-way street. They found a way to signal to their leader without words.

"If you are a leader," active-duty air force member Scott Giles, MBV '19, said, "it is absolutely imperative that you solicit feedback from your subordinates. The goal is more empowered leadership through communication."

Collective Benefits

What do the MBVs get out of this? "I think a little bit of our youth back," Seidel, a West Point graduate, said with a laugh. "Not only do these folks bring youth and vitality, but they bring a different perspective to our cohort. That we have to approach them on their level allows us to get a little nostalgic in trying to reaffirm our abilities to teach because that's what we do or did all the time with training."

A chance for valuable interaction is one of the reasons more than a third of the eighty-six MBVs volunteered their time to prepare for and attend this event on their week off from classes. MBVs drove in from across the Southland; one flew in from Louisiana.

MBVs join the program to transition from the military to business; some have already made the plunge. One is an entrepreneur who runs a security business; another is a civil engineer working on the Inglewood stadium project near campus. They all wanted to share their experiences with Marshall's newest class.

"It's important for me as part of the leadership of this program that we—veterans at USC, and I am one myself—contribute," said James Bogle, MBV program director. "The value that binds this group is service. They don't want to come here and just take; they want to give, as well. For us, it's about having an opportunity to make a contribution to the university."

GLP student leader Eugenia Hang, '22, was thankful for their contribution. "I think this is really important for the students to experience and reflect on these concepts, like integrity, communication, and so on, and to be able to see how they would affect them in a business setting in the future," she said. "One of the takeaways I got was sacrificing personal gains for the collective benefit." (Tilsner 2018)

This story describes an all-morning workshop on leadership designed and delivered by Cohort VI veterans to a business school freshmen honors class, the Global Leaders Program (GLP), in the fall of 2018. This was the second year of this exchange between a graduate business program, the MBV program, and an undergraduate program, in which veterans share their experience, knowledge, and insight with freshmen on the topic of leadership through carefully crafted activities that lead to insight about the selected concepts. The first year of the exchange is described in Chapter 5 on leadership from the veterans' point of view.

Between 230,000 and 245,000 veterans transition out of active duty each year,* and California is the state that is the largest recipient of this group of veterans as they take on uncertain new challenges in employment and lifestyle. Between 2003 and 2019, it is estimated that 4.3 million service members transitioned out of active service. In addition to being the location of a large group of transitioning veterans, California also has the most active-duty service members as well as the largest group of reserves and national guard members of any state in the nation.

It is estimated that between 65 and 80 percent of these transitioning veterans don't have jobs waiting for them upon their exit. And this doesn't take into account other life changes that transitioning out of the military initiates, which are related to this change in employment.

Each branch of service has their own Transition Assistance Program (TAP), but these typically don't effectively serve officers or senior non-commissioned officers (NCOs). This is the group that is most likely to have a bachelor's degree, earned before, during, or after active duty. A major hurdle in this process is translating one's military experience into civilian terms, roles, jobs, and careers.

With the large numbers transitioning out of active duty annually, and in the state that has the most service members—active, reserve, and recently separated—it might make the most sense, then, that a graduate-level career-transition program be started within a California school of higher education. In fact, around 2009–2010, the undersecretary of California's Department of Veteran Affairs visited various colleges and universities to assess the interest in a program that would serve this underserved group of potential students. He also visited community colleges to test their interest in doing a program at a lower level, but there were no takers at that time.

At USC's Marshall School of Business, however, he found an open reception to the idea in the office of executive education. Through a series of informal meetings involving executive MBA students (EMBA), the Director of Executive Education, who had herself completed the EMBA program with

---

* Military transition data and demographics are found in a number of sources, such as the Department of Defense bulletins, Department of Veteran Affairs reports, and the Small Business Administration reports.

an ex-marine who knew Colonel Rocky Chavez (at the time the undersecretary of the Department of Veteran Affairs for the state of California), began planning for a one-year, short program that would end with the granting of a master's degree in business—not an MBA, but a new unique degree program called an MBV.

The program's design borrowed heavily from the thematic approach to curriculum of the EMBA while adding coursework from the Lloyd Greif Center for Entrepreneurial Studies, the oldest entrepreneur program in the country, beginning in 1971. This approach allowed the faculty to offer many business disciplines within one broad course without having to offer multiple courses to fulfill the basic business requirements for the first year of an MBA program. Entrepreneur courses were added as the only elective offering in this short program, as the concept of owning and running one's own business seemed to create great interest in the veterans as they transitioned. And as it turned out during the first six years of the programs, there was significant interest in developing new businesses—both sole proprietorships and partnerships.

Transitions

At the time, the concept of transition seemed fairly straightforward. A transition program was primarily aimed at service members who were leaving active duty and joining the civilian workforce. What we discovered was that transitioning had broader meanings and so broadened our approach. Some recruits were recently separated from active duty, some had served some years ago, and some were still on active duty, a few having committed to twenty years, earning a military retirement pension. The curriculum we offered, as well as the career services we tailored for this group, made sense to these various groups who were transitioning from the military or who saw themselves needing this transition preparation even though they had separated some time ago.

The average age was between thirty-five and thirty-six in the six years we have completed, ages have ranged from twenty-five to sixty-one on graduation. We welcomed members who had been out for some time, some who have failed small businesses and who wanted to begin again, and some who wanted to change their career trajectory and focus again. For example, a number of the veterans took civilian jobs within law enforcement. Some were content to continue to grow within that field, but others wanted to take on new challenges and seek new opportunities—in other industries and startups.

Transitions in leadership has a couple of additional meanings. One is symbolic: we expect this group of veterans to take on leadership roles in their new careers and ventures. The second is related to the program's requirement that all applicants have at least three years of leadership responsibilities and performance. Military officers and NCOs all have significant leadership training and experience, so they do not need basic leadership education. With the continuing debate on leadership, its definition, professionalism, and effectiveness (see, for example, books by Kellerman and Pfeffer), working with military veterans is different because of the call to regularly learn, deliver, and assess leadership effectiveness as part of their assignments.

In fact, leadership is so critical to the military that succession planning in leadership begins very early in training programs. The assumption is that if someone in a lead position goes down or is unable to fulfill their leadership duties, the next person must step into that role without any gap in performance or unit integrity. This means leadership training is called for in all ranks in anticipation of an immediate call to move in or up. We might call this anticipatory socialization of service members of all ranks in the leadership function, meaning taking on the values, standards, and skills or a group (or rank) one aspires to join. (First defined by Robert K. Merton based on a 1949 study of the "American Soldier.")

Also, no one in the military reaches a senior rank without going through the lower ranks, whether they are enlisted or an officer. To achieve higher rank, either as an enlisted member or an officer, one must begin at the lowest rank, and then through performance and time-in-service, progress to higher ranks. This may not be the case in civilian occupations where a senior leader may be brought in from outside to take on a higher leadership position without progressing through the ranks.

Therefore, all service members are taught and experience leadership development as a rigorous part of their training. Everyone knows the requirements of the position and rank above them throughout the process—succession planning is built in from the start.

In addition to these meanings, the program focuses on the necessity of rethinking and refocusing leadership from a military to a civilian point of view. Since students know the basics of effective leadership so well, we challenge them to play bigger and bring military leadership values into a civilian context. This expectation requires a personal growth approach as well as the development of an analytical ability to identify and respond with context awareness and greater adaptability.

A graduate business degree is intended to develop leadership for business and other organizational contexts. As a professional, applied degree, it is intended to develop managers to be more effective, and to be able to take on leadership roles. Before the two role concepts of manager and leader became distinct concepts, business schools and MBA programs intended to fill the ranks of middle management with the anticipation of growing within the business or other segments of the economy. The academic field of leadership has grown in number of participants (e.g., researchers, trainers, consultants) and disciplines, and as a result, the definition, expectations, and documentation of the relationship with executive performance and integrity have become somewhat confusing (see Pfeffer and Kellerman). This confusion does not exist within the military or with veterans. The military is often the only institution that is highly regarded by the public and given credit for doing leadership right (see Gallup polls of 2006 and 2016). Unfortunately, some books on leadership don't mention the military as they discuss leadership, and this absence of attention weakens the discussion.

What has occurred in all six cohorts of the MBV program is an openness to taking a fresh look at leadership and the adaption of one's own sense of leadership to a different institutional context that varies from industry to industry and firm to firm. The students' openness to taking a fresh look at their own leadership competencies creates the opportunity for personal growth in many dimensions. Most military veterans have been indoctrinated into self-improvement as an ongoing process, so there is little resistance to taking a new look at oneself and one's context. However, more than once I have heard a student begin their statement with "I thought I knew everything about leadership, but I found out I had room to grow."

Using well-known self-assessment instruments to produce personal data helps develop a fairly complex baseline from which to grow. We add to their current self-understanding and self-knowledge new goals to develop new competencies in leadership using the "best self" concept as our guide. In addition to each individual setting stretch goals for themselves, we assign goals partners to support their efforts and support the relational aspects of leadership.

Throughout the book and program, I keep the focus on the students themselves, and their intent and ability to play bigger and aspire to greater leadership influence and impact. We do, however, identify and discuss the most effective and least effective leaders they have known. These two assignments plus their summary of their understanding of leadership could, by themselves, form the foundation for a complete text on leadership focused on "what is leadership?" and what qualities, values, and skills define the most and least effective in their personal experience.

Cohort VI

The MBV program grew from the recognition of the need of transitioning military veterans (and active-duty personnel) to have access to a graduate-level business program and the resources necessary for entering new careers or business ventures. Many MBA programs have veterans as part of their student body, but veterans must integrate themselves into a predetermined curriculum and program management designed for MBA students. The MBV program was designed specifically for veterans as a one-year program to create a more rapid, cost-effective, and efficient credentialing process and career transition, so that veterans could get into the civilian sector more quickly with a strong graduate program and master's degree.

Leaving a military environment and joining a civilian one is the most recognized use of the transition concept, but many of our students: 1) have been out of uniform for a number of years, 2) don't intend to leave the military until retirement, or 3) are in the active reserve while holding full-time civilian employment and living as a civilian. It's not unusual to have more than a dozen students over the age of forty-five in the program during any cohort, and two of our students have entered the program in their early sixties.

Some of the meanings I will attach to the concept of transition are: "a state of mind," "a personal journey of profound change," "moving from a military career to a civilian career," "changing one's vocabulary, especially on one's resumé," "moving from point A to point B on any number of dimensions in one's life," and potentially a sense of "renewal" or "reinvention of self." But I will stress that one's transitioning is frequent (maybe continuous), and may not follow a carefully planned route, and may be moving toward an unknown destination. New possibilities for life, career, and contribution, both professionally and within a community, are exciting unknowns that are frequently experienced during the program. I will explore what enables the transition and what barriers there might be to seeing it through.

The MBV program went live in the fall of 2013 with Cohort I. In addition to learning the basics of business and management and developing additional leadership competencies, the students must redesign their resumés and professional networks to effectively communicate their strengths and potential value to a new set of employers. In most cases, this process also involves understanding what options they have, what careers and jobs are available, and how to match those with their skills and experience.

As transition (out of the military) is complex, just a few days or weeks of transition instruction and discussion would not be adequate for the more advanced veterans looking for a more powerful experience to launch them back into civilian life and careers. So transition, in this case, means elevating one's credentialing at the master's level to either launch a business career or accelerate progress in a career already underway. This implies that the students within their application to the program would have to assert, and document, that they had already achieved a basic level of success and were, therefore, ready to be considered an experienced hire.

The MBV program was designed with entrepreneurship in mind. As veterans leave active service, options for their new career move are both endless and overwhelming. During the early discussion phase of the program, veterans from the EMBA program suggested more discussion of how to start a business rather than only discussing the corporate context would have been more effective. In the two entrepreneurship courses in the MBV faculty introduce students to many entrepreneurs. Taking action, customer discovery, creating differentiated products and services, and learning persistence are key to beginning to think about actually starting one's own business. Within the cohort, partners were often formed, and much support and guidance were provided by a senior board of counselors and mentors, and other individual career guidance individuals. At a more general level, it has been fairly dramatic to observe students grasp the huge domain of possibilities for lives they never considered.

After World War II, nearly half of all veterans started or owned their own businesses. After the Korean War, 40 percent owned their own businesses. Now, of those veterans of the Iraq and Afghanistan wars, only four percent have entered their own ventures, according to the Bureau of Labor Statistics. However, women veterans seem to be starting more businesses. In 2008, 2.5 percent of veteran-owned business owners were women. In 2012, that number grew to 4.4 percent—an almost 300-percent increase of the number of startups from 2007 to 2012. Women now own 383,000 businesses within the United States, as of the 2012 Census Bureau's Survey of Business Owners. This represents 15.2 percent of the 2.52 million veteran-owned businesses. (This same number continues to be used as recently as 2018–2019. See "Overview of Veteran-Owned Businesses," SBA small business series reports.)

Veteran entrepreneurs tend to be older than the general population of entrepreneurs. Seventy-four percent of veteran-owned businesses are fifty-five or older, while only 41 percent of all owners are over fifty-five. In addition to starting businesses, veteran entrepreneurs are thirty times more likely to hire other veterans than the general population, thus magnifying their impact in veteran employment and careers. These two statistics support the potential for entrepreneurship to thrive within a transitioning group of student veterans.

Principles of Program Design

Designed as a program for veterans in transition, the program needed to be efficient (short), flexible but focused, and must begin with changing one's vocabulary from a military and government focus to a business and civilian focus. In addition, a focus on personal change and changing from a military mindset to more of a civilian mindset would be essential.

The academic year 2012–2013 was filled with meetings with faculty to develop an integrated, thematic curriculum that would introduce all the basic business subjects and prepare students for some advanced work in the second semester. The program had to contain all the functional areas of business as well as the basic tools of analysis and writing. The first semester focused on organizational effectiveness and other measures of profitability, including understanding financial statements and the use and design of Excel spreadsheets. An introduction to strategy and the basic foundations of leadership based on personal growth and influence was the students' initiation to leadership and personal and organizational goals. Alongside this large thematic, nine-unit course was a three-unit introduction to entrepreneurship.

The MBV program is advertised as practical, theoretical, experiential, and professional, which means having standards of performance and continual improvement in skills and leadership development as some of the graduates' hallmarks. I challenged the students that we would expect them to lead and run something, either their own business or others', and that our goal was to improve their performance as managers, contributors, and leaders. One of the program's major selling points is the opportunity it offers to join the

Trojan family and alumni worldwide. With over 90,000 Marshall alums heavily concentrated in southern California, there would be ample opportunity to make connections, explore different careers, and apply to enter various industries along with beginning a solo venture.

The program was designed in an executive format, meaning the students could be fully employed and complete the one-year program that met every other weekend (Friday and Saturday), ten weekends during each semester. Fully employed students were expected to take off two Fridays a month, and we asked the students to confirm that with their employers and document that agreement with the program management team.

We developed a large group of business leaders to act as a board of counselors to the students, under the leadership of Greg Hillgren, a senior member of the Dean's Board of Leaders. Also, one of the board of counselors, Clint Salee, created a major mentoring board to assist the students in their career search. Early on, we also had a Marshall career service officer, Dr. John Bertrand, volunteering his time to work with the students and their resumés and job-hunting skills on the weekends we were in session. Later, during Cohort IV, we hired our own career services director, who organized an entire year-long program of career-focused inquiry and search, and worked with the already formed board, mentors, and Marshall career service office. Since the hours available for instruction were so busy, the career service program had to operate outside the instructional hours on the weekend. Lunch and Learn is generally held on Fridays, and an industry panel presents after class on Friday, ending about 1900. With breakfast beginning at 0700, the days quickly became twelve hours long.

Saturday might also include scheduling for another industry panel or speaker on a particular career-transition issue, such as resumé writing. Typically, we would schedule a cohort team meeting at the end of the weekend at 1730 on Saturday, which could extend until almost 1900, as well. One of the issues leading to these long hours was that we found numerous people and organizations willing to assist our veterans and management team, and we never lacked for volunteers to come speak to us. In fact, the supportive culture for military veterans meant managing volunteers and external assistance became a fairly large commitment.

There were a couple of campus bars across the street from the classrooms that saw a lot of our students at the end of each weekend evening. And as our sole British veteran student, Steve Pullin, suggested, there were Friday night social sessions at the "Lab *over* the street!"

As a short program preparing veterans to transition into new or more challenging careers, all its elements and curriculum needed to be in alignment with the strategy and contribute to enabling the students to focus and achieve both professional and personal growth goals. Structure, processes, values, and governance must add value and, at the same time, support, align with, and provide integrating capability to the program and its academic content. At a time when universities and other institutions are reviewing activities, processes, programs, and systems for diversity, inclusion, and equity, we designed and operate the MBV program to be congruent with these values. We provide a supportive and challenging learning environment that involves faculty as key players, but also program management and program design that are consistent with and supportive of these values as well. Demographic diversity will be discussed in this chapter, but other issues of diversity, inclusion, and equity will be discussed in this section on design. The question is, can we design carefully enough to encourage, represent, achieve, and support inclusion and equity? This type of approach is often referred to as leadership by design. Inasmuch as we can design in our values in the structure and process of the program, we can achieve consistency in our ability to achieve our goals and values without relying solely on individuals reinforcing these values.

The Principle of a Cohort, Lock-Step Program

The sense of belonging and camaraderie is both strong and critical when members' interdependency may have life-and-death consequences. Being in a cohort where everyone has a common military background and is committed to a common educational experience creates an instant bonding effect.

Where I have seen a strong reaction to the notion of unit of membership is often with the older veterans. During our information sessions, I often watch the faces of the older recruits, and watch them light up with the realization of what they might be joining. We emphasize this opportunity for membership, as cohesiveness supported by positive work norms should lead to high performance. Common membership supports collaborative behavior, sharing behavior, and helping behavior. Common membership plus a reasonable set of expectations for cohort members create a sense of pride—in the unit and one's contribution to it.

The history and reputation of the Trojan family with close alumni ties makes this a cultural outcome that is relatively easy to achieve. Also, the requirement that everyone do the same work and assignments supports that bond. Individual students may begin at different points in their academic knowledge, but having everyone go through the same requirements simultaneously helps create some equity among the students. We have offered pre-program short academic sessions that also help adjust the differences in starting points and background.

With a common experience to achieve the degree, no one is exempted from any of the requirements, and by adding a collaborative value to our collective experience, students with advanced knowledge in a subject are encouraged to help those less experienced. This has, in fact, been the case with all six of the cohorts. A cohort structure creates strong boundaries, and everyone inside them has the same risks and goals at stake. There are no different memberships, thus reducing concerns about status and inequity. We don't have auditors, which would create a second class of membership in the program, and the more advanced students aren't taking higher-level courses or electives. The entire experience is common and required of all members.

The common experience within a group of students who have a common experiential referent, the military, with a lock-step design, will reduce cultural and status differences (e.g., rank), setting the stage for a more equitable and inclusive experience. The clear-cut boundaries around the program and membership provide a consistent experience across all students. Making rank neutral adds an additional dimension to the sense of equality inside the program. Rank may be part of the first introductions at orientation, but it is held as inappropriate after that. This reduces both student hierarchy and the natural inclination to form informal social groups based on historical status. Does this work all the time? No, but it reduces the impact on the social and cultural life of the cohort, and the students understand the purpose and buy into the neutralization of rank as a hierarchical separation and external status.

In group dynamics, external status brought into a newly formed group or team will change the interpersonal and influence dynamics within the group. While we can't keep this effect totally out of the process, designing our program guidelines and values to reduce status impact will assist the democratization of the entire cohort. And, since military veterans have a strong history in needing to understand the commander's intent, they typically buy into program management's statement that this is a design and policy principle and understand that, in a civilian classroom, external military rank does not have a place in the process.

> "I feel it is important to note the uniqueness of our program and I think it is central to its success overall and our success as a cohort, is that it is rank agnostic.... It may be a small thing, but I feel that the impact is tremendous." (Troy Baisch, Cohort VI)

> "I'm not sure about the breakdown of military officers and enlisted, and frankly it does not matter, but the maturity and intellect displayed over the past year seems markedly improved more than any large collection of military personnel I have come across." (Joseph Proffitt, Cohort VI)

The Principle of a Learning Organization and Learning Community

This design feature creates a more inclusive and equitable context for learning and performing. There are two meanings of the concept of a learning community. One is attached to the basic purpose of the program: to provide a context for learning and achieve a graduate degree in business. The community piece of the concept implies closer ties among the participants rather than a stranger and more individualistic approach. The second meaning has to do with becoming more effective as a learning organization over the time within the program.

We use three devices to assess, analyze, and direct change within the community: Saturday night cohort (team) meetings, biweekly discussion boards, and formal program evaluations toward the end of each of the semesters. There are other aspects to including students in learning about our organization with the intent to change it positively,

At the program's orientation, we ask the students collectively to draft their set of expectations for how they want the cohort to perform. What should our norms be? What are our expectations for our own conduct and behavior within the cohort and for those of our membership in the MBV family? This moves the students into the area of shared governance to a certain extent, and if not shared, at least their self-governance as a learning community.

There are other values attached to this concept. Our intent is to develop a supportive, collaborative environment in which everyone can learn and be successful, even sharing tips and insights into what works in career search and how we can support one another in this search. We dismiss the notion that any of these processes are zero-sum games, where if one wins, someone else must lose. The value is that all can win, and winning is more likely if we collaborate, act as a team, celebrate everyone's success, and share knowledge and insights.

We began changing these competitive scenarios during orientation and at the ropes course, demonstrating that there is more overall winning when we literally pull together than when we pull against each other competitively. During orientation, we engage in an experiential activity that demonstrates our assumptions about individual winning and competition versus sharing the work and strategy for all to succeed. This message is demonstrated multiple times at the ropes course, and then again on the last day of the program in another low ropes activity that has the same learning: that we all can be more successful by not only working collaboratively but by viewing our tasks and mission as one that involves everyone's success, not just our own.

By assessing our progress and relationships, we are focusing on the how of organizational effectiveness, not just on the what. Students will be very task-oriented, with rapid task completion being of value. Asking for assessment along the way and focusing on how we are doing slows down the process somewhat, but it allows organization members to both learn and change when needed and desired. Focusing on process and what adds value to a group or organization is part of the change process, whether it is organizational or personal change. We teach that team process gains must be larger than process losses to achieve high performance and intended synergy. For example, training for consensus decision-making while avoiding groupthink is a process gain. The learning community is what we are experiencing while achieving our learning and credentialing goals, and then using our experience within a collaborative context to understand more deeply how to apply our knowledge to our own context and experience, and in the future.

Because it's a community made up of military veterans, we know there will be any number of sensitivities around injury and disability from combat and other sources of trauma. Inasmuch as we ask students to share personal data, stories, and aspirations, we develop within the community a sense of safety and support so individuals trust the process of being more open to examining their own paths to personal growth. That is key to increasing leadership impact. There is a trust-building process that grows slowly, but only if there is a sense of safety, empathy, and honesty that this is shared by all, or most, participants within the cohort. It is a value about which the management team is serious—that our boundaries and process are personal and confidential both within the cohort as well as what is taken out of the cohort. Finally, by focusing on both the individual and the organization (community), we deal with the inevitable tension between the individual and individual rights and the well-being and needs of the community.

The learning community becomes a laboratory for life in one's community and culture. While the tension between individual rights and community well-being will always exist, a positive way of dealing with it is through learning about the process by simulating it within a learning context, which is the final stage of the experiential learning process—applying what we have learned to other contexts in which we live and work.

The Principle of the Management Team

We use a champions model in the management team, which means we are present and available when classes are in session, and we do all of the recruiting as a team. This means that throughout the process, from recruiting to graduation, the students deal directly with the program-management team (program director, academic/faculty director, associate director, and career service director). This is difficult in larger programs, but in smaller, niche programs where one-to-one contact is important, this is a more effective strategy than outsourcing different functions to other functional activities that specialize in particular segments of the total process but contribute their expertise to a wide range of programs—for example, recruiting and admission.

Special programs with non-traditional students like military veterans are more effective face-to-face in all or most aspects of the program, and this applies to working with the management team as well as in the live classroom environment. Having added our own career services director in the past two years, we have a stronger capability of the entire cycle from recruitment and selection to career guidance and preparation. Being part of a larger organization, the Marshall school, however, allows us access to additional resources.

The other aspect of the champions model for the management team is the modeling effect, where we can model both positive team behavior and leadership, as the veterans are interested in our ability to act as role models as well as enablers and administrators. Belonging to a good team with positive performance is part of the engagement process, which has its own payoff for us as team members, as well. In addition, a team approach to management creates a lot of sharing and a sense of mutual accountability for outcomes. It also means a student can address any member of the team, who can respond to most any concern, and if not with a solution, a follow-up hand-off to the person who can solve the problem or issues. The team shares information about operational and planning issues as well as student issues. The team as a whole is usually quite knowledgeable about the individual students within the cohort, and while everyone is on a first-name basis, the students and management team typically wear name badges provided by the program.

The Principle of Physical Classroom Design

One of the more obvious design features of a program is the availability and use of space. A classroom's capacity is important; from an educational perspective, size of classrooms is important for case or discussion classes where interaction among students is expected, as well as Q & A time with the professor. For individuals who have not experienced many physical classrooms, it is even more important that they have the opportunity to engage actively in the classroom process. Tiered case rooms are common in business schools with sight lines that are clear and that visually connect all students to each other. The constraint on tiered case rooms is the location of the front of the room, or pit, where the faculty commands attention. It is difficult for the faculty to go low stage in a tiered classroom so they might focus on student contributions and leadership. It is also awkward to attempt to use a team structure during class time with tiered seating.

Using a flat case room with movable furniture allows different configurations of tables and chairs. It also allows the faculty to use the front and the back of the room, if so desired, and individuals or teams of students can take the front, side, or rear spots if presenting. In the case of the MBV, we schedule rooms that will seat a maximum of about fifty students to provide sufficient air time for these students who may not have been involved in interactive business management classes in their past education experience.

Our cohorts have been running about ninety students each, and we break them into two subsections that operate side by side simultaneously. These are still fairly large classes for the type of interactions we encourage, but the flexible classroom structure with movable furniture helps the process. A final consideration is enough space so that students who need to stand can go to the back or sides of the room without interfering with other students. Both potential fatigue and physical disability can require space to stand or, as in all modern classrooms, room for a wheelchair. Veterans in many cases aren't used to sitting for long periods, so we encourage them to stand when they need to, and we're also aware of the more recent medical recommendations that sitting for long periods is unhealthy.

From a pedagogical point of view, sitting may imply passivity, and we need to make sure that to be in an active learning mode, students spend more time being actively engaged in their learning activities. Simulations, role plays, and team and individual presentations are also desirable. As one element of a systemic analysis of space used for learning and engagement, the physical design and constraints must be assessed and arranged wherever possible to support active learning, engagement, and inclusion.

Other Diversity and Inclusion Design Strategies

Other design strategies can be used within the curriculum itself, especially leadership, team, interpersonal, and organizational topics. A few examples would include sharing self-assessment data of the diversity of values, preferences, and styles. The opportunity to work with others who don't share the same experiences, styles, or preferences creates an environment of diversity and inclusion.

Assigning students to heterogeneous teams rather than allowing only self-selected teams places students into a more challenging context to learn to work with diversity. Using self-selected teams tends to be more socially comfortable, but this implies that everyone in the socially selected team has potentially similar backgrounds, meaning their information base is potentially limited compared to working in stranger teams, where members bring different experiences, ideas, and ways of thinking. Under a stranger team design, members have to work hard not just on the project but also on understanding different points of view and ways of thinking. Also, in the MBV, the cohort puts together a profile of effective leaders and leadership that typically includes such concepts as respect, humility, service, and accountability, all of which require working effectively with people who are different and creates a sense that "we are all in this together," which embraces diversity and designs in inclusiveness. The concepts of character and integrity are also inclusive and value-based concepts that align with diversity, inclusion, and equity.

Demographics of Cohorts I–VI

One of the key differences between enlisted and officer corps in the military, in general, is the achievement of college degrees. About 85 percent of officers have undergraduate degrees, and 42 percent have advanced degrees. Military officers are four times as likely to have advanced degrees as average adults in the general population, ages eighteen to forty-four. Among MBV cohorts, 39 percent are officers, and 61 percent are enlisted and non-commissioned officers. This would imply that the enlisted applicant pool is more like the officer group in terms of post-secondary education than they are like the average enlisted service member. Within the enlisted ranks, only 7 percent have college degrees, compared to the 85 percent of the officer ranks (Parker, Cilluffo, and Stepler 2017).

Students obtain their degree before, during, or after their active duty. We have had several graduates retiring with twenty years of service by age forty with two degrees, a bachelor and a master's. Some of these are military academy grads, but many are enlisted who have earned two degrees while on active duty—you will meet a couple of them later in the book. Within all six cohorts, 14 percent entered already having advanced degrees, several of those being MBAs. Another unusual statistic about this student group is that about 44 percent are first-generation college students. In addition, 16 percent of Cohort VI are naturalized citizens, using their military service to create a path to citizenship. Both of these latter statistics represent groups of non-traditional college students.

In terms of gender, across all six cohorts we have enrolled 17.4 percent females and 82.6 percent males. The female contingent reflects the current numbers of the active armed forces, up from about 14.4 percent in 2010. The numbers of women in the military have been gradually increasing from 14 percent in 2010 to 15 percent in 2015 to 16.2 percent in 2017, but across the total armed forces including active reserve, 17.5 percent are currently female.

"The relationship USC has with its veterans and notably its female students is unprecedented. Veterans and females alike are encouraged to feel welcomed and heard, and to become primed for success. This is something I feel very strongly and have never seen within an organization before." (Vanessa Bolognese, Cohort VI)

The women members of Cohort VI

In terms of the ethnic composition of the MBV, non-white groups accounted for almost 60 percent of the cohorts over the first five cohorts and 57 percent of Cohort VI. In 2015, 40 percent of active-duty military were ethnic minority groups, with 12 percent being Hispanic and 17 percent Black. In the MBV, between 25 and 32 percent are Hispanic and 10 to 14 percent are Black. In all six cohorts, between 40 and 43 percent of students are white (non-Hispanic). Asian/Pacific Islanders consistently make up about 16 percent of the cohort and Native Americans represent between 1 and 2 percent of the students.

The biggest difference between the MBV and active-duty rosters is the larger number of Hispanic students in the MBV—about 30 percent consistently. The military has increasingly become more ethnically diverse. In 1990, 25 percent were classified as minorities; in 2015, 40 percent were minorities. However, in the MBV, the numbers are even larger, with 60 percent being minorities, including 16 percent Asian versus 4 percent in the active military. One possible explanation for these disparities is the ethnic makeup of southern California, where the white category is less than 40 percent of the total local population and the Latino population is the largest single ethnic group in the Los Angeles region.

> "I have never experienced the amount of support, guidance, and encouragement that Cohort VI gives me every day. . . . I am entirely grateful for the change I have experienced . . . since Day 1 when I walked into a room filled with diversity, strength, experience, and energy unlike ever before. . . . I knew that no matter what, I could not walk out the same way I walked in." (Rose Simpson, Cohort VI)

The students in the MBV program roughly approximate the distribution across military branches. Within the cohorts, 33 percent are army compared to 36 percent of active-duty personnel. Navy is represented by 22 percent versus 24 percent on active duty, marines are 19 percent of the cohorts versus 14 percent on active duty (an exception to this percentage occurred in the current cohort, VII, where 43 percent are marines), air force represent 26 percent of the cohorts versus 23 percent on active duty, and coast guard are represented by only 1 percent in the MBV versus 3 percent on active duty.

One of the key demographic facts is that there is only about 1 percent of the population at any point in time that chooses and is selected to serve in an all-volunteer military. By its nature of self-selectivity, this 1 percent (only about 0.5 percent are on active duty at any point in time) creates its own difference as a group. The difference between this and the other 99 percent may be the most defining characteristic, culturally, of the military. This fact is often cited by returning veterans as being the major difference, or hurdle, to overcome while trying to communicate to civilians the nature of their experience and the difficulty of their adjustment.

Summary Observations

1. Military officers as a group are considerably more educated than the general population as a whole, and are four times as likely to have an advanced degree.

2. Of the enlisted members of the military, only about 7–8 percent have bachelor's degrees, but 60 percent of the MBV Cohorts I-VI are enlisted veterans. We are attracting an educationally ambitious group in greater proportion than are serving actively, but many of our enlisted veterans achieved their degrees while on active duty or subsequently.

3. Within the MBV, 44 percent of students, on average, are first-generation students, which would imply that the military is an avenue of social mobility through higher education, combined with the data from #2, above.

4. Similarly, since 16 percent of our students are naturalized citizens, the military is also a potential route toward citizenship.

5. The MBV program is one of the most ethnically diverse programs in the university, and this represents the applicant pool and California demographics. Diversity is built into the military and, thus, our applicant pool.

6. Anecdotally, we will see that some individuals chose the military with at least one of their motivations being to escape their environment, whether gang or drug-related, or an abusive or hopeless home or local environment. Stories, many of which were shared in the application and essay process, paint a picture of family or community hopelessness and joining the military was seen both as a way out of this environment and an option to change one's life to give it greater structure, discipline, and service opportunities. (You'll meet several of these individuals as you read their personal stories.)

7. Just as education has always been a means to upward social mobility, the professional military seems to have joined that as a powerful combination for mobility, meaningfulness—both in service and in work—and for replacing a lost sense of community with a structured, purposeful, and supportive unit of membership and personal identity. So, in the case of this unique graduate program in business and entrepreneurship, dynamic routes and historical forces have combined to potentially accelerate veterans' growth, achievement, and contribution, and the continuation of positive careers and community service.

Challenges

As we discuss other aspects of the program and focus on veterans as non-traditional students and the challenges they face, I will return to some of these topics and design principles to fully build out the approach to the program and to our students. I will conclude here that the program is still in process. As we assess and review our progress, we will make changes and track its evolution going forward.

I'll end this chapter by sharing some comments by Antonio Randolph, Cohort IV, about the design of the program from a student's perspective. Antonio's personal story is at the end of Chapter 7.

The Power of the MBV Experience

"Cooperation, to some extent, can be found at every level of living existence. Some organisms and some societies have taken the liberty to advance their causes by effectively utilizing it and providing the rest of us with templates and baselines to exploit and strive toward.

In general, in a sound graduate school culture, the individual is less significant than the sum of all individuals. This philosophy is less evident and far from commonplace at the undergrad level. The assumption of the MBV faculty and directorate is that those who are pursuing graduate education will already know and/or come to realize three things before, during, or at the close of their matriculation:

1. Individual contributors are less likely to generate significant change and are rarely the source of game-changing innovation and success.

2. In order to move up the hierarchy in any organization, one must be able to influence, guide, foster, and develop people, ideas, and processes in coordinated ways using creative means.

3. The MBV coursework is far from comprehensive and only provides the foundation for each student to become cognizant and moderately capable in a contemporary organizational climate.

By deliberate design, the MBV program has no valedictorian to highlight and it does not emphasize the individual. The most prized achievements of the cohort are the corporate and program leader/professor evaluations of the capstone projects as well as the completion of the ropes course, both of which require group participation. The expressed and implied intent of the MBV, or any grad school program, is not solely or primarily to build the individual. It is to better the group (e.g., cohort, school, workforce, organization, society) and work to provide a model of what 'right' looks like. Imagine if everyone—every organization, and every society in the world—embraced this ideology. We would all be better and do better.

My good fortune landed me in the MBV Cohort IV with a tremendous bunch of individuals who, for the most part, doubled as a tremendous bunch of team players. Within this network, I had the even greater fortune and pleasure to work with a small group that made sure that I, a commuter flying in from Ohio for every session, didn't fail or fall. I worked hard to do the same for them. We all had our strengths, and we all used them to help the group toward greater good, in terms of academic and professional goals. Without these amazing teammates, there is no Antonio walking across the stage. They freely shared, openly gave, and frequently taught me something, whether academic, professional, or personal in nature. Special thanks to Takiesha, Brenda, Tracy, and Sean.

This program is a taste of what should happen and it offers an idea of what will happen if each constituent and card-carrying member of its legacy does their part and contributes their best and most cooperative efforts during and after their program tenure." (Antonio Randolph, Cohort IV.)

Now meet the first six members of the MBV alumni. I think you'll enjoy their personal stories.

Erik Bateman—Cohort V

The year was 1969. The place, Hanscom field, a US Air Force base just north of my birthplace, Boston. I was an eleven-year-old boy in a sea of adults fighting to get a better look at an object of intense interest. As I broke through the crowd, my senses were on high alert. The smell of jet fuel permeated the air as the deafening roar of jet engines started to shake the ground beneath me. It was intoxicating! I was hooked. This was a defining moment.

I was mesmerized as four beautiful F-4 Phantom jets screamed down the runway with orange and blue flame shooting out their tails. In perfect unison, the four jets broke free from the runway and arched into the vast blue sky. Seconds later, I heard another roar of engines to my right. Two additional Phantoms streaked by in full afterburner with those same orange and blue plumes exiting the engines, the ground rumbling yet again. This signified the start of the aerial demonstration by the famed United States Air Force Thunderbirds. To this shy boy, it was the greatest thing ever.

I was fascinated by aviation and, in particular, military fighter pilots from World War II. Every night at bedtime, after hearing the "lights out" command from my parents, I would be under the covers devouring yet another book about the exploits of America's aviation heroes of the Second World War. Heroes like Pappy Boyington, Chuck Yeager, and Joe Voss were my idols. Plastic models of the venerable P-51 Mustang, F-4U Corsair, and twin-engine P-38 Lightning hung on threads from the ceiling of my bedroom. I couldn't explain my intense fascination with these airplanes but it sure was real. My experience that cool fall day just north of Boston in 1969 solidified and validated that fascination and increased my desire to learn more about aviation.

Fast forward nine years to the fall of 1978. I am sitting in a conference room in downtown Boston. As I look nervously toward the door, a United States Marine captain walks into the room. I immediately notice his squared away appearance—not a button out of place or a crease in his entire uniform. My eyes move to his left chest where he proudly displays his Wings of Gold. I am at the Marine Corps officer selection office in Boston to take the aviation entrance exam, the first step in the long road to becoming a military pilot. I had driven down the night before from the University of Maine, having just started my senior year. Success on the exam would give me a slot in the naval flight training program, located in Pensacola, Florida. My stomach is in knots, my palms are sweating, and my heart is pounding in my chest. This was it. Thoughts race through my head. Have I prepared enough? Are my math skills up to par? Do I have adequate knowledge of how a jet engine works?

At that moment, my mind wanders back to the summer of 1975. Having just turned eighteen a few months earlier, I made the decision to reconnect with my biological father, much to my mother's chagrin. I was anxious but excited at the same time. I had not seen my father since I was five years old and had no recollection of that visit, anyway. As the plane began its final descent into Albuquerque International Sunport, I was full of anticipation. I had no idea what to think, as my mother had told me very little about my dad. I soon found out. As I got off the plane, I had a picture of him and searched the crowd for someone who looked like it. I recognized him before he saw me, and nervously walked up to him and said, "Dad." He was looking past me, but then our eyes locked. We both started to cry and embraced. It felt odd but wonderful at the same time. After we drove to his house, I noticed there was a great view of the airport on one side and the mountains on the other. The backyard looked out onto a beautiful golf course. The setting he lived in was impressive, but as we walked into the house, my jaw dropped. Just inside the front door, the walls were covered with everything aviation! Pictures of all of the World War II aircraft I had loved as a child covered one wall. Military citations took up another wall and pictures of pilots and their squadrons covered another. Over the next four days, I learned where my passion for aviation came from. My dad was one of the original Black Sheep, a Marine Corps squadron led by the colorful and aforementioned Col. Greg "Pappy" Boyington. The Black Sheep squadron flew the F-4U Corsair built by Grumman Aircraft, one of my boyhood plastic models. After meeting my dad, I realized that my dream since childhood was to become a military aviator. And after spending that time with him, I set a goal to become a Marine Corps pilot.

As I sit remembering this flashback, the marine captain clears his throat and brings me back to reality. "So you want to be a marine pilot, Mr. Bateman?"

I quickly responded, "Yes, sir."

"Well, it's a long road, Mr. Bateman, but if you are lucky enough to make it through the program, it will all be worth the effort." With that, he hands me the exam, tells me of the three-and-a-half-hour time limit with the usual advice to watch the time and not leave any questions unanswered. He finishes by saying, "Good luck."

Twelve months later, I sat on the flight line at the "Home of Naval Aviation," Pensacola Naval Air Station in Pensacola, Florida. I was strapping into a T-34 mentor training aircraft, getting ready for my final check ride before beginning jet training. Was I dreaming? No, this was no dream. My dream had come true. I was going to be a Marine pilot if I could successfully complete the training.

Ten months after that check ride, my father proudly pounded those Wings of Gold into my chest, and saluted his son: First Lt. Erik Bateman, the "second marine pilot in the family."

I would go on to serve twenty-eight years of both active duty and reserves in the Marine Corps and the navy. In my career, I had the thrill of landing an F4 Phantom on the rolling deck of an aircraft carrier at night. I was also fortunate to fly dozens of aircraft, including rotorcraft and prop. Finally, I served two tours of combat in the Middle East before retiring in 2006. Among my many other adventures in the military was my tenure working with the US Congress, negotiating budget line items for the Marine Corps and Navy. In the end, I went full circle with my career: I was the officer in charge of several air shows that were the first introduction to marine and naval aviation for thousands of young kids who were just like me when I was eleven years old.

Since then, I have had the pleasure of raising two beautiful children, my twelve-year-old daughter, Natalia, and my nine-year-old son, Zak. I am hopeful that one of them may choose to serve their country and even pursue their own Wings of Gold.

When I was a kid back in Boston, we would watch USC play in the Rose Bowl on New Year's Day. With the weather in Boston, it made USC look like heaven. Then, when I got my first set of orders out of flight school, I was stationed at El Toro Marine Corps Air Station, thirty-five miles south of USC. It always seemed that going to USC was a dream for another lifetime, even though many of my colleagues eventually went there. I now find the timing perfect to embark on a new path, and your MBV program is an exceptional fit. I feel my leadership ability and life experiences would allow me to be a valuable contributor to it. I would be honored to receive consideration for acceptance into the next MBV cohort.

Reflection: As I sit here just over a year after graduating from Cohort V of the MBV program, many things come to mind. In summary, my journey was very unique. I was by far the elder statesman in our group. Having retired from the military twelve years before I started the program, my experiences were significantly different from those of much of our cohort, who were still active-duty personnel.

Words cannot describe the life-changing ramifications of my experience at USC Marshall and the MBV program. Orientation was truly an eye-opener for me personally, having attained the rank of commander in the United States Navy along with having had the honor of serving as a commanding officer of multiple aircraft squadrons I thought I was fairly accomplished in my military career. As we were asked to briefly describe ourselves and our experiences, it became readily apparent to me that this was quite an accomplished group of individuals in both experience and intellect. It was intimidating for me given my own account of my accomplishments and I quickly realized that almost all my new classmates were more than capable of achieving the success I had. I found myself nervous when it came my time to talk—this was truly an impressive group.

We wasted no time before the classroom was upon us. Early on, it became apparent that the program was going to be intense and demanding; however, the art of collaboration among cohort members was not only recommended but necessary, given the diverse backgrounds and strengths and weaknesses of the cohort members. This was of particular importance to me as the technical aspects and IT requirements were strengths of most of my classmates but areas in which I needed a bit more guidance and instruction. The camaraderie I experienced was amazing and beckoned memories of the most intense relationships I had experienced with fellow pilots during my career. The academic and intellectual requirements of the program were very intense but manageable if you put in the required effort and participation. I was amazed at the program's adeptness to translate one's military experience into the ability to succeed in the private sector. This is a key component of the MBV program.

The relationships I made during the program are still strong today and have benefited me greatly in the successes I've achieved since graduation. The intense bond and pride of being part of the Trojan family is a big part of my life today and will continue to be so going forward. In fact, I have developed business relationships with fellow Trojans and partnered in multiple business deals with them in the short time since my graduation. I cannot emphasize enough the importance and power of the Trojan network and I would encourage any military member to look seriously at USC's very unique MBV program. The benefits of this experience for those fortunate enough to be accepted will be life-changing and all but guarantee many future successes. If you are considering the MBV program, please reach out and call me. I would be more than happy to spend some time answering any questions you might have.

Fight on!

Erik Bateman, Cohort V

Cdr USN Ret

Benjermen Reyes—Cohort V

"Be the change you want to see." Most quote the longer version from Gandhi. I first heard and observed this from my last active-duty commanding officer, Lt. Col. J. P. Dunne, at 2nd Bn 14th Marines in Grand Prairie, Texas. This is a quote he preached, and you saw it in his actions. It helped me realize that, if I wanted to influence change, I needed to be it first and then create the environment and situation to influence others. I already did great things, but this quote captured what I was trying to do in an easy and relatable way. It became my catchphrase.

Growing up, most would say I lived a rough life. But my life was the only life I knew, and where I grew up, it was the norm. I was born and raised in the east side of Bakersfield, California. I was raised by a single mother whose immediate family helped her to raise her three kids. My Aunt Hopie and her four kids (later it became more), combined with my mother and her three kids, made up my immediate family. We lived together, ate together, slept four or more to a bed or on the floor, fought with one another, and, most importantly, were there for each other. That was family as I knew it and I wouldn't change it. This type of living created a fire that most do not understand and fueled me to be different and better. Living in poverty and not having the means or power to choose what you ate or *if* you ate is a helpless feeling. This is a feeling a lot of kids go through and it creates a cycle of selling and using drugs, joining gangs, and turning to violence to make money or get a break from life. I wanted a break, but I chose sports because I saw what the other side consisted of.

I went left when the norm turned right. I played sports and did my home-work. As easy as it sounds, the odds were against someone like me. It is hard to do homework at night when you do not have lights to turn on or you are hungry. It is hard to play sports when every day you need to walk a mile or more with all your gear in the heat or rain. I would wonder on the way to and from practice if *today* was the day I would get in a fight because of the area I walk through. It's hard to practice at the local park if that is where the drug addicts go to do drugs, where people go to fight, where you constantly get stopped and harassed by the police because you fit the profile. It is hard to write this because it seems bad, but I want others to see a glimpse of my life and the realities I faced daily. I do not want people to look at my life and feel sorry for me or think my mother and aunt did a bad job.

I was smart, but not the smartest. Where I excelled was sports. This was the break I chose. MVPs, trophies, medals, championships, special treatment—the works. I was not the best, but I was pretty good, especially where I came from. I must admit, being good was great, but it was paired with bad sportsmanship and attitude at first. I owe a lot of thanks and gratitude to guys like Jesse Toledo (my football coach), Raymond Gallegos (one of my best friends' dad), and Charlie Rodriguez (my cousin's grandpa). They were father figures to me when I didn't have one. They treated me as their kid, even though I was not. They gave advice, looked after me, and, more importantly, called me out when I needed it. I often wonder about the impact a full-time father figure could have had on me or if it's because I didn't have one that I am where I am now.

College was not talked about growing up, but I knew I needed it and wanted to go—I just did not know how. My mother did not graduate high school, my older cousins and brothers would not graduate high school either. I would be the first one to do this in my immediate family, despite being one of the youngest. Others chose a different life that consisted of the norm:

gangs, doing and selling drugs. But in doing so, they protected and pushed me away from it. This allowed me to achieve what I feel they did not believe they could. Because of that, I knew what I did was not just for me but for my family and others.

A month after I graduated high school, I left for boot camp. I wanted out, to get away and do something different with my life. The fire that got me to this point helped me excel in the military, as well. I picked up new tools for my toolbox along the way. I quickly and easily adapted to military life. It was easy for me. I was paid, I was fed, I had my own bed. I did everything that was required of me because I knew and was reminded of what it was like when I went back home. I took care of everyone I met in the military like I had been taken care of growing up. I showed respect, but I also called out disrespect. That last part got me in trouble starting off and at that point, I knew I had to pick up rank. Not for me, but to help get my voice heard for others. A few meritorious promotions later, I was a sergeant (in two-and-a-half years), staff sergeant (in six and a half), and gunnery sergeant (in a little over ten).

This takes me back to being the change you want to see. I felt my marines' voices weren't being heard, so I did everything in my power to make them heard and take care of them. That was my new fire. I wanted leaders to be held responsible. Now, my peers, I held them responsible. I influenced change at the units I went to by my actions. Several of my marines were meritoriously promoted and continued to achieve great things in their careers. Many would say I did a lot of great things during my career from promotions, awards, embassy guard, but I believe I should be judged by what I left behind. That is why my biggest accomplishment is the success of the marines I had beneath me. I learned a lot during my time in the military and, at almost nine years of active duty, I knew it was time for me to leave. At this point, I was married with a daughter whose birth I missed because I was deployed to Afghanistan. With my work, schedule, online school, and trying to balance marriage and family duties, something had to give. I gave so much to the military, my family and schoolwork were being neglected. I took advantage of an early-out program that would help me get back on the goal that I always had in mind: completing school and helping create change.

Right before I left the military I was living in Arlington, Texas, and my Aunt Hopie was diagnosed with stage four renal cancer. I came home to help.

She passed away six months later, and my world turned upside down. This was May 2015. I continued with school online, I made trips back to Texas for the reserves and my family. Ultimately, my wife and I chose to come back to Bakersfield a little earlier than planned. After getting my BBA, completing real estate courses, and getting licensed to sell real estate, I wanted to continue my education and I found the MBV program. My thoughts were: what *is* MBV? There is no way I have a chance. Can I do it? Am I ready? Is it worth it? And, lastly, I *need this.*

I knew I needed USC not for me but for my family, for the kids that come from where I did, to show others through my actions that they can too. Be the change you want to see! I want to show kids there is another way. I came, I saw, I did—they can too, and I will help in any way I can. I believe business can be the alternative to the path most are on (drugs, violence, etc.) in search of money to gain some power back in their life. Most don't know how to start a business, what it consists of, and what it can do. I needed to learn this in depth, and I wanted to learn from the best place I knew of, USC.

The MBV program is an educational experience that cannot be put into words. From the leadership, content, professors, and peers, it is an experience I had not been a part of in my life until I did. It helped me combine everything I had learned from my past and military experience, and supplemented it with personal growth exercises, discussions, and private-sector insight that pulled out the best version of me. Business knowledge, understanding of power, real-world experiences, negotiations, networking, and credibility are a small sample of what I received during my time there. I constantly refer to the information I gained there to accomplish my goals.

My aftermath is still in the works, but I know where I am going because of my time at USC. Since graduating, I have been selling real estate but focusing more on investing. I have consulted several friends, family members, and veterans who opened or are opening businesses. I am also in the process of teaching business at the high school or college level. My end goal is to help kids like myself learn and use the power of business to connect communities in poverty with the resources they need, and create a safer city. I will do this by implementing what I learned at USC and pursuing my ultimate goal of becoming mayor of Bakersfield. Be the change you want to see! Semper fi and fight on!

Marisol Sanchez—Cohort V

The personal story of my life and early development: Imagine a little girl (age eight) lying on her belly with her chin resting on her hands, her legs bent and her feet kicking at the ceiling. Now imagine her in a trance, three feet in front of a television set, where she sees and hears a rerun of Perry Mason investigating a case. Imagine this little girl doing this night after night for as long as she can remember. Well, that was me, captivated by how Raymond Burr carried himself while portraying the character of Perry Mason, a criminal defense lawyer. I have always enjoyed court and criminal justice television programs and movies. I have a strong belief in doing the right thing and in finding justice for those who have been wronged. I have always thought that one day I would grow up to be either a police officer, lawyer, or judge.

My decision to join the military: I graduated from San Diego State University with a major in criminal justice and a minor in sociology. I wanted to join the police academy upon graduation, but when I was unable to get through a mock obstacle course, I decided to go back to school and obtain a degree in the paralegal field. I enjoyed working as a real estate paralegal for many years, but one day decided to join an electric company as a property manager. The reason for that change was because the hours worked better with my schedule and the pay was not too shabby. I was treated very well by that company, yet I always felt that I was missing something.

Then, one day in 2011, a co-worker talked to me about joining the navy reserves, which caused me to look into paralegal options in the armed forces. As soon as I learned that March Reserve Air Base (MARB) had a position for me, I enlisted and have been working there for nearly eight years. I believe that my main reason for joining was not just to satisfy an indescribable itch but because after meeting the variety and high caliber of individuals that work in the military profession, I wanted to be a part of it.

Hindsight is 20/20, right? Had I known I would have loved the service and the people I serve with as much as I do, I would have signed up a very long time ago.

My education and the MBV program: As previously mentioned, I hold a bachelor's in criminal justice, I am an ABA-accredited paralegal in the civilian sector, and a seven-level paralegal in the AF reserves. I can't help comparing my acquaintances in the civilian workforce with those in my military life, and don't tell anyone, but I favor my vets like no other. I can no longer see myself in a work setting that does not have individuals with the value system, drive, motivation, and support that military personnel possess. Which is why when I learned about the MBV program, I stopped looking at regular MBAs and was eager to apply to the program. I was extremely excited and honored when they accepted me.

In the few months I was in the program, I learned an extraordinary amount about leadership, teamwork, networking, empathy, personal and professional success. I became extremely self-aware. The MBV program not only provided me tools to become successful in almost every aspect of my life, but it created a fire in my belly and provided enough fuel to keep it ignited for 100 lifetimes.

I liken the MBV program to a house of mirrors full of possibilities. Everywhere I turned, I either saw myself from a brand new angle or opportunities (for the first time) that were always there, but I was in too much of a rush to pay attention to. It was like I was looking through a distorted reflection and not seeing what others see when they look at me, and realizing that the person staring back at me had a lot of options and opportunities.

I wish I had more time to explain my house of mirrors in greater detail as I'd love for you to experience the excitement I felt every single day I stepped into one of our classrooms. Every day, an instructor gave me a valuable nugget of data, a student shared something important, a reading assignment enlightened me, a class exercise exposed me to new information, and so on. It was heavenly.

I can't sit here and say there isn't a price to pay for admission to this exclusive club because there were sleepless nights and a high volume of material to read as well as projects and assignments to complete. You might feel there is not enough time in the day to finish them. There might be times when you feel like throwing in the towel or when someone in your life may not be as supportive as you'd like them to be. You may also miss a few personal or social events in order to finish a work project or attend a team session, and the stress may feel intolerable at times. But I promise you, you will survive. No matter what the program throws at you, I know you will succeed. I can say this with confidence because I've been through it, and because I am you.

A desire to be a better version of me started in the classrooms of this program and has continued to grow every day since. I have been enlightened as to the kind of leader that I have been and the one that I'd like to become.

I'd like to share that during the program, I admired many if not all of my peers. Each person had a unique personality and variety of skills to offer and the beauty of it is they shared. They were not selfish and did not keep their gifts (talents) to themselves. They shared them with others. They shared them with me.

No one held back supporting each other or extending themselves to make sure we all made it through. I developed a fondness for all these admirable folks very quickly. A few weeks into the program, I felt like I had known everyone all my life. As I sit here in a deployed location, thinking of my experience in the MBV program, my heart warms. I am not a very sensitive person, but when I close my eyes and think about the instructors, program directors, staff, and my peers, I feel an enormous amount of joy and pride.

The MBV experience has been one of the best academic experiences of my life. When I think about the leadership and staff and the support they provided, I not only feel tremendous gratitude, but I have admiration for them. And when I think about the instructors, I feel fortunate to have had the opportunity to have learned from some of the best minds out there. The MBV has provided many opportunities for me and continues to have a transformational impact in my life and in the lives of those close to me. Prior to graduating from the program, I was offered employment by one of our mentors, as a director for a startup company. Upon graduating, my employer began to campaign for a higher-level leadership position for me. However, I had to deploy, but upon my return, I have zero doubt that the support will continue. Some of my staff members expressed that my accomplishment motivated them to seek higher learning. I received a substantial pay increase shortly after graduation. I have been offered employment through a LinkedIn contact and an MBV peer. I do not have tangible evidence, but I swear that higher-ranking officials see me differently based on how they treat me now. It's very interesting and, dare I say, gratifying. I have also learned that this academic accomplishment has given others in my immediate circle of family and friends encouragement to pursue their goals. This list of what the MBV program has afforded me is only the beginning, and I am excited to see what is next.

In regards to continuous improvement, I have never listened to as many audiobooks about business and leadership as I do today. Most of them are from the list of books recommended by the MBV instructors. I'd also like to share that I plan to pursue an entrepreneurship degree, from USC, and that during my time out here, I have had a chance to develop a couple of business plans that I plan to pursue when I return from my deployment.

Lastly, it's important to note that because of the MBV program, my network has grown tremendously and has already begun to bear fruit which you will learn the importance of in the program. The Trojan family is truly everywhere, even out here, halfway around the world (deployed after graduation). So, fight on, my brothers and sisters. Fight on like only you know how!

Allen Rodriguez—Cohort V

My professional journey began at the age of thirteen, when I began my first summer job for the City of Los Angeles's recreation parks department. I continued summer employment over the next three years in jobs including teen counselor, park assistant, and daycare provider for infants and toddlers. At sixteen, I began working for the San Pedro Fish Market—my first full-time job—and it was interesting. Still a high school student, I worked weekends until my senior year and had various responsibilities. In the fall of 1997, I enlisted in the Marine Corps' delayed entry program and went to boot camp in the summer of 1998, which then became my career for the next twenty years. When I graduated boot camp, I was still seventeen and had the intention of doing eight years. My intention turned into a career as an infantryman, which spanned several duties and ten deployments to various areas conducting many types of operations. I retired at the age of thirty-seven, in July 2018, which was the start of the MBV and now lands me in my current position as a supply-chain operations analyst with Vyaire Medical in Palm Springs, California.

After completing my MBV, one of my short-term goals was to apply for the EdD through USC. Completing a master's was one of my long-term goals post-military retirement. I was able to move this goal forward with MBV. The program helped prepare me for the challenges of civilian employment and I feel those lessons provided by Selbie, Fast, and Shariff have helped give me a foothold in the supply-chain operations sector. I say foothold, as I see now how large and challenging this area is. This has allowed me to align future short-term goals of possibly completing the master's in global supply chain and/or Six Sigma black belt. This alignment came in part from informational interviews with Arvind Bhambri and communications with Nick Vyas. I also have reached out to American Corporate Partners to participate in their veteran mentorship program. I have been in contact with my mentor for the last two months and am very pleased with the guidance James Riley has provided so far.

I found Nate Fast's class, power, and influence very interesting and insightful. The Laura Esserman case hit close to home. Short of being a big-shot surgeon, I too struggle with blue sky thoughts and the ability to express them clearly to others. That was one of my goals from the program and now a continuous project. Telling my story while erring on the side of brevity, I am happy with the progress I have made and that I continue to improve. Another application from his class that I was able to relate with was the opening slide to session one, Pfeffer, *"As long as you keep your boss or bosses happy, performance really does not matter that much and, by contrast, if you upset them, performance won't save you"* (Pfeffer). An infantryman in the Marine Corps is a results-driven profession, maybe more so. "What have you done for me lately?" We learn to thrive in what some may call the gray area. I've seen both, performance saving you, depending on the offense, or simply the latter, performance not mattering. Nonetheless, we must know our bosses and manage up.

A tactic also learned during the power and influence class comes from Keith Ferrazzi and the bold ask. I initially saw this as arrogance and taking a stab in the dark, but after discussing the case and the classroom lecture, I understood the chess move he made here. I now understand how this can be conducted in many forms to help me make a strategic move or simply to achieve status. I understand the importance of support roles—the right ones and the power they hold.

For years as a service member, the focus has always been on others and not me. I've placed the needs of others before mine, simply as a military leader by taking care of my marines. This came at a cost: strains on marriage, and time and events away from children. Being self-focused to me always seemed just selfish. This past year in MBV has put me into deep thought about my future. I did my time, twenty years. Along the way I've lost friends and family, been beaten mentally and physically, and all for a cause I felt was right, to serve my country. I don't regret my choice and never will. It has helped shape me into the person I am today. I realize that was just a chapter in my life that has now closed. I move forward with more of a focus, a self-focus. Not to be selfish, but to take the advice I gave so many marines: "no one is going to take better care of you than you." Being more self-focused will help me achieve my goals, all the while paying it forward to help others and focus on what's truly important. For me, that's my wife and kids. They supported me for years and now it's time to return the favor. Thank you to all the MBV staff, USC alum, and partners who helped build and support such a great program to help us veterans. I thank them all for their service and commitment to support us.

Fight on!

Hovig Margossian—Cohort IV

In 1979, my parents immigrated to the US from Lebanon with their newborn daughter (my sister) to escape the civil war. I was born a year later in Burbank, California, and my brother seven years after me. My father didn't speak English, or have much education or money, but he had a good work ethic and entrepreneurial drive that he used to establish a relatively successful business, which my mother later became a part of.

My parents raised us in the San Fernando Valley where we attended various public and private schools. I was a painfully unimpressive kid—unathletic and academically below average. If I had to compare myself to a movie character, it would be Jerry O'Connell's character in *Stand by Me.* I even looked like him. I was held back a year in junior high and had disciplinary issues throughout high school. My friends and I were misfits. We stole cigarettes from the teachers' lounge, ditched school, and caused trouble.

Despite failure in the classroom, I found success on the varsity football team. Football was a brief period of my life, but it made a significant impact in ways I wouldn't understand until years after. First, I was bigger than most of my peers in school, so I was always out of place, but football turned my size into an advantage that led the team to wins. Second, the coaches were mentors on and off the field and fostered a deep sense of value in their players. The combination of the two factors was a new experience that I hadn't known elsewhere.

The success was short-lived, however, as I was expelled for the second time in my junior year and decided to drop out. By that point, my closest friends were in juvenile hall and headed to prison. I began to reevaluate my life. After a failed attempt at community college, I decided that I wanted to do something valuable, but more suited to my nature and method of learning. The military was an appealing option that I often considered, with thoughts of escaping a turbulent environment at home and changing myself. The military paralleled football with its physically and mentally demanding nature. It was also about teamwork, but most importantly, it removed me from an environment that had little use for my strengths and didn't provide an appropriate teaching approach. As someone with disciplinary issues, many people found it odd that I chose to join the Marine Corps, the strictest among the branches of service.

Marine Corps recruit training was harsh, but it was a fresh start in many ways and removed all the noise and distractions from my life. Leaders were intolerant of excuses. They commanded accountability and integrity. After the initial stage of "what the fuck did I get myself into?" I began to enjoy the challenge. The accountability factor was a catalyst for self-reflection and I realized that choice is the fulcrum that tips the scale toward success or failure. I found solace in the company of other guys with similar backgrounds, looking for a purpose. We were Kilo Company, Platoon 3054. As the weeks passed, our confidence grew, the drill instructor's confidence in us grew. If we failed, we failed together, but we challenged each other to be better. We became so good at policing ourselves that we won most of the platoon challenges and became the honor platoon. It was the first time in a long time that I was right where I belonged. It was the beginning of a decade-long career in the Marine Corps. One and a half years after graduating from recruit training, America was at war.

My military occupation was as a helicopter mechanic, where I maintained UH-1N HUEY and AH-1W COBRA helicopters. Over the years, I learned lessons in work ethic and leadership and humility by example from tenacious non-commissioned officers and some of the military's most skilled and decorated helicopter pilots. Using them as the benchmark for success, I began to adopt some of their leadership traits.

My unit deployed twice to Iraq to provide close air support to ground units during Operation Iraqi Freedom. We operated at a high tempo, providing twenty-four-hour air support to ground forces in Fallujah, Ramadi, and surrounding regions in what was referred to as the Sunni Triangle. The marines put forth an extraordinary effort that led to our unit achieving an impeccable track record for mission accomplishment. We never dropped a mission. Those deployments were true testaments to the immense struggle and sacrifice for which marines have a reputation. It wasn't lost upon me that I would likely never be surrounded by as many incredible people performing at such a high level again. After ten years, the decision to leave the Marine Corps was a difficult one. The Corps was where I pushed past my limits and forged close friendships. It was where I developed the values and work ethic that set me up for the next challenge in my life, one at which I had previously failed.

After I was honorably discharged, I used the GI Bill to earn an economics degree. Academia was a far different experience later in life, one I was then ready for. A number of factors influenced my academic success, the most significant being that I was inspired by the people teaching the courses. Their passion and deep knowledge on the subject matter inspired a new thirst for knowledge and a sense of curiosity about the world. They were similar to the military leaders I respected in the sense that they were committed to their craft and led by example.

Being engaged with the content and classroom discussions drastically changed the way I performed. During my first year back as a full-time college student, I was pretty pissed off to see that my transcript said dean's list on it. Until then, any interactions with the dean were accompanied with detentions, suspensions, and expulsions. After a few minutes of research, though, I discovered that the dean's list is a good thing in college, and I'd be on it a few more times.

I also attributed my academic success to the fact that I lived alone, which made it easy to focus on academia and curtail my social life. The campus libraries at UC Santa Cruz became my base. Academia was a different challenge that required a solo effort, and it opened up a new world. Everything about it that I couldn't comprehend in grade school became crystal clear thanks to the structured approach I learned in the military, in addition to a peaceful household and absence of distractions.

Graduating from the university was a major milestone that was followed by the challenge of finding a job. I was thirty-four years old applying for entry-level positions to begin a new career in finance, where the majority of my peers were more than ten years my junior. (Also during that time, I found the love of my life and decided I didn't have enough on my plate, and that planning a wedding would make a fine addition to my priorities).

After multiple failed attempts to get a job in investment banking, I landed my first post-military job at an apparel company based in Los Angeles that was led by a talented and successful entrepreneur. The company was small in terms of employees, so my responsibilities ranged from sourcing third-party vendors, negotiating international shipping contracts, and implementing an ERP system, to counting inventory and packing boxes for shipping. It was a great place to learn about business and entrepreneurship and it complemented skills learned in the military of being resourceful and fixing problems on the fly.

After a year, I left the company to take a position as a research associate in commercial banking. Using available information on the internet and data-management techniques, I researched local companies to determine the market for suitable clients for the bank and then created targeted marketing campaigns for those companies. A few months into the job, the sales teams to whom I provided research and marketing began to see results in the form of open dialogue for multi-million-dollar lending opportunities. After my first year, I was promoted to an officer position and placed on the executive administration team, where I was responsible for compensations, production reporting, and assisting the division's sales strategy manager with managing projects for the commercial banking division. By that time, I was married and, shortly afterward, I started the MBV program at USC, Marshall School of Business.

The MBV program focused on transitioning service members. I wasn't a poster child for the program, as I'd been out of the military for six years and the majority of that time was spent earning my undergraduate degree. However, the program brought together two institutions that played a major role in defining my life: the military and academia. The year I spent in the MBV program would become another defining period of my life, surrounded by incredible people. In May 2017, I thought back to when I decided to leave the military seven years earlier. I had a GED at the time. School was always a challenge, but I knew it was something I had to conquer. That day in May, when I walked across the stage to accept my master's degree, I finally got to shake the dean's hand. I was on his list again.

Robert Plowey—Cohort III

As a major in the United States Army, I was privileged to have the responsibility of leading our soldiers in both garrison and through multiple deployments to Iraq and Afghanistan. The experiences during my time on active duty, both good and bad, shaped me into the person I am today. After over a decade of military service, I internalized a critical set of values. I conditioned myself to have true grit, to lead by example, and to do whatever I could for my team, while empathizing with their challenges. I understand that respect is earned, not given. Remaining humble, possessing loyalty and integrity, and realizing that tactical patience is critical even after we hang up our boots, are of paramount importance. It is commonly understood in the military that we must follow before we can effectively lead. This is most certainly the case when starting a new career in the civilian world, irrespective of age or previous military rank.

I made the decision to transition from the military in the summer of 2015. This was not an easy decision. It was a tremendous change in my life. All I knew in my adult life was military service. I had no idea what I wanted to do or how I was going to do it. I convinced myself that it was going to be easy to find a good job and start a new life based on my successful military career. I was wrong, and I learned this the hard way. It was pointed out in interview after interview that I was old (mid-thirties) and that I had no relevant industry experience.

Just like every other challenge I faced in my life, I positioned myself to fully understand the environment I was attempting to enter and trained myself to dominate it. The leadership, managerial, and communication skills I developed throughout my time in uniform served as a great foundation. However, I knew I had to learn the hard business and technical skills essential to interview well, earn a job, and thrive in a new career. I also had to master the interpersonal skills required to navigate the organizational dynamics of this different *corporate* culture. This drove my desire to pursue and attend the Marshall School of Business.

USC Marshall's MBV program is a collaborative environment in which fellow veterans share personal and leadership experiences and collectively learn under the direction of a distinguished faculty. My goal was to develop the knowledge base required to begin a new career and combine it with the leadership experience I gained in the military. This was an opportunity to become a leader, not merely a contributor, in a rigorous civilian workforce. Additionally, I wanted to embrace the Trojan family and culture to develop lifelong friendships with a strong community of peers and mentors. So, I applied to and joined MBV Cohort III.

USC Marshall invested in me, believed in me, educated me, and provided me with a network as well as a specific board of counselors to advise me how to identify and accomplish my goals. In the military, especially during deployments to Iraq and Afghanistan focused on the counterinsurgency fight, our ability to adapt and evolve to myriad mission sets and disciplines was essential to success. This led me to believe that the corporate world would work in the same manner. My previous mindset of trying to do or be *just anything, for any company* was thankfully shattered at USC. I realized that it was essential to find my *true passion*. The board of counselors mentored me and helped me set up and prepare for informational interviews, which enabled me to gather what I needed to make decisions for my future.

From that point on, I dedicated myself to developing the technical and interpersonal skills required to launch my new career. In addition to the MBV curriculum, I audited as many relevant undergraduate and graduate classes I could in order to further develop and improve my fundamental understanding of finance. I broke down the different roles one can have in the finance and consulting industries to see what appealed to me. I leveraged the Trojan network, made a significant amount of cold calls, and used LinkedIn to connect with individuals in those business sectors. I made my schedule as open as possible and filled my calendar with as many meetings and informational interviews as I could.

Jim Ellis, dean of the Marshall School of Business, came into our class one day and encouraged each of us to set up a meeting with him. At my first opportunity, I got onto his calendar to meet him and thank him for believing in me and my fellow veterans in the MBV program. He had experience in transitioning into new career fields, so I requested his advice and mentorship. Little did I know, this meeting would change the trajectory of my life. Shortly after our discussion, Dean Ellis introduced me to someone who saw something in me no one else did. This individual recognized the value of the intangible skills and leadership experience honed throughout my years of service. He decided to invest in me, mentor me, and befriend me. Ultimately, he helped me confirm that I was most passionate about real estate finance. At that point, I decided to pursue a financial analyst role in that discipline.

Starting in an industry that was completely foreign to me was like hitting the reset button. As I learned in the military, I knew it was important to be humble entering my career in real estate finance as a financial analyst intern. My peer group consisted of very bright and talented twenty-two and twenty-three-year-olds who were already armed with the necessary technical skills and real estate finance fundamentals learned in undergrad. They had gained valuable industry experience and knowledge through a series of challenging top-tier internship programs. I did not have these same experiences, as I had just transitioned from active duty. Needless to say, there was a very steep learning curve.

Just as I did entering the USC MBV program, I fully committed myself to proving my value. I was determined to learn as much as I could and help the team wherever possible. I recalled from my entrepreneurial class that it is important to find the need, and I used my ears and mouth in the appropriate proportions—I listened twice as much as I spoke. By listening and exhibiting tactical patience, I eventually found an opportunity to help one of the analysts put together the summer internship program. We were a great team. He had all of the technical knowledge and I knew how to develop and implement training programs. This small task was critical to my success, and I believe it is what earned me a full-time position. It also allowed me to develop a horizontal network with my analyst class of peers who were much younger than me. These relationships were key to gaining respect at my new job. Further, fulfilling this need helped me develop a vertical network that put me on the radar of the chief operating officer. He spoke with the firm's leadership and they decided to take a chance on me as a full-time team member. To this day, he is one of my closest friends and mentors.

The internship program also put me on the radar of the CEO and president of the firm. When I had the chance to meet these highly respected and experienced individuals, they each provided critical advice: 1) learn the numbers and technical skills, and 2) earn office-wide respect. I took this advice to heart and committed to it. Years later, I continue to remember this daily as I grow within the firm.

The rest of my story is still unwritten, but I remain dedicated to achieve my goal—to be a leader in my firm. As time passes, changes happen within companies, people come and go, and opportunities are created. After roughly four years of learning the technical concepts and earning the respect of my team members, I have developed a solid understanding of the firm's business lines and organizational dynamics. I am hyper-focused on continued learning as a student of the industry. It is important to understand the various economic, geopolitical, market, and demographic dynamics that can impact our business. I am committed to finding new ways to evolve and adapt as a person, professional, and leader. This mindset has enabled me to identify and find solutions to new needs that will impact change within the firm and allow us to better manage resources, invest in our team members, share relevant information, and serve our clients. My position evolved into a hybrid role focused on both the operational and transactional areas of the firm. After a substantial amount of hard work, years of learning a new technical skill set, a new industry, and a new firm, I am finally at a point where I can leverage the intangible skills I learned from the military. This was the original goal from the outset of my journey. My experience at USC helped make this a reality.

I am cautiously optimistic about my future and I will never quit until I achieve my goals. Finally and most importantly, I understand that the best way to say thank you to the Trojan family and my mentors is to pay their generosity forward and help others as much as possible. Without their support and the unwavering love and support of my family, I would not be in the place I am today.

CHAPTER 2

IT'S TIME TO ENGAGE!

Orientation and First Meeting

They began to file in, mostly through the rear door of the classroom. Some, however, chose the front of the room. Some were dressed in business attire, some more casually, but all seemed serious and somewhat uncertain. Some knew each other, but only a few, so the rest were aware they were meeting with strangers for the first time of the roughly forty-two more times they would enter this room, or a similar room, together. I could only guess at what was going through their minds as they entered, but any guess, I suspect, would be relevant. Some chose seats almost deliberately, but others followed into a vacant seat. Forty-two men and eight women in all (Cohort III). All had substantial military experience, and in our eyes as the admission committee, substantial leadership experience.

Once all were seated, the room became suddenly quiet, and as I stood to greet them, I was almost painfully aware that fifty sets of eyes were on me in a serious, but learned gaze with focus, seriousness, and deference to the head of the room. "Good morning," I said, and the words came back to me almost immediately and collectively! "I'm very pleased to see you all here this morning!"

There are two times during the year in this business that are joyful, filled with hope and expectation. One is at orientation and the second is at commencement. The first is fresh, enthusiastic, high energy, high interest, and filled with a high sense of expectation and readiness. The last is full of ritual and a sense of achievement, accomplishment, and the sadness of separation as well as the awareness that something important and painfully dynamic is over.

But this is the first time, day one. Introductions are painfully detailed, even though there are a few who rush, seemingly not wanting to expose too much too early, or not wanting to draw attention to themselves. As I reflect on this, it's almost like saying, "I know the rest of you are important, more than I am, so I won't take any more of your time." There is strong interest in who is in the room. What is each person's branch of service, rank, years of service? I always encourage personal comments, but at this first introduction, I'm more accepting of shorter versions. Later on the second day, I will ask that they pair up and introduce each other, and at that time, I insist they share through their new friend something positive about themselves that we couldn't find out in any other way. It takes an hour the first day to go around the room, and I never go row by row since each individual won't listen very well if there are only four or five left in their row before it is their turn. This means it's also the first time I ask for assertiveness. You choose when you want to introduce yourself. This can be awkward if several become assertive at the same time. But, I'm also introducing choice into the mix early along with assertiveness. For the first day, even with introductions, it's too easy to wait for instructions or to take your turn.

Each person must have their presence acknowledged by their new group of peers to whom, in a very short time, they will feel a strong connection through common membership. To me, this is the beginning of group identity in the cohort. Identifying with the group is a strong process dimension that will create support and cohesiveness. Early on in the life of the cohort, I intend to foster a spirit of collaboration rather than one of competition. This is important to me, as the argument for a spirit of competition in a growth-focused environment can be exciting, and can bring out the best in the participants. But I have chosen collaboration to build a strong peer group of support for all members regardless of age, rank, or experience. Also, if we are to develop a supportive and caring environment for learning and growing, each individual needs to know that the others are there for them and that we as a group, a community, are bonded together to support each person's success.

This is also the time where the issue of rank is acceptable to be identified. But in this year's work, one's military rank will not be discussed or determine any other structural relationships. We cannot control what people think and feel, but we can set expectations about not bringing past rank issues into this civilian classroom setting. What branch of service one has belonged to, we have found, is always a source of some fun with each other and an opportunity to exercise some well-known stereotypes humorously. This first student introduction session is placed intentionally at the beginning of orientation to immediately signal the importance of who is in the room along with program management and some faculty. The focus is on the participants and their awareness of, and ultimately their closeness with, the other veterans in the room who make up the roster of a new cohort.

Cohort III Classroom
Rich Schmitt Photography

Veterans as Non-Traditional Students

Another reason for doing an initial quick introduction of each student is to drive awareness that this is a face-to-face experience. Many of our students have extensive experience of several (or many) colleges, mostly online distance learning. We signal early that one's presence is not only mandatory, but valued. We value each person's choice to be with us each weekend, thus focusing attention on the use of presence that will contribute to our leadership discussion in the next weekend we're together. We go face-to-face throughout our ten months together during the weekends we are in session. Much work does get done between these biweekly sessions through the use of collaborative software and other electronic means, including entire communication boards that everyone joins, but when we're together, we interact, collaborate, and, especially, get to know one another fairly deeply within this short-term graduate program.

Non-traditional also means these are not students taking a break from top-tiered undergraduate programs to work a few years and then go on to other top-tiered schools for a graduate degree—in our case, an MBA. While we typically have a half a dozen or more military academy grads, most of the undergraduate schools our students attended are lesser-known schools and schools that have historically served the military population, many of which have branch facilities on military sites. What I have seen with these veterans is a strong personal commitment to learning, growth, and achievement, and in many cases, their undergraduate degrees are earned over multiple years and multiple schools. What comes through on their application concerning this long-term quest is determination and perseverance, often in the face of incredible adversity. Having been involved in different roles in graduate business admissions since 1975, I have great respect for intense commitment to achieve both certifications and personal growth.

Their veteran or active-duty status also makes them non-traditional students. In the total population, there is just over 7 percent who qualify as military veterans—between 20.4 and 22 million people—and their numbers decline every year. Adding active-duty and ready-reserve numbers together, there is still less than 1 percent of the population in service at any point in time in recent years, and these numbers are also declining. In 1980, 18 percent of the population qualified as veterans. With the draft ending in 1973, the military became an all-volunteer organization, with active military declining from 3.5 million in 1968 to approximately 1.3 million now. This means that veterans are becoming a smaller portion of those of a traditional age group for college. (See reports from the Department of Veterans Affairs, Department of Defense, US Census Bureau.)

Many universities are recruiting veterans and increasing their veteran-focused facilities and activities to attract them to both undergraduate and graduate studies. For example, at USC, we have about 1,300 veterans in both levels of higher education, with the recent addition of a Veterans Resource Center, and the creation of housing especially for veterans. I should also add that when we use the term veterans to describe our program, between 15 and 20 percent are active-duty military at any point within the cohort. We typically have three or four who separate from active duty during the ten months, but the rest continue on active-duty status either until their enlistment is completed or they are eligible to retire after twenty years of service. Active reservists and members of the national guard are often seeking their twenty or more years of service as well while attending the program.

In regular graduate or undergraduate-level classes, I would usually have about 5 percent veterans in each class, about two out of forty, which could set them apart from the other students. In the MBV program, all students are veterans, which creates a different sense of comfort and belonging for each student. It could be argued that the veterans would have a better chance for growth in a more diverse environment, but in this common background setting, the students understand their common values and experiences and go to work quickly with each other. And one of the common values is self-improvement, so there is much support for their personal growth and sharing of their transition difficulties. One of the other differences with this group is medical. Many have experiences with combat trauma, including PTSD, MST, and TBI, plus also sometimes serious hearing loss. While we don't directly address these conditions, we provide a supportive, caring context for learning and growing. The veterans are sensitive to each other, and will typically move in to assist where either requested or sensed. The cohort is both very caring and somewhat protective of each other even while humorously competing with each by branch of service or other typical (mostly) male challenges.

Challenges

Leaving the service and seeking civilian employment has several, somewhat unique, challenges, especially for those who have attained senior rank and status, those retiring after at least twenty years of service, and those who had no previous experience in the civilian work environment. The following are some of those challenges that are somewhat unique to military veteran students.

Uncertainty: Leaving a highly structured environment and life for one that has both enormous opportunities as well as unknowns is a major disruption. This uncertainty is heightened with a physical move and often a reintegration with one's family after long periods of deployment. The high degree of unemployment upon leaving the military is by itself a source of uncertainty.

Family issues: Depending on how much separation has been the norm in the family, reintegration, not just into civilian life, but with the family can be a daunting challenge. This factor isn't so challenging if the family has been able to live together in a number of the assignments, which is often the case. For example, garrison troops stationed in Camp Pendleton, California, may be part of a broader military family community on base compared to other service personnel subject to frequent deployment to combat zones or at sea. Health issues often exacerbate problems of reentry. Many of our students are either divorced or in second marriages, some of which are a result of long deployments and physical distance. Emotional distance within marriages is often cited as a problem when one of the spouses has been away for significant time and has been exposed to significant combat stress and is experiencing difficulty either feeling or expressing emotions with their spouse or family. In fact, even being open to this issue within families is difficult and requires acceptance that it exists.

Financial issues: Depending on whether one is retiring and receiving a pension or completing a tour of duty and enlistment, one is thrust into an uncertain state of financial security. Given the federal support for veterans in education, most of the cost of our program may be taken care of through their participation in some form of the GI Bill, e.g., the Post 9/11 GI Bill. And if they have full access to the Post 9/11 financial support, they also receive a housing allowance that financially is quite helpful, and if not replaced upon graduation from our program, leaves a large hole in their financial stability. The university now has sufficient funds to engage in Yellow Ribbon funding for as many students as can qualify. This is joint funding between the university and the Department of Veterans Affairs (VA) matching funds.

Losing one's identity and one's sense of membership: One's identity is much clearer in the military, especially in dress uniforms, where one's name, rank, years of service, unit, certified achievements, and recognition for one's contributions, achievements, and awards are highly visible. In working with veteran students, this loss of membership and identity is a difficult hurdle to overcome, and as was mentioned earlier, the cohort model helps create a unit of membership for all the students who share the common experience of military service. Often one's identity has been shaped by serious responsibilities and major leadership duties, and the abrupt ending of this as part of one's identity can create a sense of loss.

Translating one's military experience into civilian terms and meanings: One of the most difficult transitional tasks our students have is to translate their military service and resumé into a resumé that is understandable within a civilian environment and organizational culture. There are many characteristics of command that can directly translate to a civilian context, but it is difficult to demonstrate the relevance and usefulness of many military functions and jobs (MOS, military occupational specialty, categories) to a civilian and business context. We spend considerable time during lunches and evening career sessions assisting in the rewriting of resumés and translating experiences and competencies to fit a civilian audience and context.

Loss of sense of purpose beyond self: One of the three most frequent losses I hear from veterans is that of a sense of purpose beyond themselves. In an all-volunteer military, everyone has not only taken an oath to serve and to protect, but they have also voluntarily given up their rights to individualism and, to a certain degree, individual freedoms. This loss is replaced with a sense of purpose to which they commit themselves within a team context. Getting used to seeing one's own well-being as a sense of purpose is difficult at best, and many if not all our veteran students are either engaged in non-profits or volunteerism of some nature to another cause. Often, it is to serve other veterans and their needs subsequent to their military service. It's impressive to listen to these students discuss both their current community involvement as well as their aspirations to contribute more to their communities. This is one of the strengths veterans carry into the communities in which they live.

Health issues: Health issues, while frequent, aren't always visible. We know we have students with PTSD, MST, and TBI, but these issues aren't typically discussed. In some cases, it's fairly visible in the behavior of the student as they might withdraw from interaction or not attend class. But usually it is not visible to us, even though we conduct the classroom and cohort to provide support and caring for those in pain. A number of our students are supported financially through voc rehab, which provides full support for those who qualify with service-related disabilities. Usually, these disabilities aren't discussed, but we may know of them through our discussions of financial support alternatives at the beginning of the program. The university is well equipped to assist the veterans through the process of qualifying and accessing these various forms of financial support.

Loss of self-confidence: One of the least obvious consequences of leaving a position for which one is highly trained and proficient is the acquiring of new competencies during a time of uncertainty and search for a new employment commitment. This is often the case with more senior veterans, who have for some time had serious responsibilities and major achievements and contributions to their service, the country, and to those under their command. Couple this with the issue of uncertainty of direction, and the process to attain this level of competency often creates at least hesitation, if not avoidance. In addition, given that these students are non-traditional, developing confidence in intellectual achievement and cognitive and skill mastery over new material is difficult, and getting started is often slower than hoped for and slow relative to the speed of this ten-month, fast-paced program.

"The most positive change is the confidence we developed this year—namely, the poise that is required to be an effective leader in business." (Anthony Garcia, Cohort VI)

". . . MBV is a tremendous journey of professional development, personal growth, and bonding with an incredible team of cohort-mates, instructors, staff, and the many selfless individuals who support the program." (Troy Baisch, Cohort VI)

Different Times, Different Responses

As I mentioned in the prior section, losing one's military identity upon separation can be a challenge as one begins transitioning to a civilian identity. This identity issue has been more amplified with an all-volunteer professional military. When the military draft still existed, people could serve out their enlistment and still maintain their civilian identity to a certain degree. Jobs were held for servicemen and women when they returned, and since everyone was expected to serve, there wasn't such a distinction between those who did and those who didn't. The ready reserve and the national guard still retain closer ties to their civilian life than active-duty personnel. Also, if one is or was in an elite unit and in combat, one's identity was most likely stronger with one's unit and others within the unit than those who provide a supporting role. However, even a supporting role in a combat zone creates strong identity ties with one's unit and one's contribution within the all-volunteer military. Add these additional identity roles, units, and experience to the fact that at any point, only a small number of the American population is engaged in active duty or active reserve and national guard units. This creates a special class of membership and citizenship.

Being able to join an exclusive, all-military background cohort reignites many of these feelings of both membership and exclusivity. At the end of WWII, when service personnel returned home and there were not a lot of jobs waiting for them, the GI Bill provided much-needed support. The GI Bill of 1944 was signed before the end of the war to not only ease the transition home, but to provide assistance to veterans to head off the complaints after WWI that veterans weren't supported very well.

The GI Bill had a profound effect on colleges at the end of the war. At the peak of the use of the GI Bill in 1947, 49 percent of college admissions were veterans. Between 1940 and 1950, the number of college degree holders nearly doubled in the United States. (See Smith-Osborne 2019 for discussion of veterans' benefits.)

Veterans were also offered low-cost home and business loans to ease their transition in being able to own a house and prepare for a new career. And for those who were in the large group (almost half of the returning veterans) who wanted to start their own business, it offered help in securing financing. Of the 16 million returning veterans, 7.8 million used the education benefits from the GI Bill: 2.2 million went to colleges, and 5.6 million engaged in other training and other educational institutions. Because of the time the GI Bill took place, most of the bill's proceeds went to white men. The military wasn't desegregated until 1948 by executive order of the president, four years after the GI Bill was signed, so the proceeds were not evenly distributed to Black veterans and women veterans. Often, Black veterans wanting to go to college were referred to historically Black colleges and universities (HBCUs), thus swelling their student bodies to capacity. Because of Jim Crow laws in the south and discrimination in housing, Black veterans had difficulty buying homes and receiving business loans because the states had some control over how the GI Bill was administered and whether any protections were built in for non-white veterans. (See, for example, Weber 2017).

Today, under the Post 9/11 GI Bill and other legislation, there are almost a million veterans receiving educational benefits. There are 53 percent of these veterans in public institutions, 27 percent in private, for-profit schools, and 20 percent in private, non-profit institutions. In 2017, there were 4 percent fewer recipients of GI educational benefits than the prior year, but there is some speculation that a strong job market might have had some effect on this number. Four of the top ten schools in total veteran enrollment are for-profit schools with the University of Phoenix number one, with the largest number of veteran enrollments. They have held this position since Post 9/11 benefits began in 2009. The benefits favor public institutions in terms of limits on tuition assistance, so private non-profits have the smallest enrollment of veterans to date. As a private, non-profit institution, we work hard to supply as much of the total cost of the MBV program as we can, since the GI Bills were not intended to pay for all of the private-school tuition. We have been quite successful in making sure that all students have as much financial assistance as possible using such programs as Yellow Ribbon and scholarships.

Employment Issues and Assistance

One of the biggest issues facing veterans as they exit the military is the question of their next job or career. As mentioned earlier, translating one's military experience and specialty into civilian terms is at best difficult. Our experience in the program is that senior veterans have difficulty and identity issues facing the civilian job market because of the feeling of starting over. A forty- to forty-five-year-old veteran typically can't begin at an entry-level job, and the pay and status issues would not match their most recent experience in the military. A senior officer or senior NCO who has had considerable command responsibility and recognition will find it difficult to integrate into any industry at some lower level.

> "Veterans taking entry-level jobs and starting over in education may create dissonance with previous military roles equated with clear status and identity, and this may have a negative impact on veterans' self-esteem" (Keeling, Ozuna, and Millsap 2019).

The employment numbers aren't bad, however. In 2012, post-recession, the unemployment rate for veterans was 12 percent, 9 percent in 2013, 7.2 percent in 2014, and 5.7 percent in 2015 for males and 6.4 percent for females (Keeling, Ozuna, and Millsap 2019). Median salaries comparing veterans with non-veterans have an interesting twist. Controlling for demographic variables, male veterans' median income was 11 percent higher than their non-veteran counterparts, while female veterans' median income was 14 percent higher than their civilian comparison group (Batka and Hall 2016). This is good news for our students to know that, on a comparison basis (controlled for age and experience), veterans actually earn greater incomes, in general, than comparable civilian groups their own age.

There has been a big effort on the part of many corporations and cities to hire veterans, and many of those jobs are lower-level jobs. However, the current culture is demonstratively more helpful to veterans in their search for employment than in prior years, especially than for the returning Vietnam veterans. While specific groups will experience difficulty in finding jobs and careers, the aggregate numbers are strong. What unemployment numbers don't expose is how many of the potential workforce are no longer looking for work, and how many veterans are underemployed.

With a full-time career service director, we have a strong focus on the educational component of job preparation, exposure to career opportunities within the economy, and individual mentors for the veteran students. Ninety days after graduation, 88–91 percent of our graduates are employed. This outcome will be discussed later when we do some summing up. The difference, however, between our student cohorts and full-time MBA students is that most of the MBA students are seeking entry-level jobs. In the MBV, 30 percent of our students were hired into new jobs, 29 percent started new ventures (does not mean they are not employed in addition to their new venture), 15 percent were promoted in place, and 33 percent stayed in the job they were in when entering the MBV, including some active-duty personnel. With the average age of 35-36 in the program, some of the veterans have been out of active duty for some time, so are looking to continue to do what they are doing or to advance within their current employer's organization.

Our career service director develops and runs between forty and fifty career events a year, and the students get trained by career professionals in resumé writing, networking, interviewing, and self-assessment. Other programs they may attend, for example, are dining etiquette and dress for success programs that draw comparisons between military and civilian expectations.

The program spends all available time outside curriculum instruction on career search activities, including increasing personal and professional self-awareness, strengthening networking skills and awareness of career opportunities, learning to focus strategically on career opportunities, enhancing job-search strategies, developing positive interviewing skills, and how to negotiate and close on a job offer. An additional piece to this process is for alums to return in the future cohorts and share their experiences and provide suggestions to the next group of veterans as to how to transition successfully.

The ease with which the program attains volunteers to assist with the veterans' growth and reintegration issues has been amazing, and a turnabout from historical perspectives from prior conflicts. Business leaders, primarily from the southern California region, are eager to engage with our students and assist their transition wherever possible. Not only are there business executives, owners, and managers in helping roles, we have been fortunate to have some successful senior business owners act as individual advisors and mentors.

Additional Learning Community Values

I introduced the learning community concept earlier and discussed a process issue of paying attention to how well we do as a learning community and where we need to improve. At the beginning of the program, we spend considerable time with the students, developing their own expectations and standards regarding how they want the community to be, and what the standards are to which they will hold themselves accountable. It is important to develop some self-control and self-monitoring values and expectations for our spending a year together, and how we want to represent the cohort, program, school, and university. I've included the set of expectations from Cohorts III and IV as examples of the kind of work the students do with each other. We ask at the end of the exercise that everyone agrees to be held accountable individually and as a community to perform against these values.

As program management, we are explicit about our expectations and standards, especially as they concern academic integrity, but also attendance and participation in both the life of the cohort and within the classroom. While not much time is spent in actual monitoring of these expectations, the fact and process of creating this agreement is where the value exists. Our intent is to create awareness at the community level, as well as self-awareness and self-monitoring. The process is also a way to be more inclusive and enabling of both their contributions as well as their personal standards of decorum. We have had instances of reminding individuals or the cohort of some specific agreement around our behavior, but not many. The more difficult situation is to get agreement about general and interpersonal behavior when we are not in session, but together socially or otherwise informally

MASTER OF BUSINESS FOR VETERANS
COHORT IV
Expectations and Aspirations

"We, the members of Cohort IV recognize that excellence and success can be achieved through efficient teamwork. The heart of what we believe to be the foundation for our success is embodied in four core values that we agree to uphold and exemplify, starting with focus which is the pillar principle that aligns our vision:

I. Focus

i. We commit to a higher purpose than self and dedication to excellence.
ii. We will be present, aware and engaged in all sessions.
iii. We will be the model of accountability and leadership.

II. Open-minded

i. We will be good listeners.
ii. We will be transparent, challenge bias, embrace growth, and give honest feedback.
iii. We will be courageous, creative, and trust our abilities.

III. Unity

i. We will be cohesive, supportive, encouraging, and make lasting relationships.
ii. We will build the MBV legacy and leave USC better for our having been students here.

iii. We will practice togetherness, be team-oriented, and be 80 in 80 out.

IV. Respect

i. We will use the 'golden rule.'
ii. We will respect our differences and our different opinions.
iii. We will give constructive criticism."

COHORT III
Our Expectations and Commitments

"Members of Cohort III have agreed that the following expectations and principles will guide and direct our behavior as graduate students in the Marshall School of Business. We will strive to be leaders and role models in both academic and professional communities. While we remain considerate of our impact on others while striving to achieve our personal goals, we will always be mindful of creating a positive learning environment to advance the common good of the cohort.

We commit to living up to the following expectations and principles:

We will hold mutual respect for each other regardless of our differences and opinions. We will not belittle nor bully others in the cohort.

We will sacrifice for each other and invest in one another's growth and well-being.

We will be supportive of each other's efforts and goals and encourage each other.

We will express empathy and understanding with each other, and maintain courtesy in the classroom and our relationships.

We will operate out of teamwork and cooperation, and learn from one another.

We will be open-minded, flexible, and slow to judge each other.

We will create a safe environment for expression while maintaining confidentiality.

We will commit to working hard as individuals and as a group.

While committing to working hard, we will express enthusiasm, but always have fun!

We will support open and honest communication and act in a civil manner while resolving conflict.

We will resist forming social cliques that might hurt the overall cohort dynamic.

We will focus on personal growth involving moving beyond our comfort zone.

While increasing our marketability, we will represent the MBV program and USC positively.

We will hold ourselves and each other accountable for our performance, agreements, and conduct.

We will fully take advantage of opportunities offered to us by USC and engage in activities offered by the university and others.

There is not a rigid dress code, but we expect good judgment in balancing comfort with professionalism.

> We ask that the faculty challenge us academically while providing an excellent program in graduate management education; we ask that faculty be accessible to provide guidance, feedback, and support."

In both cohorts, the values of teamwork, support, respect, and accountability are apparent. In Cohort III's agreement, there is an awareness that social cliques may form in groups of this size and with different service identities and rank differences, and a recognition that the need to continue to resist such sub-groupings is important for the overall cohesiveness and integration of the cohort. The importance of involving the entire cohort into setting and maintaining these integrating principles as a program design feature is to have both program management and the entire student cohort feel responsible for the strong dynamics of the cohort and the values of the community that support our commitment to everyone's success and well-being.

> "The cohort: the most remarkable change overall, is one I've noticed more recently. We went from a large group of individuals to a cohesive MBV family who care about each other very much." (Sion Detra, Cohort VI)

Values of Contribution, Assertiveness, and Taking Initiative

These three values can be compared between military and civilian culture. One is the difference between compliance and contribution. Another is between showing deference and being assertive. A third is waiting for instructions versus demonstrating initiative. I'll discuss those briefly here, but they also play a big role in our leadership expression and growth.

In most organizational contexts, the idea of compliance with expectations, directions, and policy, rules, and procedures is basic. However, civilian employers are going to expect, if not demand, contributions from their employees, in addition to merely compliance, especially if they are hired with advanced degrees or certifications. The demand to add value from day one is often overlooked when candidates are job hunting. Hiring someone because they fit the culture and demands of the job implies that they can make a contribution to the mission with their talent, experience, and education. And in the military, the consequences of not obeying a lawful order can be serious, so compliance is primary, but going beyond compliance to genuinely make a contribution to the achievement of the mission is expected in most organizations.

The second and third comparable values are to be appropriately assertive and take the initiative to solve problems and to make a contribution. Veterans have learned to give deference to higher-ranking members, and this behavior is valuable in civilian work as well, but not to the exclusion of taking initiative and taking action where and when those skills are appropriate and demanded by the context, the mission, and one's role.

How deference, waiting for instructions, and compliance play out in the classroom will determine how much transformational growth and competence development each student achieves. We encourage students to speak up, participate, analyze cases with others, and be open with ideas and opinions to create a dynamic learning environment in which students express themselves and learn to build on each other's ideas and comments to reach better outcomes and solutions. Setting personal goals to be more assertive in the classroom is a positive step to change one's own dynamics and the dynamics of the classroom. Compliance, giving deference, and waiting for instructions can be seen as passive behavior that is detrimental to achieving organizational goals, and in the classroom, learning and growth. Other design issues, such as the classroom arrangement, are also part of this discussion as we encourage strong participation and assertiveness that takes into account the other students in the room. (See Hae Hwang's story at the end of Chapter 3 for a strong example of personal change in this dimension.)

Other values, both at the individual level and at the community level, will be discussed within the chapters on leadership. For example, issues of courage, humility, integrity, empathy, service, and support for other members of the cohort will be discussed in chapter four.

Other Early Experiences Intended for Community Development

Once we're into the first semester and the students are familiar with one another, we take the next step in team—or in this case, community—development. And, for this purpose, we go outside of the classroom, changing the learning dimensions, bringing the entire group together as one, and engaging in a day-long ropes course. This type of learning is intended to be quite different from a regular classroom environment and employs a different learning strategy. Rather than explain the purpose and approach, then the theory, and then the practice, experiential learning reverses the sequence and engages students in an activity that is compelling and challenging, and then debriefs the experience, distilling learning from it, engaging students first, asking them to describe their experience, offering suggestions to those following them for success, and then much later, possibly, attempting to identify where the learning might be used in other contexts.

Other purposes are actually to have some fun together, get to know each other better outside the classroom, and interacting so everyone benefits. And in this case, it is the cohort as a whole that will benefit from engaging, observing, debriefing, and developing closer bonds with its members. Additionally, the experience will assist in their identifying with the cohort, and with the cohort as a unified community.

Pre-event assumptions run the spectrum from "this will be fun, and outdoors, away from the classroom" to "this is trite; everyone does this," "I've done many of these; no problem," "these events are a waste of time," and "I believe I know everything I need to know about leadership and teams, so what can this teach me?"

> "I thought it would be another day of mundane physical adventure, not the spiritual and emotional gauntlet it proved to be . . . but after enough obstacle and ropes courses, I thought I'd seen them all. I was wrong." (Alex Hesselgeser, Cohort III)

> "The beauty of the MBV program is that the academic rigor is accompanied by experiential learning and team-building events that give

> students the opportunity to apply what they've learned in practical, hands-on exercises and projects that help reinforce the learning and provide context on how it can be applied in the real world." (Troy Baisch, Cohort VI)

Chapter 1 began with a story of volunteers from the MBV program (Cohort VI) designing and running a four-hour outdoor experiential training session with the freshmen honors students (global leaders program) and the topic of military leadership. In Chapter 5, I include the outline from the first MBV/GLP experiential session that took place in October 2017 (Cohort V), which spells out the leadership approach the Cohort V volunteers used to introduce the freshmen to military leadership principles and values. This document is a straightforward outline of four key principles: humility, sacrifice, tactical competence, and ownership/accountability.

This collaboration was about three years in the planning, and Professor Carl Voigt, the faculty member in charge of the GLP Program, was able to provide dates for us in both 2017 and 2018 to conduct this outdoor low ropes experience for the freshmen honors program. Professor Voigt is a good colleague of mine in Marshall's management and organization department, and we both agreed that having our veterans share their leadership expertise and experience with freshmen would be a valuable addition to both programs. Our program had no difficulty obtaining volunteers. About two dozen Cohort V students participated, led by Andre Gomez and Bruce Voelker (you'll meet Bruce later in the book), and about thirty-two veterans participated the following year, led by Nick Seidell. Travel distance made little difference for the veterans attending. The first year, students came in from all over southern California, including San Diego, China Lake, and Palmdale; in 2018, one student traveled from Louisiana (on his off weekend) to participate. Our problem with the veterans who join the program is not how to get volunteers to contribute to special events, but how to manage the large numbers of them who want to be involved, sometimes more than we need. This phenomenon existed throughout the first six years of the program, and in my opinion, was one of its most visible and unique characteristics.

The following is a statement by Cohort III graduate, Bob Plowey (introduced in Chapter 1), using the metaphor of life as a marathon to illustrate his MBV experience. I like the marathon as a metaphor, and use it frequently in the classroom for both what we do regularly, and also how to prepare for the long haul of living, working, contributing, growing, and staying in the arena and on the field of play.

> "The marathon of life we are running is just about to begin, and the MBV program was the best training regimen for race day. As I loom across the start line, nervously waiting to begin the first leg of the race, I reflect on July 24, 2015. Our orientation seems like yesterday. Our last class session took me back in time and allowed me to reflect on my personal growth and the growth of our cohort since that day. WOW! As I blink and open my eyes, my tunnel vision subsides. Moments before the shotgun start, I notice that I am surrounded by Ty, Vinny, Alex, Destiny, Greg, Danny, Ray, Kiefer, Michael, Robert, James, Dennis, and Hae. Then I notice Bryan and Moe standing on the sideline holding a huge MBV sign and cheering us on, and I realize I am not alone in this race. This bolsters my confidence, and I am ready to run!" (Robert Plowey, Cohort III)

Jackie McKenna—Cohort VI

I was a military brat from the day I was born until my dad retired from the army during my senior year of high school. Back then, I was a reserved kid, partly due to my upbringing and introversion. Like everyone else, I had leadership potential, but in my case, I lacked confidence and preferred to be in the background.

After high school, I attended college at a local university thanks to an ROTC scholarship. Like many college students, I did not know what I wanted to be. Thus, I opted to listen to others whom I thought knew better than I did and declared nursing as my major. By the end of my sophomore year, my disinterest in nursing and ROTC came to a head, and I was ready to leave both programs. After external pressures and persuasion, I remained in college and selected sociology as my major as it would allow me to complete a degree within four years and commission as an army officer.

Throughout college, I slowly pushed out of my comfort zone as I was entrusted with a set of responsibilities that helped me develop my leadership skills. Toward the end of my undergrad, I gained some self-confidence; my eight-year military career would further increase my confidence level and my leadership abilities.

It wasn't until I was twenty-six and twenty-seven years old that I was truly challenged as a leader. I was a newly promoted captain, company commander to 120 individuals, and in the midst of my divorce. I was challenged mentally, emotionally, and physically. After command, I was burnt-out. Realizing I needed a remedy, I began to read self-help books to feel whole. As I became self-aware of both my faults and strengths, I reached a point where I needed to leave the military.

I am forever grateful for my army career and experience as I believe I am a better person and leader for it, but I thought I could put my interests and skills to good use in another profession. After several months of introspection and reflection, I submitted my request to transition from the military to pursue a second undergrad in computer science.

Attending school full-time was thrilling. However, after the second semester, I felt a sense of emptiness, a lack of purpose, which I equated to not having a job. Additionally, I began to question myself on whether I was a leader. Did my military uniform make me a leader? Did I behave a certain way in the army because if I did otherwise, I would have been judged and seen as a poor leader?

At the end of my second semester, I stopped attending school to become an analyst. While an analyst, the gnawing thought of my not being a leader led me to challenge myself in my role as an analyst. After three months, I was given the title of deputy team leader. A month later, I put in my resignation due to the work environment and mundane work. For the second time, I decided to pursue computer programming, but instead of the traditional university route, I would attend a four-month coding boot camp. I thoroughly enjoyed it. I felt appreciated. I had the opportunity to be creative and collaborative within a team while developing new ideas that could help people and on some occasions be the leader of the group. After the completion of my coding boot camp, I started my first position as a software developer.

After a couple of months of feeling stagnate, I decided to pursue a master's degree in information technology management. My initial plan was to attend an online program through Northwestern, but a couple of months prior to my first class, I saw an online advertisement for the MBV program and signed up for the information session.

Afterward, I submitted my application because I believed the MBV faculty were more interested in my success, unlike Northwestern's faculty. I wish I had attended the MBV program during the first year of my transition out of the military. It helped me civilianize myself as I learned about the job-search process, tools, and networking, while gaining business acumen. I enjoyed the program's emphasis on leadership as I've strived and struggled to be a good leader. For me, the MBV program was another support group of highly skilled professionals who had the knowledge, connections, and experience to elevate me and my cohort to the next level, whether it be from pursuing a higher-paying job to higher education. In the end, the MBV program was a door that opened itself to many other doors.

It has been one month since I graduated from the MBV program. It's also been one month since I started my new position as a product manager. It's too early to say what will happen next in my life or career, but I will continue to learn how to be a proactive leader and a good person. I have had my ups and downs, my pivots and divots, but the one thing I believe will be unchanging is my interest in being a leader.

Lou Moreira—Cohort III

I am 38,000 feet in the air as I write this—flying to NYC for a job interview with one of the biggest hedge funds in the world. I ask myself, how did I get here? Well, it sure has been a wild ride in this thing we call life. My name is Lou Moreira, and I am a proud USC Trojan, MBV Cohort III, aka the GOAT. My life started in Portugal, where I was born. After waiting patiently for seven years, my parents finally got their green cards and immigrated to Boston in 1989. I was five years old. Growing up in Boston and spending my summers in Portugal made for a very fun childhood, but the one thing missing was never getting to play organized sports. For as long as I could remember, I counted down the days until high school to finally play football. It was what I looked forward to the most.

Playing football was everything I had thought it would be, and by my senior year, I had been offered several athletic scholarships. I played receiver, I played safety, I was even the punter. In my senior year, I made all-state. But I knew I wouldn't play football in college as football was not the priority—I had fallen in love with track and field. It was during my sophomore year during pre-season track practice that Coach Dickerson caught me jumping over hurdles just for fun. He stopped me and said, "Luis, do that again," and so I did. The rest is history. I went on to win four state championships (indoor and outdoor) and finished sixth at nationals my senior year. My greatest accomplishment in athletics—breaking the Massachusetts division 1 high school state record in 2001—still stands today, almost two decades later. Every March I go online and check (because we can do that now) and see that, yet again, I am holding it down. It always puts such a smile on my face.

Out of high school, I took a track scholarship to Northeastern University in Boston. I had a terrific freshman year, winning rookie of the year and being awarded for scoring the most track meet points at the conference championships. Although this felt gratifying, something was not right. I was having trouble with my grades and had zero drive to be there. I gave it another go, and it was all downhill from there.

Here is when things changed. Later that fall semester, I was watching Dick Wolf on television. He was talking about the troops in Iraq and Afghanistan, and that's when it hit me. Watching footage of American soldiers fighting the War on Terror made me realize all along that's what I wanted. The subconscious mind is an amazing thing—suddenly it all made sense. Throughout my childhood, I watched every single war movie and loved them all. There were so many good ones: *Forrest Gump, We Were Soldiers, Platoon, Hamburger Hill, Full Metal Jacket, Saving Private Ryan, Black Hawk Down.* I would always tell myself after watching, "I would so do that for my country if needed." But it never hit me to do so. Running track in college was all I wanted. Serving in the military never crossed my mind—let's be real, I was too busy winning state championships. But in all reality, watching the troops on television was the wake-up call I had been waiting for.

This is when things get real. In January 2006, I walked into an army recruiter's office, and I said, "I want to fight the War on Terror and serve my country, and, oh, I also want to jump out of planes like my dad."

The recruiter looked at me a long time and realized I wasn't joking. He replied with "OK, son, we can do that. What's your name?"

Three weeks later, I was shipped to basic training and, in one year, I had boots on the ground in the Taliban stronghold of the Helmand Province, Afghanistan. Back up quick—I graduated basic training as the soldier leader of the cycle, nominated over 350 basic trainees, and was acknowledged by the commanding general. But of course my mother had to ruin that by embarrassing me in front of him, with all her kisses and joy: it was a dead giveaway I was a momma's boy.

From there, I went to airborne school, wrapped that up, and got assigned my first and only duty station: the 82nd Airborne Infantry, Ft. Bragg, North Carolina—also known as the center of the universe. All we did was train and deploy for the next six years. I was a tough private and got in trouble often, but my leadership was able to figure me out. Physical punishment, mopping parking lots, weekend duty—none of it had any effect on me. That all changed when my corrective training was to not allow me to do PT. Yup, my sergeant took away the gym, and it worked like a charm. Watching my battle buddies getting ready for the gym drove me crazy. Watching my battle buddies get back all pumped up ate me alive. This went on for an entire week—basically forever,—and I changed for the good. It was like night and day.

Fast forward six years: I had made sergeant in three years, staff sergeant in four, and was getting out of the army with twenty-seven months of combat and a bronze star. I never expected to receive a bronze star—as far as I knew, I was just doing my job.

After getting out of the army, I did not go back to Boston. Between my best friend and comrade and a girl (why is there always a girl involved?), I moved to Dallas. I had grown so much from my time in the military. I became a true leader, I was responsible, I was driven and had goals to conquer. As I transitioned back into civilian life, I went straight to work. The GI Bill was too good to be true, and I will forever be grateful. After knocking out my bachelor's from Southern Methodist University in applied physiology in three years, I still had one year left on my GI Bill, but hold on. During my time at SMU, I started a personal training business from the ground up, solely through grassroots marketing. Between college and working as a trainer, bodybuilding was my pastime. I competed in several bodybuilding competitions along the way and managed to win the Texas State Bodybuilding Championships, earning the title of 2014 Mr. Texas— and that is pretty cool. Bodybuilding resonated back to my time in combat. Any downtime we had during our re-fit between missions, I was pumping iron. Most of the guys played video games, but that was never my cup of tea. My leadership never had an issue with my whereabouts—I was either on my cot reading bodybuilding magazines, in the chow hall eating, on the phone calling Mom, or demolishing the weight room like an absolute savage. This planted a seed in my head that I would compete in a bodybuilding competition after getting out of the army.

By December 2015, I had finished my bachelor's and did not want to pursue bodybuilding any further. In all reality, I was sick and tired of not being able to wash my own back. Being an athlete was all I knew, and I refused to think that I would just find a corporate job and let life go by. I pondered for some time and could not figure out what to do. The NFL was out of the question as I hadn't played football since high school. But something special happened as I was watching the Winter Olympics: the sport of bobsled. I saw these guys, they were big, they were fast, they were explosive—right up my alley. And the craziest part was that I already had a friend on the team. Years prior, he had attempted to convince me to try out for the team—he'd even mentioned the Army World Class Program, where they have active-duty soldiers in various sports, bobsled among them; however, I was not interested when he proposed it. Getting out of the army, getting my education, and competing in bodybuilding was my focus.

But after watching it on television years later (I'm seeing a trend here with lifetime realizations through television), I said, "That's it!" After spending some time on Team USA's website, I saw they had a combine for tryouts, and I immediately began training for it. I had to lose weight and re-learn how to sprint again from being a bulky bodybuilder. It was a very difficult road, but I managed to get picked up on the Team USA Olympic Development Program. My rookie season came in the winter of 2015–2016, which was also the start of the MBV program.

Let's back up here. Remember the girl I told you about? Right. She introduced me to MBV. Although I had one year left on my GI Bill, grad school was never on my horizon. After applying, I got accepted and attempted to juggle the MBV program and my rookie season as a bobsledder. You're probably thinking that I am nuts and that there was no way I could simultaneously do both, and you're right. It was extremely difficult. I missed lectures due to training and races and finished my first semester with a 2.9 GPA, putting me on academic probation due to not having a 3.0 average. Taking on the challenge of managing both endeavors was overwhelming, but there was no way in hell I was going to quit or not succeed. The start of the MBV program was nothing short of amazing. Right away during orientation, I met so many amazing men and women. I mean, how cool is this, I get to be in a top grad school business program with all veterans. As my rookie season came to an end in February 2016, I was 100 percent all hands on deck focused on MBV. I didn't miss a single session and finished the spring semester with a 3.4 GPA, graduating with all of my classmates in June 2016.

My experience with the MBV program will be one that I will talk about for the rest of my life. It was by far the best educational experience I could ever get. It taught me how to deal with real-life experiences that I would one day face in the corporate world. But the most crucial takeaway I got from the MBV program was how to convert my military leadership experience and qualities, and how to transition them into a corporate environment. So many veterans get out of the service and have no idea how to do this. Then they get lost and go down a rabbit hole of depression, lose their sense of purpose, and immediately question why they even left the military. Also, I met and made some lifelong friends. I still visit Los Angeles every year to catch up with them and attend the MBV tailgate.

A last note on bobsled. After graduating from the MBV, I was then 100 percent focused on making the 2018 Winter Olympics. After moving to the Olympic Training Center in upstate Lake Placid, New York, my training was better than ever, and I officially made the National Bobsled Team for the USA. I spent the next two years competing and going on tour with the team. My best placing was eighth at the World Championships in Kogneeze, Germany, in a team event. This is where my heart gets crushed. Although I qualified for the 2018 Winter Olympics, I did not travel with the team and compete. They left me out, and I will forever have that bad taste in my mouth. But I must say that I am at peace with it and that, with time, all wounds do heal.

February 2018, I am officially retired from a short bobsled career as a professional athlete and have come to terms with the idea that I will find a job and work for once. A resumé is a person's billboard, a reflection of the applicant in the eyes of the reader, and I felt that without work experience my resumé was very strong and the anchor to it was my MBV degree. Feedback from potential employers all revolved around my grad school experience. I loved being asked about it, I'd instantly light up and memory after memory would come to mind. From role-paying HR situations in communications class ("You can't talk to people like that—there's something called HR"), I learned so much and had tons of laughs along the way. From all of our group work and presentations to dissecting case studies, to creating entrepreneurial business plans and learning how to manage a balance sheet, the curriculum was a home run. I gained so much knowledge from every single course, and the experience overall was astounding. It is still carrying over today.

My first job didn't last long, it was a B2B inside sales job and I was miserable. Chained to a desk composing emails and making cold calls made me very unhappy. I was the saddest I'd been in years. From there, I found an outside sales position through LinkedIn as a remodeling consultant for an exterior remodeling company. That is where I currently work, and landing the job was easier than stealing candy from a baby. Sitting down for an interview, I was yet again asked about my graduate school program. Between talking about my military experience and my time with the USA bobsled team, nothing came and sounded as professional as when I elaborated on the MBV program. It has been almost a year in this role, and ultimately I am not happy. At the end of the day, I do not see myself with this company in five or ten years and want to take the necessary steps to have a fulfilled and prosperous career.

That puts me right back to this very seat, 38,000 feet in the air. After landing a line of communication via LinkedIn with a top hedge fund and several Skype interviews, they decided to take a shot on me and fly me up for an in-person interview. Even though I have zero experience in the industry, my leadership experience, my perseverance to see a challenge and conquer it, and ultimately my MBV graduate degree in business propelled me to get this opportunity. I am more confident than ever and feel that I can work hard, learn, and add value to this firm.

If you made it this far, it means I have grasped your attention and in fact, my story is interesting. Thank you for reading. If you are wondering if you should apply for the MBV program, it is really simple. IT IS AN OPPORTUNITY OF A LIFETIME!

Fight on!

Lou Moreira

Jhoana Crespo—Cohort II

There have been multiple experiences in my life that have shaped who I am today. For starters, I was born in El Salvador, where I was raised by my maternal grandmother and grandfather until the age of eight, at which point my mother petitioned for us and brought my brother and me to the United States. Although I was young, I still remember what my life was like in El Salvador, and because of that, my appreciation for what my life is today will never leave me. I understand struggle, challenges, and difficulties because I lived it first hand and, if nothing else, that experience helps me maintain perspective in my life. Education is extremely important to me, but not necessarily in the sense of sitting in a classroom and learning from books, although that's a great way to expose yourself to information. Exploring different cultures and learning how others think and process information can tell us so much.

When I joined the army as a fresh-faced seventeen-year-old, I had no clue what life was like outside of California. It was eye-opening and exciting to learn about life in the Midwest. Through that, my interest in learning by exploring and traveling was sparked. There have been multiple situations in my life that either taught me a lifelong lesson about myself or sparked a never-ending interest in me to pursue something further. Completing basic training was the first time I contemplated my approach to challenges and the takeaway and personal lessons learned. Accomplishing that, considering I was only seventeen and the first in my family to join the military, and going into the process by myself with not much background or understanding, was something I was proud of at the end. It made me realize I was capable of a lot. Similarly, deploying to Iraq two years into my service was another experience that served as a pillar for me at a time in my life that helped shape who I am. Getting accepted into and graduating from the MBV program is a more current experience I look back on as a key accomplishment that assisted me with the biggest growth and development I've undergone in the shortest amount of time. The foundation I got while attending the program has led me to grow exponentially as a leader, mom, wife, and in all aspects of life, which is incredible to me. My biggest takeaway from the program was my newfound mantra, which I've lived by since graduating: leave fear behind.

My husband first found out about the MBV program and thought I would be a great candidate for it, but because I've been in the army reserves my entire career, I didn't meet the initial three-year active-duty service requirement, and he ended up signing up for it after attending an info session. Not surprisingly, he was accepted and was part of the inaugural cohort. When the active-duty service requirement was dropped, my husband insisted I submit an application for the following year. I ended up getting in and got the opportunity to be part of Cohort II. I remember my husband talking in awe about Professor Turrill's ability to effectively break down what leadership is and expand it to new levels, especially to a group of veteran military personnel, some of whom had years in key leadership positions. Looking back now, I realize that my growth and development as a leader truly began during my time with the MBV program. I learned to look inwardly at my default behaviors and biases and set those as my starting point for change, as opposed to looking at the outside variables, like subordinate or superior behaviors and personalities. Understanding that I only have control to change my behaviors and actions changed my approach for dealing with difficult or challenging situations or individuals. It's so easy to do the opposite, especially in the military, because we're based on a rank structure and I don't have to consider others' views if I don't want to so long as I outrank them. But that approach is so limiting in the long run because your influence won't be as impactful and the chances of getting buy-in from others is unlikely if you're only using your rank and position to attain it.

My favorite thing about the MBV program is its focus on transitioning, and for most of us, that meant going from the military into the private sector. That focus was extremely beneficial for me personally, because the way we conduct business in the military, it's easy to forget that that's not how things work on the outside. After the program, I had a better understanding of how to package and sell the skills I'd picked up in the fifteen years I've been in the army and expand from them to continue to develop and grow. Today, I'm a first sergeant at one of the largest HR companies in the army reserves, with about 300 soldiers in four different locations, plus a couple elements overseas. It is one of the most challenging positions I've had to date. On top of running the company part-time, I started a new position with USCIS in a completely new field for me. I remember having a sense of calm when I first started, as I felt absolutely prepared to take on every challenge that came with starting a new job in the civilian sector and taking on a first sergeant position. As I reflect back to the last two years of being a first sergeant, and I think about the multitude of issues that came my way and my ability to navigate my way through, I can't help but be thankful for my time at USC with the MBV program.

Among the high points of the program for me were the relationships I built during the short period we were there. There were so many personal growth lessons that were learned that will never leave me. Looking back now, I realize the foundation I received there has served me in all aspects of my life since graduation. The fascinating part for me is that I continue to grow exponentially. I remember having a conversation with Professor Turrill in which I shared what I thought were some of my weaknesses, and his response was something to the effect of "Well, the good thing is you're aware of them." It was so simple, I almost didn't know how to respond, but I remember thinking about it for a long time after. And while it did make sense at the time and I understood what he meant, I have a much higher appreciation for his words now. Growth for me started with awareness. Once I looked inward and acknowledged my weaknesses, I was able to work on areas that needed sharpening. It seems like such an obvious concept, but it's not always easy to admit you have areas you have to improve. Something amazing happened for me when I allowed awareness to flourish. Once you become aware, there's no going back, which is why I feel like I've seen more growth in me since I've graduated than any other time in my life. That conversation with Professor Turrill early in the program served as an aha moment from which I've been able to build and positively apply to all aspects of my life.

Our last session together left a lasting impression on me. There were many memorable moments that day that ended up serving as the final nudge I needed to take a leap of faith and leave fear behind. Afterward, I decided I was ready to operate differently by letting fear fuel me instead of stop or slow me down. For a long time I wanted to explore running my own business and, after graduation, I finally took the steps to make it official, along with a couple of my classmates. The lessons learned from taking that leap of faith led to new levels of growth for me. Not only did it serve as a reminder that fear is a liar, and that we are capable of more than we give ourselves credit for, but I also realized that running my own business was not for me, at least not in the industry I chose. The lessons I learned from that venture were immeasurable. Finally taking a leap of faith and investing in myself and taking a chance on my dreams opened up a whole new world for me, mentally. The idea of leaving fear behind left such a lasting impression on me that it's a lesson I've put emphasis on and have passed onto my young daughter. It is a topic we discuss regularly, and I see how it positively affects her as she processes and takes on the obstacles she encounters in her world. It liberated me and gave me the confidence to take chances and conceptualize and implement big ideas in all areas of my life. It's helped me change how I approach challenges. I'm no longer intimidated or overwhelmed by difficult situations; instead, I approach them with excitement because I know there will be a bigger lesson learned once completed. I view everything as an opportunity to learn, and the outcome almost always leads to growth. The idea of leaving fear behind was by far the biggest lesson I picked up during my time at USC.

Sadao Nakachi—Cohort V

I had all the elements to succeed, but obstacles would create speed bumps. These speed bumps turned out to be disguised opportunities in hindsight. A Peruvian-Japanese immigrant, I arrived in southern California at age three. I was taught by my father that hard work, studying, and exercise were all elements required to earn a prosperous career and be a healthy person. I learned Japanese, Spanish, and English when not at elementary school and was an honor student leading into high school. I had issues paying attention in class and was innately loud and disruptive. Near the culmination of my junior year in high school, my parents had had enough of my behavior and decided it would be best that I enlist in the army to get straightened out. I contracted in the army's split-option program that allowed enlistees still attending school to divide up their training. I would attend basic combat training (BCT) in late June 2000, during my summer vacation, and return to finish my senior year in high school.

At age seventeen, I reported to Fort Sill, Oklahoma, for boot camp (BCT). It was an experience unlike any other in my life. I saw strong and flexible men adapt to the training and excel, and I saw others who would break mentally, cry in their bunks at night, and pray to be released from their contract. The majority of my platoon were men who were easily five to ten years my senior. It was eye-opening to see some grown men broken, while others were rebuilt into warriors. I thank my drill sergeants, Gill and Mitchell, for molding me and unlocking a hidden potential within everyone in our platoon. Fort Sill was my Yale. I had learned to be comfortable with pain, stress, and the unknown. I learned to redirect agony into a personal drive that could help me grind onward and tackle my goals.

Upon graduation, my parents noticed the difference in my behavior, discipline, and character. I didn't hang out with my old friends anymore, I got a job after school to help with rent, and I completed high school without issue. Things were finally shaping up. Little did I know that the following year after enlisting would behold the largest terrorist attack on American soil ever seen.

I served fifteen years in the US Army Reserves, which allowed me to meet high performers from various fields, especially while attending leadership development courses (PLDC, BNCOC, WOCS). Thanks to great military mentors, amazing colleagues, and a strong work ethic, I was able to reach the rank of sergeant first class (E-7) and transition to become a warrant officer. I stayed in the field of transportation for the duration of my military career, performing in the role of gun-truck operator for my first deployment (2004) and as senior transportation manager for my sophomore deployment (2008). My efforts garnered me the bronze star for meritorious service, a combat action medal, and the Army Commendation Medal.

I learned of the MBV program thanks to not one, but three graduates: Jesse Cabrera, Kiefer Maddex, and Tracy Valenzuela, from Cohorts I, III, and IV, respectively. I knew all the graduates from working in the army and held them in high regard as intelligent and exceptional leaders. At the time of preparing my application, I had worked eleven years as a registered nurse in the emergency department. I was so excited to submit my graduate application that I expedited my bachelor's nursing program and completed it in eight months, instead of the prescribed twelve.

Graduate studies at USC Marshall's School of Business were inspirational. I gained a new voice. It's life-changing in the most positive way possible because you're constantly unlocking talents through assignments that push you out of your comfort zone. I learned that I'm a voracious reader when it came to learning about strategy, innovation, power, influence, and leadership. It allowed me to combine my military and critical-care nursing experience with graduate business concepts and knowledge. It has made me a valuable and unique nurse within my health-care organization.

Since graduating in Cohort V (2018), I have walked away with a renewed sense of purpose. I learned from mentors I met during the program that I needed to give back. I would go on to create a professional development program in my emergency department at Kaiser Permanente to help nurses return to school for their advanced degree. Since its inception, the program has helped twenty nurses enroll back into school with tuition almost completely covered and captured a 20 percent increase in bachelor's-prepared nurses in a department of 225 nurses. The program caught the attention of our hospital's Magnet & Professional Growth Council, where I am now co-leader and assist nurses in creating their own approach to professional development programs within their departments.

I applied and passed the certified emergency nurse (CEN) exam to obtain my specialty certification in emergency nursing. I currently sit on USC Marshall's alumni association executive board as the professional development champion. I also hold a position as a social media influencer for the board of certification for emergency nursing (BCEN), helping promote specialty certification and higher standards in nursing care. In spring 2020, I am scheduled to present an alumni life class in collaboration with the USC Latino Alumni Association to newly attending USC students. It's an honor and privilege to give back when possible to an institution that has opened so many doors for me.

Becoming a Trojan has provided me peace of life. I retain my position as an emergency nurse and now have the flexibility to take on stretch assignments that appeal to my interests and strengths. I don't kill myself for a paycheck, I am able to spend time with my wife and kids, and I have created a network that is rich in knowledge and friendship. I have USC, the MBV program, and the army to thank for that.

Greg Gombert (with Destiny Savage)—Cohort III

My career began one summer day back in 1985 while driving down Florida's Interstate 30A with my father. We were cruising the southeastern seaboard on vacation. I didn't know it at the time, but this kid who grew up next to Lake Michigan would eventually go on to serve in the navy depicted in a highway advertisement posted alongside the 30A. The sign had a warship with a sexy bow wave caressing its prow and the tattered, sun-bleached billboard read: "What have you done for your navy today?"

What did I know about the navy while still in high school? I knew they sailed ships and that they would pay for college. Next thing I knew, I was headed to Notre Dame, USC's arch-nemesis, on an NROTC scholarship.

I have served my country for twenty-four years, during which I had a very successful career as a military leader, including command of an AEGIS guided missile destroyer and then an AEGIS guided missile cruiser.

My role as a commanding officer was similar to that of a chief executive officer. I led, directed, and was accountable for the operation of a 9,800-ton AEGIS warship and oversaw the professional development of 364 sailors, while ensuring we carried out the navy's mission of serving as a global force for good. I planned, coordinated, and led all financial planning and budgeting while obviously also directing all engineering, combat, surveillance, training, cyber, and logistics operations, including Typhoon Yolanda Humanitarian Assistance/Disaster Relief operations with international partners, non-governmental organizations, FEMA, and the State Department.

Most commanding officers with as much experience as I had also enjoyed serving as ambassadors or attachés for international relations efforts with countries such as China, Japan, South Korea, Singapore, Brunei, Malaysia, the Philippines, Peru, Brazil, Chile, Panama, Saudi Arabia, Oman, Kuwait, and Bahrain. While we focus on interoperability for all maritime security matters, we also make lifelong friends.

As my navy career was on its last leg, retiring was an afterthought. Generally speaking, it's not in my nature to "take a powder" and coast. From a practical point of view, I was getting married to my eventual MBV class-mate and would be a stepfather to two kids!

I knew I had to get my rear in gear, hit the books, and get myself to a business school, while setting up a new professional network. I probably would have landed back at Notre Dame and my alma mater's Mendoza School of Business if not for Destiny's suggestion that I look into the MBV program she'd fortuitously discovered at a job fair in San Diego while chatting with the program's director. Destiny, as you will read, is a Trojan. I'm her arch-rival (and vice versa), but I still love her, and have to say her discovery, regular advice, and help changed my life in so many ways.

Now, I left the navy a pentathlete of sorts, conversant in strategy creation, planning, policy development, budgeting/financial management, and field operations. Incidentally, most of my operational experience included nine deployments addressing international security threats and supporting overseas diplomatic strategies and initiatives for the navy, Office of the Secretary of Defense (OSD) for policy, the State Department, and key allies and partners.

I sensed I needed instruction that incorporated all of the necessary (and contemporary) components of running a company, small business, or non-profit. In other words, I wanted to graduate with a comprehensive portfolio of business knowledge that I could apply straight away.

As I began the MBV program, I was a little nervous about having to recreate myself and start over. It wasn't like I was accustomed to going to school and taking courses that would flip my perspective on things in life. Frankly, the most challenging component was the elaborate and extensive self-exploration and self-assessment. Looking back, it was absolutely unnerving but essential, so I could anchor myself to my strengths, build more effective relationships, and relate to my peers in the business community in a more emotionally intelligent way. Thankfully, my belief in leadership as service developed while I was a Boy Scout (and Eagle Scout!); and my time at Notre Dame and my service at sea helped immensely.

Personally, my favorite classwork included business strategy, negotiating, finance, communications, marketing, and entrepreneurship. The ropes course was a blast—I overcame some fears on that day. USC's network is an underpriced perk, and I appreciated the career events, one of which got me my job at Smart & Final, while also providing engagements with hiring managers and careerists from other industries and companies.

Ultimately, I finished the program with a lot of love for my MBV Cohort III classmates. I miss them every day. We took care of each other, leaned on each other, kept each other honest, and as a family, pushed each other to make the transition. While I don't want to let myself down, I definitely don't want to let my cohort down.

Speaking of classmates, I attended USC with my wife, Destiny. She's now a double-Trojan, having completed the MBV program and a public policy degree as an undergraduate.

We are one of just two couples to complete the program together!

Given Destiny's job and her ongoing hunt for her next job, plus my job hunt, career events on and off campus, networking, and our kids, we had to serve as our own study group. We kind of always knew we'd do the program together because we were transitioning at the same time.

It was a good thing I had my sidekick with me for the academic work. The program is as much about time management as it is academic and class project work. Every other week we were jetting up to USC, working our butts off with little to no sleep, and then returning to San Diego to rest and reconstitute. As usual, Destiny set up our weekly homework and research schedule, which also incorporated our carpooling-mates. There is a PMP certification in project management, and we have to say we earned it in every respect. Every two-week interlude was all about cost, risk, and schedule.

At the end of the program, which was ten and a half months in hyperspace, each of us had to write a lengthy paper looking forward, a piece that was as much a reflection on our past (the good, the bad, and the ugly) as it was a focus on our aspirations.

Destiny and I went our separate ways for about one week and just started writing. You get an outline and some general guidance. I think she followed the guidance; I did not. That I didn't would come to no surprise to some of my classmates (and old friends).

The two of us did enjoy listing the behaviors we would leave behind. Old baggage—some of it emotional, some of it psychological, and, generally speaking, some of it just plain impractical and counterproductive. It was with this section of the final assignment that we collaborated. Basically, we had to list and describe attitudes, beliefs, and behaviors we needed to leave in our wake.

In summary, we have some work ahead of us. We started the MBV program looking to learn some new things, make some new friends, and join USC's network. By any measure, we stretched ourselves and started to brand our accomplishments.

This all happened in the face of some very strong headwinds associated with the storm in our personal life. I really thought about giving up. The dips were deep and long. I guess you could call the program a productive distraction. Destiny disagrees; she was all jazzed to get back to her alma mater and make new friends.

Together, we came to realize that what USC was really trying to do was make it so our leadership styles are an expression of our best selves. Wherever we are, we have to step up and lead. We promised to lead and, in doing so, give back. USC gave us a hand up and we will never forget.

Michael Chavez—Cohort VI

In the beginning: My name is Michael Frank Chavez, and I am a graduate from Cohort VI. I am the eighth of ten children by the same parents and, yes, we grew up Catholic! My father was a painting contractor and my mother was a homemaker. All ten kids had eight years of private grade school, and half also attended private high schools. That adds up to 100 years of private-school tuition! To say that it was a financial sacrifice is an understatement, but my parents believed that it was their responsibility to provide a solid education base to give us the best chance for success in whatever direction our paths took us. Due to financial constraints, we rarely went anywhere on vacation and didn't have much opportunity for paid entertainment. Like a few of my siblings, I became a voracious reader. I had a healthy imagination as a child and loved comic books, which became a gateway to graphic novels and eventually novels. These stories transported me to faraway places and all manner of adventures. I would regularly stay up far past my bedtime enthralled in the latest story. My father, Frank S. Chavez, was also a veteran who worked twelve- to fifteen-hour days painting houses in the blistering sun with a positive attitude and a willingness to do the dirtiest parts of the job without complaint or hesitation. Working alongside him from the early age of six taught me the value of hard work and maintaining the right attitude. It also motivated me to do well in school in order to avoid such intense physical labor!

For the most part, school has been fairly easy for me. By reading so often, I expanded my vocabulary and boosted my reading speed and comprehension. I would consistently be among the first to complete in-class assignments, and I tended to read ahead in most subjects to get a feel for what was coming next. That said, I did struggle quite a bit in subjects that required a high degree of memorization, such as history and Latin, and I tended to procrastinate on assignments until they were due since I knew I could rush it and still get a good grade. Little did I know that I was setting myself up for quite the challenge in future undergrad and graduate courses!

Military Life: I signed up for military service during my senior year in high school and delayed my entry until the end of that summer. Boot camp pushed me well beyond what limits I thought I had and I began the process of discovering and honing my strength: physical, emotional, and mental. My time in the army began my first real education on what true leadership is all about. "The quality of a leader is reflected in the standards they set for themselves," said Ray Kroc, the American businessman who made McDonald's famous. This quote exemplifies what I have always looked for in a leader. One leader who stands above the rest during my enlistment was my first sergeant while I was stationed at Ft. Wainwright, Alaska. He not only would participate in physical training at 6:30 each morning, even at sub-zero temperatures, but would complete laps around the company formation as we ran our six miles, all the while yelling that he was willing to do twice as much as he expected of us even though he was twice our age. He also made it clear that he would happily transfer us to another base if we didn't want to stay, and he pushed us to define our career goals and did everything he could to help us achieve them. He had sky-high expectations of us, and I tried every day to not let him down.

Civilian Life: I have been out of military service for twenty-one years now. During this phase of my life, I experienced triumphs and setbacks like everyone else. While I felt a clear sense of purpose while in the military, I have struggled to find one in my civilian life. I made a successful career in business development for engineering firms, but did not find much challenge or satisfaction in it. In the year I turned thirty, I chose to go back to school to obtain my bachelor's degree in business to further the career I fell into. I joined a few clubs at Cal State Fullerton, and the one that made the most impact on me was the Student Veterans Association (SVA). I felt the familiar (and almost forgotten) bonds of kinship, and developed strong friendships with fellow veterans.

I continued on with life and the same career for years, until my older brother passed away unexpectedly in his sleep. This forced me to reevaluate where I was. Like him, I worked long hours, slept little, ate unhealthily, and exercised very infrequently. It was a wakeup call that I needed to change in order to avoid a similar early end. It also made it clear that I wanted to do more with my life; I wanted to make a positive impact on others' lives. I began to shift my focus away from working long hours and more into volunteering and spending time with family. Eventually, one of my veteran friends from SVA, Jim Hodgson, talked about how he was going back to school to obtain a master's from USC. He explained that the program was specifically designed for veterans, particularly those seeking to transition to civilian life. This was the first I heard of the MBV degree, and I was eager to learn more. He also shared that it was a cohort model in which the class remained together and the professors rotated in, resulting in closer friendships among the students. There were several financial aid options, including the GI Bill and USC's extremely generous scholarship program. Best of all, the program lasted only ten months! I was impressed with everything I learned and decided to attend an informational session with my wife. It was there that I met James Bogle and Professor Robert Turrill. Almost immediately, I felt their sincerity, and that they truly cared about the program and those enrolled in it. That was it. I was sold. I applied for the next cohort and was accepted.

A Major Step (Part 1): About three months prior to beginning the program, I established a YouTube channel, Uncle Mike Reads, reading and reviewing children's books to foster literacy and critical thinking skills. It began as a passion project that filled me with purpose, combining my love for kids and love for reading. I never envisioned it becoming more than a side hobby, and enjoyed finding my personal style. The downside was that I began this project and commitment right before grad school! I was concerned about being able to leverage both while also working full-time, but I decided to give it a shot. Little did I know that this one decision would change my life.

MBV Life: This experience has been nothing short of transformational for me. While I excelled at traditional academic courses like accounting and finance, I was surprised to find that courses like leadership, entrepreneurship, and communications were far more challenging for me, particularly leadership. Prior to this, I had held a simplistic view of leadership and thought I knew as much as I needed to about it. From the first class, I knew I was out of my element and that this was not going to be a cakewalk. I quickly learned that my style of leadership was not particularly effective or adaptable, and thus began the arduous process of identifying and building my leadership skills.

The biweekly discussion board assignments asked me to open up and share my thoughts and struggles with leadership. I resisted at first as I am a very private person who does not easily trust others. I was encouraged by those brave individuals who shared their deepest thoughts, and began to do the same. Eventually, it got to a point where I looked forward to posting, and I began to reply to others' posts. This became a valuable avenue to get to know my classmates on a deeper level.

This program pushed me out of my comfort zone and prompted me to do some deep soul searching. I realized I was not happy at my job/career and wanted to tap into my need to do something with a purpose. Networking has opened many doors and opportunities for me to do this, from working with the Congressional Medal of Honor Foundation to connecting with authors and publishers of children's books.

The program has been exhausting, educational, and simply transformative. The staff are nothing short of exceptional; they consistently have gone out of their way to help in any way they could. In summary, it has been an honor and privilege to be part of Cohort VI. I have witnessed personal and professional growth in so many, which has inspired the same in me.

A Major Step (Part 2): Earlier this year, USC held a book fair on campus during one of my class days, and I casually walked over during my first class break to see what it was all about. There, I had the opportunity to meet and speak with a couple of authors, and the book fair was all I could think about when I returned to class. I made a decision to meet as many children's authors as I could and spent most of the rest of the day doing just that. I met dozens of people who shared my passion for children's literacy and connected strongly with a number of them. I received a ton of encouragement from various authors and publishers, and some even gave me copies of their books for free to cover on my YouTube channel.

I felt energized and motivated like I had never experienced before. For the first time, I felt like I could turn my passion project into a full-time occupation. Since then, I have been building my network and laying the foundation to make this work. I now volunteer for the local library and am seeking a board position for Reading is Fundamental of Southern California (www.rifsocal.org). I have partnered with another classmate to establish an after-school program teaching leadership and character development to elementary schoolchildren. With my YouTube channel, plans are in place to connect to children's hospitals reading to kids as well as military bases to reach children of service members.

In conclusion, my life has been completely transformed. The MBV program gave me the courage and skills I needed to take this leap and follow my dreams and passion. I made some lifelong friends, gained a handful of amazing mentors, and am venturing out into the world, confidently stepping out of my comfort zone to live my life to the fullest.

CHAPTER 3

ON THE HIGH ROPES—"CLIMB ON!"

We gathered in the flat, grassy area of the park, rather slowly, but by 8:45 a.m., we were ready to go. Philip, our trainer, directed us into a circle, shoulder to shoulder, with no second row. It's always cool in the morning at the Culver City Park, and many of us were wearing extra wraps, which we would shed as the day heated up.

I kicked off the introduction to the day's activities and tried to set a serious tone plus high expectations of what we could accomplish together that day, including getting to know everyone better and in a different way away from an institutional environment, and, of course, to have fun.

> "Today is about a couple of different levels of understanding and insight. First, there will be individual, personal challenges, for each of you, but the challenges will most likely be different between you. Pay attention to your response to these challenges as much as you do the outcomes. We will discuss both the outcomes and your response to the challenges.
>
> The second objective today is to learn to support each other, both giving and receiving feedback and encouragement. This is not a competition. This is a shared experience, a common experience on which we can build.
>
> Third, today is also about community-building. We are developing our identity as a group, as a cohort. This identity will serve us well throughout the year as we face many challenges in the various academic areas.

So, today is both paying attention by each of us as to our responses to physical challenges as well as supporting one another interpersonally and as a total group, the cohort. Use today for your own purposes, gain as much as you can from the experience. Take time to reflect throughout the day as well at the end of the day on what various activities mean. What learning or take-aways did you gain? We'll do some debriefing throughout the day and at our final wrap-up, as well. And don't forget to have fun!"

A Moment to Remember Senator John McCain

In Cohort VI, the ropes course day was September 8, 2018, two weeks after Senator John McCain's death. I had spent much of the prior weekend listening to and watching John McCain's memorial service. He had died of brain cancer on August 25, and his memorial service began on Wednesday, August 29, and concluded with his burial in the Naval Academy's cemetery in Arlington, Virginia. It seemed to me that, in this audience of eighty-six military veterans, we needed to say something before we began our outdoor training experience to acknowledge the passing of one of our heroes, not just as a military hero, but also as a major contributing citizen to the state of Arizona and the country at large. When we left the campus the last time we were together, one of the students at the very end of our cohort meeting on Saturday evening informed us of Senator McCain's passing, but we were already leaving the room, so there was no time for a response or comment. So I felt we needed to pause before we began the day's activities to reflect on the man, his life, and his contributions to his community and our nation, and to reflect on his final gift to the country.

Senator McCain had known for about a year that his illness was terminal, so while he treated it, he began making arrangements for his leaving. So, here was a case of a person taking control of making the arrangements for his own memorial and funeral and asking certain people who were important to him to speak on his behalf there. As I watched the speakers and services, I became aware of my own sense that something else, something very important, was taking place. I had this strong sense that McCain had consciously designed an intervention for all of us as his last act on this earth. He used his last opportunity to solidify his legacy through what I would describe as a lesson in organizational and cultural design, a design for how we might approach our disagreements, politics, and problem-solving and planning capabilities. I don't recall seeing or experiencing anything like this, which was so intentional and so directed at leaving us with his last hopes and directions for a better life together.

I shall use some organizational design concepts that I feel are both important and aligned with what he meant to do, to leave us with a lesson that, if accepted, would be a more effective strategy for moving forward in our common challenges as a country, regardless of how fractured we had become.

First principle: "Collaboration does not mean compromise." It has become common to accuse members of one's own political party of compromise if there is even a whiff of collaboration across the aisle. In design terms, collaboration, where both parties are representing their own point of view while listening to the other party's point of view, is the best framework for negotiation and problem-solving. Compromise is actually a fallback position if the collaboration breaks down and bargaining takes over. Compromise is used to allocate a known resource, while collaboration has the potential for increasing the resource. McCain instructed us in this by having major representatives of both political parties eulogize him at his death. They collaborated in recognizing his citizenship and contribution, thus increasing the opportunity to see his life and contributions in a much larger scope and with much more relevance to an increased number of divided citizens.

Collaboration is used within organizations to solve larger, more difficult problems and exploit opportunities where there are major differences for approaching a task. It's a more powerful approach to seeking consensus on difficult issues. Consensus is more powerful than either using a majority approach or assigning the tasks to a group, or decision-making by a single individual. Using collaboration, we invite differences in perception, knowledge, and forecasting ability to combine talents, knowledge, and best efforts to achieve more optimal solutions to the problem or opportunity confronting us. McCain's principle of collaboration was not just to be used in his memorial service, but was intended to direct us to a more inclusive and robust approach to setting our future direction in our country. In design terms, collaboration and consensus are integrative devices to pull multiple points of view into the best outcome. Also, both design concepts create acceptance and buy-in that would not necessarily be achieved when important and strategic decisions are made by an individual or by a single group. While collaboration and consensus are time-intensive, the payoff in terms of both quality of outcome and buy-in by multiple constituents is big.

Second principle: "We can integrate our efforts forward through our common values." There are different ways to integrate efforts within organizations—for example, through common authority structures, team or individual liaisons, or common goals. But one of the most powerful methods is to test our assumptions and decisions against an agreed-upon set of common values—like honesty, valuing the individual, and protecting freedoms—as well as community. Dedication to human rights, democracy, and equal justice, and respect for the dignity of all people are among the values upon which we have agreed in the past that can be used to integrate efforts toward common goals.

McCain listed a number of these values in his final letter to the American people, emphasizing them as our "common causes." These values form the core of organizations and our national culture, and, therefore, become some of the largest integrating forces binding us together in our daily lives.

Third principle: This principle is very apparent when working with veterans, and may reflect McCain's own military background, but it is also used in many other contexts, as well. This principle is "service to a purpose beyond self," where we not only operate out of self-interest, but contribute to a larger mission or purpose. Contribution to the larger good and to our common purpose is a larger idea than just serving ourselves and developing a total focus on our personal portfolio of assets, achievements, or awards. While common values unite and direct all of our behavior, a purpose beyond self is aspirational and takes us outside ourselves to achieve greater unifying efforts and outcomes. If there emerges an agreement on this common purpose beyond self, this purpose (or mission), itself, becomes an integrating factor across groups.

Three comments were made within the eulogies in the Saturday memorial service that captured the essence of these principles: "see past differences in search of common ground," "commit to something bigger than yourself," and "when all is said and done, we are on the same team." McCain left us these guidelines and design principles as his last intervention to help us move forward as a more unified country, one that is united by values and common cause rather than fractured by different political agendas. It would have been easy and appropriate to have focused just on McCain the person and his contributions, but by taking charge of the memorial itself, he turned it into a lesson in civics and in how to design a shared commitment to a common good and common future. My reflection on what he did as he exited was that he was very intentional in directing our attention to strategies and designs that are well-known to us in the service of more productive, growth-oriented, and satisfying citizenship. I felt both instructed and grateful. I felt I had received his intent.

After my brief remarks, there was a moment of silence, followed by applause from the cohort. We began our day then, as I introduced Philip Folsom. Throughout the day at the Culver City Park ropes course, a number of the veterans came up to me and commented on our recognizing the passing of Captain McCain, and were pleased that I had addressed it and spent some time on it. And, for myself, I was still overwhelmed by my personal insights into the intervention Senator McCain had planned and enrolled so many others in delivering after he was gone. Rather than leaving us with our grief at his passing, he left us with inspiration and direction for our collective future.

Philip Folsom

After introducing Philip as our trainer and guide for the day, I shared the fact that he and I had worked together for about fourteen years, so I knew they would benefit from his insights and approach to the day. He introduced his team of trainers and provided his introduction and objectives for the day's activities.

Philip is an army veteran, himself, and has done considerable programming and training with veterans in various contexts, our program among them. He related well to our MBV students. He provided his own objectives for the day along with an introduction to the course, safety guidelines, and information on differentiating the process from the content of the day's activities, the how and the what, focusing on what our responses might be to the activities, and how we approach personal challenges emotionally and deal with our own sense of identity, self-concept, and self-control. Many of the activities are structured around what looks to be an individual or interpersonal challenge, but are actually group challenges.

One major learning objective of some of the activities is not to assume rules of the game that have not been made explicit. If there isn't a rule covering an activity or experience, don't assume there is. The point of this is that we often put self-limiting constraints on our activities and efforts that really aren't there, thus limiting the possibilities of the outcome. One of the more interesting self-limiting constraints is assuming you can't ask for help, that you are alone and should be able to solve the problem without help. Helping and asking for help were major themes of the day.

> "The premise of experiential learning is that it allows participants to both explore and discover the operating system that is running unseen under the hood of all individuals and teams. This operating system, which consists of core beliefs and a whole set of assumptions about how the world works, is often revealed as malleable and therefore capable of being improved. In short, choice is a function of awareness, and experiential challenges that are well facilitated suddenly give students and teams access to the manual controls of their life. In addition, it is usually the case that people tend to engage with similarly challenging activities in the same predictable ways. Fear is fear, regardless of whether it is of public speaking, conflict, or doing a high ropes course event. The common variable in all situations is the person or team. This universality allows for the experiential challenges to stand in as a metaphor for all other challenges the students or class face."
> (Philip Folsom)

There are typically four different activities in the low ropes segment of the day, all with their own stories and insights. Competition versus cooperation is another major thread of learning throughout. Some activities are done with half the participants blindfolded, relying on communication from their partner to survive or win the activity. None of the activities is intentionally obvious as to the point of the game's solution. Explicitly expressing your personal goals in a group context, and then organizing around those goals to achieve them collaboratively, is common. One of the major highlights of the low ropes half of the day is Philip Folsom's rendition of the Hero's Journey (see Joseph Campbell), which is inspirational, insightful, and comforting in its references to fear of change, accepting the challenge of the quest for personal growth, overcoming the difficulties of real personal change, and returning to share one's newly developed gifts with a community as a more complete and mature person, ready and capable of contributing.

One of the most effective activities is to break into teams of about ten. Each person writes their personal goals (for their life, career, program) on a card, and then everybody lies on their backs in a circle and places their goals at the top of their heads. Then the ten form a group inside a smaller, tightly defined circle, and the task is for each individual, with help from the group, to retrieve their set of goals from inside the circle, which is their body length away from their goals left on the ground. Each individual in turn leans out of the small circle, supported by their teammates to reach their goals on the ground. If anybody falls or steps over the tightly defined circle, they must start over. The challenge is for the group to develop an optimal strategy, number of people helping, positioning, stability, etc., while the individual leans out to reach for their goals. The symbolism is not lost on the veterans. One needs a support system to achieve one's goals. Leaning out is difficult and risky without the proper strength and support of your team or support system. One doesn't succeed alone. Secondly, the entire team must retrieve their goals before the activity is finished, so all ten team members must accept help from other members to succeed, and everyone must successfully retrieve their cards for the entire team to succeed. Of the morning activities, this is the one that is most often remembered and discussed by the veterans after the day is completed.

"This activity is called 'Jewels.' It involves a predictable sequence of discovery that almost all groups have. First, there is a collection of individuals looking at their own unreachable goals. The group often begins to question the overall activity and wonder if they are being set up to fail. Second, the group reorganizes into friendship pairs or triads of previous relationships or proximity. The small group vainly tries to support the individuals in leaning out to reach and retrieve their goals. It is rarely successful. Third, the group coalesces into two main teams, often divided by gender or some other binary division. This is fairly successful at first because the individuals have much more resource support, but invariably one individual fails for some reason (often self-sabotage), and the rules of the game require everyone to restart at the failure of any individual. Finally, it becomes apparent that for everyone to succeed in their individual goals, the people must help each other. This reciprocity is the core of tribe, honor, and sustainable success." (Philip Folsom)

Two of the veterans shared these comments after this event:

"During the second group activity, where we had to write down a goal, place it on the ground, and then work as a team to pick it up, I learned that I have to trust and allow people to help me. I am so independent and so used to doing things on my own that I don't allow people to help me who truly want to, and I also have a hard time asking for help." (Natalya Turner, Cohort III)

"The exercise of retrieving our personal goals as a collective unit high-lighted the values of trust and interdependence while reinforcing the necessity of group support. I realized how calloused I had become to these values. The symbolism of this exercise emphasized the sig-nificance of forming trustworthy relationships and strengthening indi-vidual and group bonds. I learned that while personal goal-setting is uniquely individual, the support structures necessary to achieve and sustain these goals share common themes . . . but I was surprised and humbled at how the entire cohort effortlessly and seamlessly came together to support one another." (Ray Kim, Cohort III)

The morning activities all point to the collaboration and success of the team and/or the total community. Don't make assumptions that all activities must be competitive. Pay attention to the actual goals and rules of the game before any assumptions are made and acted on. The second major learning objective is asking for help, developing a support system that helps everyone in the team achieve their goals. Philip stresses, "The day of the lone wolf is over!"

> "Similarly, the idea of the lone wolf being a glamorized or idealized example of masculinity (e.g., Rambo, the Lone Ranger, and many others) is a death sentence for many veterans trying to transition back into civilian life and assimilate into a pride-based culture that celebrates the individual. The truth is that the lone wolf is not howling at night to celebrate his freedom. He is howling because he is starving to death, and he is desperately asking if a pack has room for him. In the military that is called 'popping smoke' to signal distress, and it is not often allowed in our civilian world." (Philip Folsom)

Ray Kim summarized in his evaluation of the session:

> "A lone wolf dies. I can personally attest to the validity of this adage and the message of solidarity. Having attended leadership/team-building courses, I viewed the ropes course with slight skepticism, but walked away on Saturday afternoon with a renewed understanding of camaraderie and humility." (Ray Kim, Cohort III)

The day represents a rich photo opportunity, and it is not unusual to have at least one expert photographer in the group chronicle its activities in order to share when we meet again in two weeks. I encourage this and set aside some time when we reassemble to see some photos as a reminder and a link to our outdoor experience. Usually, we post a set of photos to a special site available to all members of the cohort. We may also use these photos as a promotion to the next cohort as to the nature and activities of this full day's training.

On the high wire at the Culver City ropes course

I also formally evaluate the day in written form on the discussion board the following week, asking for evaluative comments on the individual, interpersonal, small-group, and community-level outcomes of the day as each individual sees them. We will spend a few minutes debriefing these comments in the next class without taking too much time from the faculty and content areas. I've learned that spending time reflecting on, evaluating, and debriefing these types of activities is critical for learning and reinforcing the experience. This is similar to what they have known as after action reviews, so there is little resistance.

After lunch back at the grassy area and picnic tables, we move to the high ropes course up the hill, where the afternoon is also broken into about four different activities or challenges, some individual, some with a partner.

> "The ropes course is particularly powerful because human beings are only born with two innate fears, and one of them is a fear of falling. This universal fear, which we all share, is therefore a great opportunity to attach a more relevant fear (inadequacy, asking for help, vulnerability) to the experience so the learning can be transferred and integrated into the students' careers and life. Veterans in particular have learned to 'turn off' their fear as it can negatively impact a mission. Unfortunately, emotions do not get 'turned off' individually, and by shutting down our fears we also end up shutting down our joy, compassion, empathy, and so much more that make us human and make life worth living. Rebooting this healthy emotional landscape is scary and uncomfortable but invaluable to a life fully lived and filled with healthy relationships, joy, and appreciation." (Philip Folsom)

The rock climb is with a partner and the partners are linked together by a safety rope as they help each other up the wall, finding hand and foot holds to boost them to the pinnacle of the wall. This is the most physically demanding challenge of the afternoon, forcing a lot of stress on forearms and legs. About eight to ten of the others are tied to the ropes stabilizing and securing the climbers, and it is also their job to assist and encourage the climbers in any way they can. The power of encouragement is strong, so the supporting crew keeps focus on the climbers while responding to the trainer's command of walking backward or forward, depending on where the climbers are on the wall. The wall is about fifty feet high, so it is a rather daunting feat to make it to the top where a cowbell, eager to be rung by the successful and exhausted partners, awaits the climbers. At the top, the two sit for a moment on the ridge, turning around and gazing appreciatively at the Pacific Ocean in the distance. Culver City Park is situated such that at the top of all the events, one can literally pause, breathe, feel a cool breeze, and appreciate both their success and the view.

Once the climbers have reached the top and taken in the view, they rappel down the rock wall quickly, as their support team walks forward and the trainers guide them back to the ground. "What helped? What stopped you? What created your momentum to keep climbing? What advice do you have for the next pair? What would you like to share with the group? Did you feel encouraged?" After several hugs and more high fives, the climbers share their ideas and reflections with the entire group before the next pair ascends the wall.

The second and third challenges involve partners again, either balancing on a rope or a log stretched across a space thirty feet above the ground. The partners meet in the middle of the log and navigate an exchange of positions for each person to go beyond their partner. This typically involves some awkward hugging, some grappling, and often falling before success is achieved. Being upon the log is more difficult than it looks from the ground. Students feel alone at each end of the log and often hug the vertical pole for stability. I once had a student freeze up while wrapped around the vertical pole for over twenty minutes before we could talk her down to safety. Coming down involves stepping off the log while being suspended by ropes attached to a harness controlled on the ground by one of the trainers. With two people aloft at the same time, there are two trainers guiding the supporting ropes and safety of the individual.

The cross-beam activity usually produces numerous humorous videos and photos, awkward hugs, hip dancing, falls that appear painful (but aren't), and an occasional vocal solo! On the ground once again, there is more debriefing, hugs, high fives, and moments of high relief. What helped, what were the barriers to success, and what advice would you give to the other team members?

The final challenge is the leap of faith, an activity in which each person in a harness climbs a pole to reach a small wooden platform about thirty feet up. When the climber reaches the top, they must find a way to get up on the platform, which is about three feet long by fifteen to eighteen inches wide. One is typically seated first on the platform, and the challenge is to stand on a single pole that has a tendency to move from side to side as one tries to stand and also when one is standing. This activity brings out the fear-of-falling instinct quickly, and many climbers want to come down rather than continue.

The team encourages the climber. The trainer talks to the person alone on this unstable pole, tells them to relax, breathe, think about their goal, get themselves under control before leaping for the ring. The ring, a liberated Porsche steering wheel, isn't too far away, and is actually closer when one is on the pole than it looks from the ground. The steering wheel (the ring) represents the goal of the individual, and it is reachable by leaping for it. Before ascending, the trainer charges the individual to express their goal. What do you deeply want in life? See that ring as representing that goal, and realize it's within your reach if you focus on it, get intentional about reaching it, steady yourself on the pole. The pole isn't shaking; you are. So, get yourself under control. Being calm before you leap creates the conditions most optimal for your success. Grab the ring and hold on. Your team supports and encourages you. Your belayers move in accordance with keeping the safety rope taut, but not too tight. The trainer talks to you, calming you, questioning you about your goal, about your intent, and about your taking control of this event that leads to your success.

> "It was the leap of faith that was by far the most memorable. I am terrified of heights. However, I was forced to calm my nerves and become one with the surrounding environment, a talent I didn't even know I possessed. . . . It was enlightening to hear a fellow veteran identify the numbness I'd been feeling over the past two years, who could help me identify the issue and accept my fear and feelings." (Kiefer Maddux, Cohort III)

> "Zen (the trainer) asked what I planned to get from this. He said it seemed that I was going to 'power through' the exercise. I had to explain that I felt like I needed to face my fear and no matter how much I wanted to. I could not just power through it. I can't lie about it, and it is no secret that I was terrified up there. Had it not been for my

teammates supporting me, I would not have had the courage to stand up on that pole and ultimately leap to the ring." (Moe Duran, Cohort III)

"What I gained was more spiritual than I had expected. As I watched each of our team members do the leap of faith, I learned from their experiences. But one particular comment struck my interest. Alex mentioned that he regretted not staying in that moment of turmoil just a little bit longer—that there are few opportunities for us to experience the inner turmoil in a safe environment. I was intrigued by this notion and slowed down my entire process when it came to be my turn. What I gained was an understanding of myself that I hadn't known before. It is difficult to explain, but I realized I am more powerful and more capable than I had ever thought. I felt empowered!" (Unknown, Cohort III)

"It was the conversation with Zen (the trainer) where he mentioned that the only time I smiled was when I grabbed the ring. He then asked if I could relate that to my life in general. This shook me a bit. I think there is a lot of truth and reality in that. After some reflection, I think that often I am so focused on a goal that I don't enjoy the experience of getting to it." (Daniel Lowry, Cohort III)

"The leap of faith taught me to just take life one step at a time, no matter how long it takes me, no matter how scary it may be, no matter if I fall. Just keep moving forward." (Natalya Turner, Cohort III)

When the individual stops shaking, the pole becomes quiet. Encouraged to relax, focus, and get committed to achieving the goal, the team counts backward from five before the individual jumps, with arms outstretched, eyes focused squarely on the ring as the goal, and grabs it with both hands and swings! Not everyone succeeds, but many do, and I've noticed an interesting phenomenon. If the first person gets the rings, it is more likely that the next individual, in order, will also be successful. It's not a scientific observation, but I've observed this leadership-modeling behavior a number of times in the almost fourteen years I've been engaging in this ropes course.

The leap of faith!

Focused and determined

Again, at the end of each jump, congratulations and hugs are delivered, and even more emotion is expressed than on the other events. This event seems to move powerful emotions in many of the participants. Many get emotional even before climbing when they have to own up to some of their deepest aspirations that have been blocked before. It's interesting that career goals are ostensibly the topic, but over half of my students over the years talk about personal goals, and usually deeper personal goals than one would normally discuss in such a group, but the trainer on the leap of faith is excellent and experienced in staying with the individual until they tap into some of their deeper and driving motives and goals.

One such example took place in spring 2007, when one of my MBA students, who just happened to be a career air force officer in her mid- to late thirties, finally broke down and declared that what she most wanted as her personal goal was to have a baby with her significant other. They had been hoping for some time with no results. I had never seen her emotional in the classroom. She was always under control, but the trainer encouraged her to be a little more open and deal with what she really wanted to achieve. After the group supported her in her tears at the moment, she climbed on, focused on the ring, verbally expressed her goal of creating new life, and jumped. Once down, she debriefed her experience and her feelings that were by this time perfectly OK with her and with her support group. Sometime later in the semester, she approached me at the end of one of the class nights, and said she just wanted me to know that she was pregnant.

The afternoon is getting late as everyone completes all four challenges in their teams of ten to twelve for the day. Philip gathers us in one large circle to do the closing comments for the day.

Going around the circle one by one, each individual shares the one insight or comment that best represents their experience to them. It is serious, but upbeat. Comments about trust, team, commitment, giving and receiving help, collaboration, enabling, exciting, and of course, fun, are common. The trainers usually distribute a small token of the day's activities and achievement, and we finish as I thank Philip and his trainers, and encourage all to reflect and anticipate where these insights might be useful. I encourage them to leave and spend some more time with each other if possible. Most of our veterans who travel for the weekend go home on Sunday, so they still have some time on their Saturday night to continue their reflections. Local students will tend to head for home within an hour or so.

Members of Cohort VI at the ropes course

It's typically a memorable and very effective day for the cohort to come together as an entire group, and to leverage their feelings, emotions, and insights for use in their own development and—happily for me—the cohort itself. My experience has always been that after the ropes course day, the class goes better, the dynamic feels more positive and helpful, and individuals feel they know each other much more deeply. The day at the ropes course interferes with the stereotype that the classroom is only for cognitive development. Along with important personal insights, students learn to relate to one another more congruently.

> "The main instructor [Philip] spoke our language and made more sense to me in his few short discussions than most people have in the eleven years I've been out. It made sense to me, and I found it very therapeutic. I have struggled in the civilian world and felt that I don't belong. There are switches turned off that haven't fully been turned back on and my personal relationships with civilians (including my family) have suffered. . . . I'm proud and thankful to be part of this program. The ropes course helped bring the group closer together. We all benefited from it and will continue to do so." (James Galindo, Cohort III)

> "Looking into my classmates' eyes and saying the words, 'look at me, breathe with me' or 'I appreciate you and who you are' [Alex to Natalya] live in a realm outside of words. They live in a place inside your heart that is exposed by fear, uncertainty, and triumph. This course not only exposed me in this manner, but followed through with an atmosphere of support and learning that allowed me to capitalize on the momentum. What made it so special was how this atmosphere was generated by my fellow classmates. They are a special group of people. . . . The ropes course was yet another affirmation of what an incredibly selfless group we have in the cohort. The amount of support everyone showed for one another was incredible." (Alex Hesselgesser, Cohort III)

> "[Philip] rightly notes that in the military we seek ways to mask vulnerability in order to project toughness and garner respect. As Philip and some other students have mentioned, vulnerability is actually a strength in the corporate world. Showing vulnerability can help endear

you to peers and subordinates and make people feel more comfortable approaching you." (Alex Hesselgesser, Cohort III)

"I can't count how many times I have jumped from a perfectly good airplane, but even I have to admit that climbing on top of that pole just seemed greatly unusual. I think that many of us found something during that leap that we may have lost somewhere along the way. I think that very thing was faith itself. I know this is what I felt. Every individual became a 'teammate' that day, and it was truly amazing to witness." (Ty Smith, Cohort III)

Ty Smith—Cohort III

I grew up in East St. Louis, Illinois, and I was the oldest of five children. I say "was" because I am now the oldest of four. My younger sister Antinia passed peacefully in her sleep on November 11, 2015. Unfortunately, my mother's grief had only just begun, as she would also have to endure the loss of my nephew Rashan nearly two years later. I was raised primarily by my mother and stepfather; he's really my dad. I mean, he's the only one that I ever had, and he did the best he could with what he knew during that time.

For decades, East St. Louis has been decaying in poverty and riddled with gang violence, trapped in a way of life not created by the people condemned to endure it but *by* others, *for* them. East St. Louis is a really hard place to grow up, but it is my home, and I love it. My family never had much, but we are awesome, nonetheless. I always tell people that once my family accepts you, it's 'til death do us part. I'm not kidding. I have plenty of family members who are actually the former partners of a cousin or an aunt. My family loves unconditionally and I am who I am today because of the special pieces of themselves they each gave to me somewhere during my first seventeen years. They are also the reason I work tirelessly to become the man I know I can be.

I joined the navy when I was seventeen. I knew there was nothing good waiting for me in East St. Louis, and I had a calling. When I was twelve, my mother and I watched the movie *Navy SEALs*, starring none other than Charlie Sheen. It was at that point that I made the decision to someday become a Navy SEAL. Not to mention, and most importantly, I was not ready for college at that time. In cities like East St. Louis, education isn't as encouraged as it should be. I had no idea of the value of an education until I began to seek an education. Then I quickly learned that its real value is self-preservation with all of the bells and whistles; it was the way to everything I would ever want. My naval career was an absolute dream. I was a very fortunate sailor in that I was always able to find my way into a good deal. My first significant duty station was in La Maddalena, Sardinia, Italy. That place will always hold a special place in my heart. But when 9/11 happened, I was reminded of my calling, and refocused on living my dream. I checked into the Naval Special Warfare Center in February 2002, just five months after the terror attack in NYC. My indoctrination into the ways of the special operations community began with Basic Underwater Demolition/SEAL school, or BUD/S, for short. Nearly a year and a half after that, I was in Afghanistan for the first time as a brand new Navy SEAL. My career in the SEAL teams is where I truly began to learn what leadership really means.

I retired from the navy after twenty years of service, including six tours to the Middle East. During the closing years of my career, I was given the opportunity of a lifetime. I was given the responsibility of leading what was, in my opinion, one of the greatest SEAL platoons in the history of the teams. I will always look back on my time with SEAL Team ONE, ECHO Platoon as very special, and in the most precious way. During the tail end of my career, I was given the opportunity here and there to focus on my education, and ultimately completed a bachelor of arts in organizational management from Ashford University; a university at which I now sit on the board of trustees. Also, I earned an MBV from the University of Southern California, Marshall Business School. Six months prior to graduation and the start of terminal leave from the navy, I launched Vigilance Risk Solutions, a San

Diego, California-based security and risk mitigation company that specializes in conflict and violence prevention.

As I was about halfway through my undergraduate degree, I was really beginning to realize how much I actually loved education. I was also beginning to realize that I was even pretty good at it. I remember distinctly developing a new kind of confidence. Then one day, I ran into a good friend and SEAL teammate who told me about the MBV program at USC. I went home that night, did some research, and nearly immediately realized that the program was for me. Although at the time, I was planning to join the FBI after I retired from the navy, I also had aspirations of someday becoming an entrepreneur. I loved the fact that I was able to see just how entrepreneurship-centric the program is by reviewing the curriculum online. I was also excited about the fact that I was finally getting the opportunity to experience graduate school in a brick-and-mortar environment. Most importantly, I was excited to be given the opportunity to give my family the ability to say that we had a male academic in the family.

I learned a lot about business and entrepreneurship during my studies at USC, but I think the most valuable parts of the program were more experiential than academic; at least for me, that was the case. While I was completing the MBV, I was also going through a very dark period in my life. My heart was pretty much in a perfect emotional storm.

Not only was post-traumatic stress finally catching up with me after a career of dispatching evil people on behalf of this great nation, but I found out I had received another invisible wound that was as damaging as anything visible could ever be. Living with PTSD and traumatic brain injury (TBI) is proving to be a never-ending mission in which the enemy I'm planning for is of the highest skill and has been trained by the severest school known to man. It has impacted my life; in some ways, it has harmed me. But, I can honestly say that I'm in a much better place now than I was during the MBV program. I truly believe that my MBV cohort and faculty lent a hand in the healing I've accomplished thus far. I'm grateful.

Other than my life, I'm grateful for regarding the entrepreneurial mindset the MBV program gave me, and how it has advanced my leadership potential. I was a good leader when I was in the SEAL teams. I led my men into harm's way; we faced the enemy on even turf, and we erased them. I brought my men home *visibly whole*. I was a good leader. But as a new entrepreneur who is finding a way to survive my first time at creating a business from scratch, I now have a completely new skillset to pass down to my sailors when they are ready to transition from careers in the military. They don't have to transition alone, the hard way. My mentorship of my sailors doesn't have to end just because I'm retired from active duty.

When I think of my highest points during the MBV program, I recall one time in particular. The ropes course is a team- and leadership-building physical obstacle course that MBV students have to complete twice; once during the first semester, and again during the second semester. This evolution would prove to be very special to me, but not solely because I was navigating the course with a cohort that had become more like a family to me than a cohort. This time was special to me because of something that happened at the first ropes course during the first semester that caused what happened during the second semester's course. During the first semester's ropes course, I had spoken with the MBV faculty and had received permission for my wife to participate. Even though this course was particularly designed to build teamwork and leadership within my class, I made it personal to me and that was selfish.

Philip Folsom, owner of Philip Folsom Programs and co-founder of Human Kind, was leading the event and he did not particularly agree with my wife participating. In my opinion, he didn't agree for reasons that I now understand to be an obvious contradiction to the goals he had built into his program. When I confronted Philip about his emotions, it was exactly that, a confrontation. My communication offended him, and I was being a bully. I'm ashamed to say that, but I know there's growth on the other side of my admission. But I have to defend myself at the same time because I was not myself. At that time, I was someone else. I was stuck in the perfect storm that had become my burden of post-traumatic stress. Not only was combat beginning to catch up with me, but the deaths of my sister and nephew were also nearly fatal to me. When I had finally come to the resemblance of a starting place to where I feel I am now, I realized how I had behaved, and how it must have affected Mr. Folsom, and was very disappointed with myself.

During the second semester, I was in a much better place. I was beginning my transition in leadership. Although I had a very long way to go (and still do), I was at least able to see the sun again. Near the end of the second semester, and very close to commencement, we met with Mr. Folsom and his crew again. As before, the ropes course was both challenging and fun. And, yes, I bonded with my cohort, and it was awesome. But the most important thing that happened to me that day was a very short, but in some ways everlasting, conversation between Philip and me. It wasn't even really a conversation—more like an encounter. Philip approached me with a genuine look of both humility and pleasure and simply said to me, "You're different now. Your entire energy is different. You look good, man." In that moment, I knew exactly what Philip meant, and I was relieved.

One of the most important lessons I have ever learned is empathy. I believe it is one of the best qualities a leader can have. You never know how the briefest of encounters will affect another person. You never know what another person has going on in their life. So be very careful as to how you treat people, regardless of who they are, how much they have, where they're from, what color they are, what they believe in, what their sexual orientation is. You never know how that interaction might touch them. It could be the difference between their giving up and refusing to. When I first met Philip, I was in a very different place. Maybe I was even considering giving up, in some way or another. I might have even still had one foot in that place during my second encounter with Philip. But what I got from Philip during that second encounter was what I would now call positive market feedback. It was proof I am not and won't ever be out of the fight, and I have serious gratitude for that. With honesty, I can say that I am a much more empathetic leader now than I was a few years ago. And my appreciation for that growth is immeasurable. Thanks, Philip.

I'm very fortunate to have completed the MBV program. When I first applied, I knew that I was curious about entrepreneurship, but really I was focused on getting hired by the FBI. I wasn't quite ready, or at least I didn't think I was ready, to tackle entrepreneurship. So I have to say that of all the things I took from the MBV program, it is the entrepreneurial spirit that completely altered my future. The feeling of being at USC is difficult to explain—you have to experience it. But it is a very special feeling. While I was at Marshall Business School, my entrepreneurial spirit caught fire and

I decided to take the leap prior to graduating. I'm really happy that I did, because for now, I am a successful entrepreneur.

Very close to commencement, I remember Professor Turrill asking us what it was we each wanted to leave behind as our graduate school education came to a close. I knew exactly what I *needed* to leave behind. For a long time, I've felt as if I was walking around in the eye of a storm. Years must have passed since I last saw the sun, and I mean *really* saw it. I had allowed post-traumatic stress to creep up on me like a thief in the night and consume me. I never even saw it coming. I just looked up one day, and it was there. Well, during my time in the MBV program, I went through a transformation. I was forced to confront the fact that I had become someone else, but that I didn't have to stay that way. So I utilized my time learning from people like Professor Turrill and James Bogle. Some of the lessons I took away from those conversations help me in my decision-making process to this day.

During the MBV program, I learned to think much more critically. That gained insight helped me become more mindful of myself and my emotions. That mindfulness gave me back a little more control when I was in the midst of one of my downtimes. I felt like I was no longer in the dark, and that I had a better understanding of post-traumatic stress, and how I could learn to live with it. So as I left graduate school, I decided I no longer needed the storm in which I had been consumed; I left it behind.

The personal growth I experienced in the MBV program was nothing shy of tremendous. And I have to admit, it feels really good. For example, during my time in military special operations, I learned to speak a very secret language. That language is the language of military acronyms. The military has an acronym for everything. I'm serious. You name it, and the military has an acronym for it. I never knew that once I transitioned from the military, I would need to learn how to speak like a civilian again. That meant needing to learn to speak business as well. I needed to learn the language of an MBA. I definitely learned how to speak MBA during my time at Marshall Business School. I also never considered how powerful of a step that would be in my overall transition. In fact, about two months ago, I was out to dinner with several former SEAL teammates, and one of them was telling me about some close quarters combat (CQC) training he had been doing with a local SWAT team. He was telling how he had to explain to them that there was no need for them to be moving so quickly through the kill-house. He said, "Unless it's HR, there's no need to go that fast." When he said that, I caught myself off-guard because the first thing I thought of when he said "HR" was human resources, not hostage rescue. I laughed out loud.

Since leaving the MBV program, I have continued to run VRS. I launched VRS just a few months prior to graduating from USC. We work primarily in the middle market, and many of our customers are public companies. We even work with a few Fortune 500 companies. We have grown from a company of three to a company of fifteen. I'm extremely proud of the company I've built and that my entrepreneurial spirit started at Marshall Business School. It feels good to be happy; I'm sure I am a much nicer person to be around. At least that's what my wife keeps telling me. We even had a beautiful baby girl, Josephine Rose Smith, named after her two great-grandmothers, came into the world on May 20, 2019, and saved my life. Thanks, Jo Jo. Daddy owes you big time.

Hae Hwang—Cohort III

I was the first in my family to join the military. I grew up a Korean immigrant, and the military was where all Korean men went—not because they wanted to, but because they had to. It was never a place for women. I watched my uncle pay off his college loan after having his second child; I told myself I would never get a loan. The military was a great option for me to continue my education when my parents couldn't afford it, but of course to my dad, it was not an option. I needed to convince my dad. The storyline I came up with was that, as a minority living in Koreatown, Los Angeles, I would never be able to compete with the majors. I would never be given opportunity equality as white people. But with military experience, I would be given an opportunity without being labeled a minority or a Korean-American. I would be an American soldier who served the country. It worked!

The eight years I served in the army taught me how to be resourceful, take initiative, organize and prioritize, and adapt quickly. It was quite different from my expectations. Then I was thrown into the job market with nothing but military experience. I quickly realized this was not enough. I needed to further my education to compete with the needs of the market. I was introduced to the MBV program and attended a job fair USC hosted for veterans. I was so nervous that I cried while being interviewed by James Bogle. Of course, I thought I did not have a chance of getting accepted, but I was. I knew I needed to make the best of this opportunity. I still remember hearing from previous cohorts on orientation day how important it was to have a study group and how much we would enjoy the leadership course. I started an Excel spreadsheet and collected everyone's contact information. By the end of the orientation day, it had gone out to everyone, and the study groups were already starting to form.

As a full-time graduate student with no daytime job, I also volunteered to create an assignment sheet, which was shared by the entire class to help everyone organize and prioritize what needed to happen in the two weeks between our meetings. Without realizing it, I was being challenged and encouraged to take a lead role. When I started the MBV, I had a tremendous fear of failing. Failing from the standards I set for me, and completely afraid of talking to someone I don't know because I feared they might not like me. Networking took a tremendous amount of energy for me, and I lacked confidence. I learned through the courses, discussions, and case studies that I enjoy problem-solving. I remember many classmates struggled to understand the accounting lectures and homework. I made study guides, cheat sheets, and study sessions to go over the materials together before the final. I never thought I was a leader, but I was evolving through the challenges I faced in MBV and learned how to recognize the problems and come up with solutions.

Fear of failure, procrastination, becoming too emotional, afraid of making new friends (networking), and being passive were a few things I wanted to leave behind as I was finishing the MBV. Networking, confidence, and emotional intelligence were goals I listed to continue to develop. Since I graduated from MBV in May 2016, I continued to work at DreamWorks Animation, but have transitioned into a different role. Due to the major M&A of NBC Universal and DreamWorks, I was left without leadership just one month after taking on the new role of HR coordinator. I needed to learn quickly, make quick assessments, create efficient processes, make executive decisions, figure out my resources, and network with different departments to find solutions to major corporate changes. I needed to communicate with employees and different members of leadership. I also needed to learn new systems and understand different organizational structures. Case studies from the strategy classes allowed me to understand the organizational structure and business model of NBC Universal. Accounting, finance, and corporate finance class allowed me to understand the different finance languages used to communicate the business operation. The communication class allowed me to understand emotional intelligence and how to adapt communication in different situations with employees, coworkers, and leadership. I can continue to list how the MBV program developed and amplified what I learned in the army and, best of all, allowed me to realize where I am and understand my potential.

It has been a little over a year since the M&A with NBC Universal, and major leadership change at DreamWorks and my direct department, HR, I had to learn to adapt and proceed. I have learned to create organizational charts, develop creative solutions to difficult and sensitive employee issues, and network across departments to provide seamless service to DreamWorks employees. I have learned the new HR processing system, created multiple efficient procedures to do what was once done manually, researched and provided information to leadership for effective decision-making, and hosted weekly orientation sessions for new employees. Unique to the entertainment industry, I have had the chance to work with a few different local unions, with whose representatives I have networked to understand how unions support our employees and how to communicate effectively with them.

The networking growth channeled out to mentoring as well—to Korean USC undergrads. I was invited to be one of the panel members to the club called KCOSO, Korean Career Oriented Student Organization's event, where I talked about what I do at DreamWorks, how I got there, and what I would recommend to the student. I have continued to provide mentoring and encouragement to KCOSO students and regularly attend their events. It has been an amazing experience.

I can say the MBV was one of the best decisions I've made and the only thing I regret, looking back to 2016, is not taking the time to network with different clubs and mixers or taking advantage of time to do more informational interviews and get introduced to leaders in different fields of businesses. The program gave me some amazing friends who challenge me to be better every day. I continue to challenge myself daily to learn something new and to raise my hand and stand in front of people. It still scares me, but I enjoy watching myself grow.

Troy Baisch—Cohort VI

My name is Troy Baisch. It's taken over forty-five years for me to be able to proudly say, "I am a Trojan!" On New Year's Day 1973, the USC Trojans demolished the OSU Buckeyes 42–17 in the fifty-ninth Rose Bowl. I was nine years old. The sportscasters on TV kept talking about the "Men of Troy," which I thought was pretty cool because most of the time I was getting teased for having a weird name. But now here were all these fans at the Rose Bowl cheering for guys with the same name. I knew I wanted to be a Trojan and to attend USC more than anything else in the world. But as I got older, it became an impossible dream. I lost my way because I lacked the confidence to succeed.

As a youngster, school was easy for me. I was a straight-A student through elementary and junior high school, but then got complacent. In high school, the work became more challenging, and my laziness impacted my grades. As my academic performance suffered, so did my confidence. I made poor choices and worse friends. By the time I was a senior, my future appeared to be a dead-end job and community college, if I was lucky. No way was I ever going to go to USC!

I graduated high school in June 1981, and, despite my mediocre performance, was accepted by Chapman College in Orange, California. I enrolled for fall 1981, and dropped out after one semester. I went to Cal State Fullerton in the fall of 1982, and dropped out after one semester. Quitting became a habit. So did a lot of other really destructive behaviors. Reflecting on that time in my life now, it's a wonder I'm still alive. After a few more years aimless and adrift, I decided that a radical course change was necessary if I were ever going to live up to my potential and achieve anything meaningful.

I enlisted in the navy at age twenty-three and began recruit training on September 17, 1986. My first navy memories are of eighty recruits waking up at 0300 to the sounds of crashing garbage cans and screaming drill instructors. Everyone was terrified and disoriented by the sudden shock. It was our first lesson, and an important one: bad things often occur when you're most vulnerable, and you must be able to overcome that initial shock, gather your wits about you, and do your duty.

The navy changed my life. It became the one thing at which I'd succeeded that was challenging and required honest effort. Hard work and success turned out to be as habit-forming as mediocrity and quitting had been for me earlier. The navy also changed my worldview. Traveling the globe and living overseas enhanced my appreciation for all we have in the US, and also gave me a deep and abiding respect for other cultures and customs.

I owe much of the success I enjoyed throughout my career in the navy to others. I had leaders and mentors who showed me the way and challenged and encouraged me to do my best, even when I believed I wasn't up to the task. I was often sent to jobs I didn't want in places I didn't want to go, but the tours I thought would be the worst turned out to be the most personally and professionally rewarding. Getting outside my comfort zone was necessary for growth. It also taught me that the people who have your best interests at heart are often the ones making you do the things you'd rather not. I retired in December 2016 as a chief warrant officer 4 after thirty years of service.

When I retired from the navy, I wasn't really sure what I wanted to do professionally, so I decided to go back to school and finish once and for all. I'd been taking classes off and on while I was on active duty and I had over 230 units, but only an AA to show for it. I took a few classes at Park University while at Camp Pendleton in the '90s and enjoyed their small class sizes, so I decided to re-enroll and finish my undergraduate work there. I graduated from Park in March 2018, with nearly 270 units.

As I neared completion of my undergrad work, I gave some thought to going to grad school because I wanted to teach part-time at Mira Costa College or Palomar College, and maybe at Park University Camp Pendleton. I was looking at a number of graduate programs, but USC and MBV were not among them. Then a really weird thing happened.

I was at home one day when my doorbell rang. There at my door was my doppelgänger neighbor, Jason Witt from MBV Cohort V. At the time, he and his wife, Melissa, lived at the same house number I do, but one street over. I live on San Helena Drive; they lived on San Tomas Drive. The FedEx and UPS guys are constantly getting our houses mixed up, but I'd never actually met Jason before. He was looking for his iPhone delivery. He saw all the USC memorabilia in my house, and asked if I went to USC, and I told him no, I'd always wanted to go and was a huge fan, but had never had the chance. He told me about MBV and invited me to attend an information session. So even before I attended USC, the Trojan network was already a powerful resource!

The first information session I went to was held on campus in February 2018. James Bogle did the bulk of the presentation, and he convinced me the MBV was right for me, but I was still unsure if I was *ready* for USC. Despite the success I'd enjoyed, I still had doubt I could actually do it. Then Dr. Turrill gave us his thoughts on the program, its history, and its future. He talked about the Trojan family and service to others. It made a pretty powerful impression, and I determined then and there that I was all in. It's one of those moments I'll remember for the rest of my life because I realized in an instant that something I'd wanted to do for over forty-five years was actually possible, so long as I was willing to take the leap and make it so. "You can't win if you don't step onto the field."

It's funny how things work out. Back in June 2010, I suffered a heart attack while I was on transfer leave between duty stations. It was really a blessing in disguise. I was young enough to survive it, but old enough to know I couldn't just put things off until someday, because someday might be too late. As soon as I was on the path to recovery, I went to the local tattoo shop and got Tommy Trojan tattooed on my left shoulder. I believed it would motivate me to finally get to USC one day because if I didn't, I'd look pretty stupid laying in my coffin with a tattoo of Tommy Trojan on my shoulder and nothing to show for it. When I sat in that information session and listened to James and Dr. Turrill, I thought: *I need to do this right now or I'm going to regret it for eternity—literally!* I spent the next two months mercilessly pestering Jamie Saure with admissions questions, and I'm now convinced she is the most patient person on the planet.

To say that MBV was an incredible experience for me is a gross understatement. When I retired from the navy, I thought I'd never have the opportunity to experience the same kind of camaraderie and esprit de corps I'd had in the military. MBV provided that, and much more. The quality of the instruction is exceptional, but I could have received quality instruction in any other graduate program at USC, or at any other top business school, for that matter. The people and relationships that come with MBV are what make it so special. Every day, I think about those people and our time together. Every day.

The real blessing of the Trojan network isn't that there are people you can call upon all over the world when you have a question about something, or you need some kind of assistance. The real blessing is that there are people all over the world who trust you and will call you when they have a question or need help with something because you're a Trojan and they know they can rely upon a fellow Trojan to help in a time of need.

The opportunity to bond with such a diverse group of veterans is something that can't be found in any other program or any other university, and the benefits it provides are tremendous. Having a mixture of professionals who were long-separated from the service, recently retired or separated, currently transitioning or remaining on active duty and of varying experience from junior enlisted to field-grade officer all in the same room and on the same team was the secret sauce that made the program such an enriching experience. Three big takeaways for any leader, whether seasoned or aspiring: (1) you *can* teach an old dog new tricks; (2) that young guy/girl who doesn't know anything knows a lot more than you think they do; and (3) asking for help is not a sign of weakness.

When I began my journey with MBV Cohort VI in July 2018, I wasn't sure what I wanted to do, but I knew what I *didn't* want to do. I was not interested in entrepreneurship, and I did not want to work for the government ever again. So now, a year later, I'm happy to report that I've started my own company, Charlie-Six Group LLC, and I've taken a term position with the Commerce Department to manage the Census Bureau's local office in support of the 2020 census.

Cris Pacheco—Cohort VI

My name is Cris Pacheco. My story begins growing up in the city of Chino all the way through high school. I went to Ontario Christian for the entirety of my academic career except for my junior year, when I went to Chino High. This was due to the financial crisis that swept away my parents' business as well as my father passing in 2009. I was always a decent student and had a full-ride scholarship to attend Cal Poly Pomona in 2010.

Long story short, I was exposed to partying and had such a great time that I forgot to go to class and put no effort into school. I thought academia was mundane and obsolete as I was making money on the weekends hosting events in downtown Pomona. I was very involved with organizations (LBSA) and growing my entertainment business, but not with going to school and completely putting it on the back burner was terrible for my sense of accomplishment.

My mother kicked me out in 2012 (when I was twenty), and I ended up living in my car for a month and a half in various places in Orange County. Any parking lot was my home to sleep—good thing I had a 24-hour fitness pass to be able to shower! I was lost during this time, but luckily had a job that allowed me to network and work with great leaders.

As a way to recover my career, I turned to trying to be a firefighter by attending Santa Ana College. It was during this time that my confidence started to rise as I was succeeding in classes, finally! Once I went to my first firefighting job fair, along with 10,000 others in Long Beach, I realized patience would be needed—something I did not have. Luckily, another classmate, Nakisha Reed, was a veteran who advised me that I could really make something of myself in the Marine Corps.

In April 2014, I reported to MCRD in San Diego for boot camp. I did very well and was assigned to be an amphibious assault crewman at Camp Pendleton. During this time, I had gotten jumped out in Los Angeles, which required reconstructive surgery of my whole jaw. I also met my lovely wife, Lee. While I was enlisted, I was able to finish my undergraduate studies with National University and graduated in 2016! This was a huge accomplishment, which went along with being a competent marine and leader. In May 2016, I started my digital marketing company, Surge Digital. During this time, I also purchased my first home with my wife in San Juan Capistrano, where we currently live. Drinking ceased in December 2016 as well, which has helped all my mental issues I was having, by the grace of God. I had recovered my career and my life.

As a transitioning veteran in 2018, I hit the ground running by growing my business and being accepted into MBV at USC! This was a very stressful time as I was constantly working, studying, and commuting. USC was the greatest component that has ever happened to my career! All the connections, opportunities, curriculum, resources, and football games allowed me to be successful in business and in the classroom (dean's list both semesters with above 3.7 GPA). This was a great confidence and competency builder for my future and my family's future. I feel a great sense of accomplishment to have graduated from a prestigious institution like USC, and from my dream school. USC has put my life into an upward trajectory, which I hope to continue to give back as well. Currently, I am serving as the founder of the Trojan Cannabis Network by bridging the gap between alumni and industry professionals in the hopes of creating opportunities in business and advocacy (volunteer). Thank you to all the staff, faculty, mentors, and students who have made my experience a beneficial one! If you are reading this, please do not take anything for granted! I was lucky life didn't go into a deeper spiral and will be forever grateful for where life has taken me. Confidence and competency were goals I accomplished at USC. Thank you for letting me share my story. I hope this can bring value to someone.

Lester Ciudad Real—Cohort II

I grew up right outside of Manhattan in an urban/suburban part of New Jersey. Like many kids in my neighborhood, I grew up poor with not much expectation of becoming more than a blue-collar worker. My parents were both immigrants who did not get past sixth grade. My mother taught me a lot about hard work, and I believe she is the reason behind my strong work ethic. I was not the best student in grammar school or high school, but I did enjoy playing sports and being part of teams. I found out early that being part of a team is special, and that goals and accomplishments are attained together, not as individuals. As I reflect back, I would say this is one of the reasons I decided to go into the military.

I remember always being intrigued by the military. As a kid, I played soldier with my friends. As a teenager, I began to learn about military history and the different branches. I was instantly intrigued by the Marine Corps. Their reputation as the toughest, most accomplished, and best dressed solidified the deal. I knew in my heart that one day I would support, defend, and risk my life for this country and what better way to do than as a United States marine?

When I was in high school, I thought about going to college, but my grades and guidance were not leading me to a four-year university. There was a moment during my final days of my senior year of high school where the faculty posted the names of all the graduating seniors and what university they would attend. As I read my peers' names and college acceptances, I was happy for them, but sadly my name did not have a college next to it. It was at this moment that I realized I had not fully taken advantage of my opportunity, but also that something needed to be done. After high school graduation, I attempted to enlist in the Marine Corps, but due to certain circumstances, could not. I needed to figure out what I was going to do. I got a job working in a warehouse through a temp agency. I worked from warehouse to warehouse, getting paid minimum wage, taking the bus back and forth to work. This lasted about six months. I realized then and there that I needed to do something with my life, or I would be stuck in what I felt was purgatory. So I quit my job that day and enrolled in community college. It was the beginning of my long journey.

My goal of becoming a United States marine was always on the top of my mind, and I always reminded myself I would accomplish this goal, no matter what. When I enrolled in community college, I did so with the intention of completing an associate's degree and then transferring to a university.

Since my education journey began, I have earned two master's degrees from the University of Southern California and a bachelor's from Hawaii Pacific University. I have had several people ask me what degree I am most proud of. I pause and, with all my bearing, say my associate's degree from my community college. Most people are astonished and ask why. I tell them it's simply because it was the toughest degree to get. It took me three and a half years to earn my degree. I commuted by bus sometimes up to two hours each way. There were times I had to walk several miles to catch a connecting bus because I missed the last bus. I worked full time, and most semesters went to school full time. There were some semesters I could only go part time, which delayed my completion. In addition to my circumstances, I also was fighting my environment. When most of my friends were hanging out and doing what most nineteen- and twenty-year-olds do in my neighborhood, I was commuting to school or working. It was one of the toughest goals I accomplished. It taught me persistence, perseverance, and to keep on going no matter what. To prove to myself and everyone else that I could do it when so many believed I couldn't. When I received my diploma in the mail, I had tears of joy. At that moment, I knew I could accomplish any goal I put my mind to. The following semester, I enrolled in a four-year university in New Jersey to finish earning a bachelor's degree. Not much changed. I still worked full time and went to school full-time, all with the intention of graduating college and commissioning as a second lieutenant in the Marine Corps.

It was early February 2007 when I decided my real goal in life was to be a US marine. That dream was beginning to wither away. I was twenty-seven, and realized if I did not take action then I would never reach my dream. I paused my college education and enlisted in the United States Marine Corps. I swore in on June 2, 2007, and was shipped off to Paris Island, South Carolina.

It was midnight when I arrived on the island. The bus doors opened and the drill instructor yelled, "Get off my bus!" We were directed to stand on the infamous yellow footprints. The yellow footprints signify many things, but mostly the transition from civilian to marine. I had made it—or I thought I had. I still had thirteen weeks of hell to get through!

I have talked with many marines about their experience at Paris Island. A few claim boot camp was fun. I disagree. It was extremely tough, and it took every ounce of me to get through it. I don't think the physical aspect was the toughest. I believe the mental part was. Speaking candidly, quitting did cross my mind. But I then reminded myself why I was there and what was waiting for me at the end. I completed the goal. On August 19, 2007, I earned my eagle globe and anchor and the title of United States marine. Outside of my son's birth, it was the proudest moment of my life. I'd done it! But I realized soon after that it was only the beginning.

The Marine Corps was one of the best experiences of my life. It taught me how to be a leader. But more important, it taught me how to follow and be humble. My first unit was HMH 363, a helicopter squadron. My MOS or job description was a 6042, also known as an IMRL asset manager. My responsibilities were to manage aircraft equipment, everything from a small wrench to cranes and motorized equipment. After a few months at the squadron, there was an opportunity to volunteer to be an air crew/machine gunner on the helicopter. I applied for the chance to help out any way I could, but first I would have to qualify. About eight of us requested to take part, but only five made it due to the physical and educational portion of the qualification. It was extremely tough, and I barely made it. It was December 2009 when I got pinned with my aircrew wings, which happened to be a couple weeks before we were to deploy to Afghanistan.

Boots were on the ground February 2010, in the Helmand Province. We were flown in to Camp Leatherneck in a C-17. It was a little nerve-wracking when the C-17 had to do a nose dive in order to avoid enemy incoming fire. At that moment, I knew our lives would be forever different.

Flying in Afghanistan was a great experience. The air crew members were on a rotation schedule. We would fly outside the wire four to six days a week for up to ten hours at a time. We were responsible for transporting troops and gear in and out of Forward Observation Base, sometimes in really hot areas. Taking enemy fire was a normal occurrence. My first deployment was a great learning experience for me. I was tested in many different ways. I learned many skills, both hard and soft, and a lot about myself. I would take all of this with me for the rest of my life. I successfully completed my first combat tour, and would be back in the sandbox a year and a half later.

My second tour, I was attached to a C13 squadron. I was no longer aircrew and only focused on my primary MOS. This tour was a little different in that we were beginning to slowly pull out of Afghanistan. You could see the downsize on a weekly basis. The danger was still high, as there were many base attacks in 2012 throughout Afghanistan. A lot of my downtime was spent in the gym and studying for the GMAT exam so I'd have options if and when I decided to get out of the corps. My second deployment came to an end, and I was on my way home again.

It was 2013 when I arrived back in San Diego from Afghanistan. It was a pivotal time in my life as I had to make a decision whether I was going to reenlist for four more years or get out of the Corps and begin a new career as a civilian. It was a very stressful time. I was debating if I would put an end to one of my life's dreams. The decision came down to two options. I would reenlist for four more years, which would put me at twelve years of service. I figured if I reenlisted, I might as well stay and complete the twenty years for retirement. The problem with this option was that I saw the rest of my career in the military and wasn't sure that was the way I wanted to finish my time in the Corps. The other option was to get out, get a master's degree, and start a new career where I could follow other interests. I decided to go with the latter. I soon began researching MBA programs. It was at this time that I stumbled onto the MBV program.

The MBV is a one-year degree specifically for veterans. I like to think of the program as an executive MBA for veterans. For many of my classmates, this graduate program was a transitioning program. For others, it was an opportunity to improve the hard skills required for the business world. In terms of transitioning from active-duty service member to civilian, the MBV was like those yellow footprints I once stood on in Paris Island. It was a transformation that began my career in the business world. The MBV at USC not only provided me with the hard skills I needed to succeed in business, but allowed me to build some great relationships. I still maintain close relationships with many of my former classmates. It's important to express that I had never been part of, nor will be, a class, cohort, or program that had such camaraderie and support for one another. In the military, brothers-in-arms stick together; this holds true outside of the military as well.

As I was transitioning from the military, I didn't know what I didn't know in terms of what industries and career paths were out there, but I knew I had an interest in real estate and finance. I began to network and do informational interviews. Through my networking, I met a former navy officer who had been in the original Cohort I of the MBV. While he was still in the program, he was also interning at Goldman Sachs in New York. I was intrigued for two reasons. The first was that he was commuting every other weekend between New York and Los Angeles. The other was that he was able to intern at one of the best investment banking firms in the world. He introduced me to the internship program called the Goldman Sachs Veterans Integration Program, also known as the VIP. I decided to apply to the VIP, even though I doubted I would make it to the first round of interviews. A couple of weeks later, I received an email stating I had made it to the first round of interviews, which was a phone interview. I like to think I was a little lucky during the phone interview as my interviewer was also a veteran marine who was stationed in Hawaii around the same time I was, so we built rapport instantly. He recommended me to the next round. The next round wasn't so easy. I was invited to interview in Dallas in what they call a superday. It was four back-to-back thirty-minute interviews with two interviewers. It was very challenging, but many of the interview skills I had learned were all due to the MBV and the Marshall School of Business. I prepared endlessly, rehearsing and predicting what they would ask me. I wanted to go into that interview and capture it, and that's exactly what I did.

About a week later, I received a phone call and was offered the opportunity to be part of the 2015 VIP Cohort. Three out of seventeen interviewees were the only ones to receive an offer. I credit much of my success in this endeavor to the MBV for not only preparing me for this opportunity but also giving me the confidence that I could succeed. I was an enlisted guy who competed with mainly officers, many of whom had done their education at one of the academies (e.g., West Point, Naval Academy, and the Air Force Academy). The internship program was a very competitive program that had some of the most accomplished veterans I have ever met in it. I was honored to have been part of this elite group.

In February 2015, I began the internship. I spent one week in New York and seven weeks in Dallas. I commuted every other weekend from Dallas to Los Angeles to make it in time for class. I put in long hours at Goldman Sachs to come home and finish up work for class. It was exhausting. I was offered a full-time position at Goldman Sachs after the internship, and I accepted.

I graduated from the MBV in May 2015. It was one of the most gratifying moments of my life. Prior to the MBV, I was trying to find myself. I had all these preconceived notions that because of my background I would not be able to work for a large organization like Goldman Sachs, or that because I didn't go to a big-name school as an undergraduate student, I could not compete with those that had. Through the MBV I learned that is not the case. It does not matter where you start; it matters where you end. It took a long time for me to realize that. That I am just as good as the next guy or gal. I will always be grateful to the MBV, Cohort II, James Bogle, and Robert Turrill for making a success of every veteran who steps foot into this great business program. I owe much of my success to the MBV and USC, and for that, I thank you.

Delilah Johnston—Cohort IV

Upon being accepted into the MBV program, I was already in an established career with the City of Los Angeles without any intentions of becoming an entrepreneur. My goal was to complete the program with hopes that this new educational accomplishment would make me more competitive in promoting to a management position.

The MBV program provided me with more than an entrepreneurial understanding. The leadership course was instrumental in my personal growth and developed my approach to situations, both professionally and personally. The business acumen I obtained through the many courses has provided me with a skillset to run a business, but also allowed for a different perspective in my current career. This knowledge has separated me from my peers, who lack an entrepreneurial background that shows itself when overseeing projects, budget analysis, or innovative ideas. The learned emotional intelligence competencies have helped me obtain better results when trying to achieve a win for work projects by shaping my approach to situations and personalities.

My personal reflection since graduating the MBV program has been very positive and beneficial. The USC network was instilled in us at the start of school, but I didn't realize how useful and powerful it was until graduating. In retrospect, I wish I could have utilized and grown my connections more before graduating—something I'm working to catch up on now. I am dedicating time to stay connected with peers in my cohort and attend functions when possible. The MBV program has made changes and influenced me professionally as well. Those higher up in my organization have noticed the differences in my ability to manage, resolve, and implement improvements for efficiencies. The credibility of this degree has made me a top contender for the next level of management in my career.

Eddie Arambula—Cohort IV

"I am my own king on my own chess board," I would say when I was growing up. My parents emigrated from Mexico when I was a child and always told me I could be whatever I wanted to be. I just had to work for it. My youth was full of ignorance of what went on outside of my studies. When I was in high school, I began to notice the financial struggles my parents had. I remember not taking my graduation picture because it would cost fifty dollars and my parents did not have the extra money for that. I wasn't upset—I just realized the difference between needs and wants and that our allocation mostly went toward basic household needs.

During my freshman year in high school, I was presented with my first life challenge. In the spring of 1997, I tried out for my school's baseball team. I had only played intermittently during my childhood. My parents worked a lot, so my brother and I didn't have much time for extracurricular activities. Needless to say, I was not very prepared for high school baseball. The coach said, "You don't have what it takes to make this year's team." Of all my friends, I was the only one who was cut. Being a good student did not translate to success on the baseball diamond. At my young age of fifteen, I considered it my first failure. I decided I had a choice to make: give up on my dream of playing baseball or work on my skills and try again next year. I watched all the home games from the stands and cheered my friends on, wondering what lay ahead.

That summer, I worked on my baseball skills with a few of my buddies. I was determined to make the team the next year. I went to the park daily and continued to work diligently on the tools needed to play baseball. My friends hit countless ground balls and fly balls for me to catch. They threw batting practice to me until the sun went down. It was a most memorable summer. I worked harder than I had ever worked on any skill. I made the team the following year and played every game until I graduated. I batted .441 and stole twenty-three bases as the starting catcher. Unbeknownst to me at the time, the drive and determination I had would be the answer to many of my challenges to come.

The year 2001 was remarkable for many reasons. I graduated from Gardena High School with honors, I was accepted to a university, and I had a job. Being the first in my family to finish high school and enter an institution of higher education was a worthy accomplishment, but there was more to come that year that would make it tough for everybody. Being your own king on your own chess board means that you are in control of yourself and the surrounding environment. Maybe I didn't know what I was really saying when I came up with it. Perhaps it was just a way to think that I was in control of my destiny.

September 11, 2001, was a day like no other. I was in the student lounge of Cal State Fullerton early that morning, hanging out and waiting for my first class. On the two television screens there, I witnessed the events unfold and watched the towers come crashing down. I remember seeing students crying. I was in a daze, only seventeen years old and not understanding what was to come. Next, my parents lost their jobs in the recession that began in 2001, after an unprecedented ten years of growth. Nearly eight million people became unemployed by the fourth quarter of 2001, up by more than two million from a year earlier. It was a challenging situation for my family. I was in college and working, while my younger brother was still in high school, and my parents were both unemployed. Furthermore, my college experience was not going well. I felt out of place by the drastic change in demographics and the lack of Latinos around campus. I started missing classes, and my grades began to drop. After graduating from high school with honors, I finished my freshman year at Cal State Fullerton with a 1.67 GPA.

As the days went by and my parents' savings depleted, I took it upon myself to find a way to help out my family. I went to my local US Army recruiting office and got the information I needed to make a sound decision. I shipped out to Ft. Benning, Georgia, in the summer of 2002, for basic infantry training. I was eighteen years old. Another first in my family. No one had ever served in the military. It was a mentally and physically tough sixteen weeks, but I had the drive and determination to succeed. Plus, the biweekly paychecks were holding my family together and keeping them out of poverty.

The decisions I made in my youth shaped what I have become. My education did not end in the spring of 2002. After a few years in the service, I decided to go back to school part time. At the time, I never imagined that after almost a decade, I would have completed two bachelors and two master's degrees. I enjoy studying, learning, analyzing, and writing so much, I am in the application process for a PhD program. Once again, that drive and determination helped and guided me toward achieving my goals.

There are many reasons I chose to pursue the MBV. As a previous graduate student at USC, I was very impressed with the rigor, professionalism, and quality of the staff. Furthermore, there is no program in the nation like it. It is designed solely for veterans like myself, to successfully transition leadership and managerial skills into the private sector. Although there is no other program to compare it with, I am completely confident in USC and the Marshall School of Business to conduct a program fitting of its reputation. Lastly, the comfort of joining a cohort strictly built of veterans is a most beautiful thought. The opportunity to not only share a classroom but also personal experiences in a supportive environment at USC is the most important reason for pursuing this degree.

Highlights of my experience with the MBV program include the relationships that were built, nurtured, and maintained there, professors and students alike. A year later, I remain in contact with many classmates as we continue to push each other in a positive direction. We discuss our goals, whether personal and professional, and troubleshoot hurdles along the way.

The diversity in service, ranks, and military occupations was also a plus within the program.

Additionally, the faculty created a program in which it is OK to feel vulnerable and reach far outside your comfort zone. It is a safe place. It is in that zone of discomfort where we grow the most. Football tailgates were also a favorite. Once again, spending quality time with classmates and faculty outside of the classroom was always a plus. Great memories are remembered and missed, as we know that those moments spent as a complete cohort have come and gone. We know how difficult it may be to have a reunion where everyone is there once more. From a leadership and development standpoint, I realized I had many traits, skills, and experience that were transferable. Through assessment tools like the career leader report, I gained further understanding of those skills. During class projects and assignments, I continued to establish additional leadership competencies.

High points of my experience in the MBV program included the ropes course and leading multiple projects during entrepreneurship/marketing class. The ropes course was designed to help identify fears, biases, behaviors, and baby seagulls. As the day went by, I excelled in managing and controlling a fear of heights. Being more comfortable than other classmates, I felt a duty to help those in need of help. I felt pretty confident as I completed all the obstacles until I got to the rock wall. Cecilia and I decided to race each other up the wall. We climbed as fast as we could and were side by side until about ten feet to the top. I was fatigued and got stuck on an obstacle I could not reach. Cecilia got to the top and cheered me on. I tried and tried and tried to reach the next rock. I could not do it by myself. I realized I needed help. It took a few minutes to realize that I could either ask for help or be stranded there, unable to reach the top. I was so close. I swallowed my pride and yelled down to my group, "Team, I need some help!" They replied, "We will help you!" and up I went. It was a special moment. I realized I had help—all I needed to do was ask. After that realization, I was more comfortable with the MBV program. I reached out to classmates and professors as I needed help. I didn't feel like I had to figure out everything on my own. The ropes course showed us we were stronger together, and stronger we became. Key takeaways from the program that influenced my decision to continue my education beyond the MBV included my interest in theory and research, leadership, and my comfort within the academic setting.

I honor those men with whom I served by doing the best I can each day. Those men who gave the ultimate sacrifice are my heroes. They will never be forgotten. As I continue on my journey, I will hold their memories close, for they give me strength. I owe it to them, just as much as I owe it to myself, to utilize my gifts and continue toward my goal of completing a PhD, hopefully becoming a professor one day. [Eddie is currently in the PhD program at Texas State University, RBT.]

The MBV program pushed me well beyond my comfort zone. As a result, I became a better speaker, more in tune with my leadership and management skills, and less hesitant to ask for help. I also gained an entrepreneurship perspective.

I still keep in contact with numerous classmates who are at different stages of their career or military service. I've also contacted friends I served with to inform them about the MBV program, its benefits, rigor, and quality. Since the program ended, I have also noticed my increased awareness, patience, and communication with my autistic son. I have tried to influence him without using so much authority, and it has helped keep open lines of communication. He enjoys my openness to negotiating certain situations, as well. I am very proud of both our progress. We will continue to grow together and to nurture the father-son dynamic.

Since completing the MBV program, I've moved near Austin, Texas. My wife secured employment as a structural engineer, my kids are well adjusted to their new home and school, and I have found the direction in which I'd like to proceed. I continue to set short- and long-term goals (personally and professionally), to network, push myself out of my comfort zone (speaking about myself), maintain contact with classmates, and, most importantly, take care of my mental, physical, and emotional well-being. Although I realized most of my network and support system was being left behind in Los Angeles, I have diligently worked on attaining one here, as well. Lastly, I know that all I need to do is ask for help and the MBV family will come to my aid.

CHAPTER 4

UNDERSTANDING LEADERSHIP

Men of Cohort V in the Los Angeles Coliseum during the singing of the national anthem.

> "It is not the critic who counts; not the man who points out how the strong man stumbles, or where the doer of deeds could have done them better. The credit belongs to the man who is actually in the arena, whose face is marred by dust and sweat and blood, who strives valiantly, who errs, who comes short again and again, because there is no effort without error and shortcoming. But who does actually strive to do the deeds, who knows great enthusiasms, the great devotions, who spends himself in a worthy cause, who at the best knows in the end the triumph of high achievement, and who at the worst, if he fails, at least fails while daring greatly, so that his place shall never be with those cold and timid souls who neither know victory nor defeat."
> (Theodore Roosevelt 1910)

The quote above from Roosevelt's The Man in the Arena speech is the most frequent one veterans employ in the papers they write in the leadership section of the MBV program. I use it here to foreshadow my approach to leadership within the program, as well as to recognize that it seems to resonate with a number of veterans.

I begin with self-awareness, self-knowledge, self-control, and personal growth under the umbrella concept, "Leadership is the expression of our best self."

> "At bottom, becoming a leader is synonymous with becoming yourself. To become a leader, then you must become yourself, become the maker of your own life. All of the leaders I talked with agreed that no one can teach you how to become yourself, to take charge, express yourself, except you." (Bennis 1989)

It wasn't until the end of Cohort III, in May 2016, that I began to understand deeply that the responsibility for leadership had its roots in our best sense of self, or an idealized self. It's not just a prescribed set of role behaviors. It's not just matching a particular style with a certain situation. It certainly isn't random, and no one currently believes that leaders are born, not made. And while charisma may be useful in some cases, it can also be dysfunctional in others, and is not a requirement of having influence and impact in service of achieving goals. It's more an intersection of mission, people, context, and character. The only one over which the individual has control is their character, their concept of their best self.

How, then, does one achieve one's best self? What are the aspirational goals one must develop to guide one in self-development and self-improvement? Becoming one's best self is a 'being' statement. If we look at one of the army's guides for leaders, "Be, Know, Do," we see both of those modalities highlighted, but the army leads with the being imperative right up front. This isn't always so clear in other leadership texts or guides. Most leadership writing provides directions for what to do to succeed in leading organizations, but most don't mention people in the organization, except to label them followers. When one considers leadership as an influence and impact process, it opens the idea up to all players, not just formal leaders. This implies that everyone, through their presence and actions, is in the process of influencing others and potentially creating an impact with their influence. As the concepts of followers and subordinates imply, there is a hierarchy where some, by role and title, have more authority and influence than others. Observing this process, I may be led to the conclusion that if I'm not the leader, I'm also not responsible for initiating behavior or for outcomes. If I should become the leader, then I will take responsibility, but until that time, I will comply as necessary, and probably keep my head down so as not to make a mistake or to suffer criticism.

When engaging students in developing their own leadership abilities, I avoid focusing on how to be a good follower. I want each individual to focus solely on their ability to influence and have impact through their behavior. I also avoid using the concept of leadership as only a superior role and position within a hierarchy. Everyone is capable of leadership, and everyone is capable of having influence and impact within a context. This is where I place the focus on developing. In reality, this process of influence goes on constantly at work as well as in other contexts, and everyone is involved in it.

It is important to grasp the idea that we are all always influencing others within any context with our presence and behavior, rather than focusing on either hierarchical position or compliance as leadership. In an all-military context and classroom, compliance is ingrained in everyone's behavior. In fact, non-compliance to a lawful order is punishable under the Uniform

Code of Military Justice, so it is non-trivial. So we know about compliance. As students begin to transition to other contexts and roles, the idea of contribution begins to move in on the concept of compliance, where one is charged early in one's career to add value. And should one begin a business, then the idea that leadership is taking charge of both the context and performance is organic.

If one is in a context that is team-based, then adding value and contributing is not only valued, but required of a good team member. As we use more and more collaborating structures and behavior, the concept of contributing becomes more demanding. This is often difficult for students to accept, as in many team project environments, I frequently hear, "I'm not the leader, so I will do what is asked of me or what is delegated." So high-performance team environments require members to be at their best at all times, sometimes initiating and influencing and sometimes being influenced and helping to carry out the decisions of other members.

Good team members know how to facilitate their team's performance as well as to build on each other's ideas and contributions. All of these behaviors are learned competencies and contribute to the overall performance of the unit. When we operate from the perspective of our best self, we have the competencies to move in and out of a lead role, assist others, and contribute to the performance outcomes of the team, as a team. One's leadership then involves knowing when to step up, when to support, and when to facilitate. In a recent article, "The Four X Factors of Exceptional Leaders," one of the factors is "They play well on teams they don't lead." (Reimer, Grant, and Feuerstein, 2018). The authors contend that candidates for the C suite don't have to continue to try to be the smartest person in the room, but to develop their own team members and play well with other teams they are not on. But when helping others develop their own leadership and influence competencies, we recognize that all these behaviors have influence and impact.

Our focus as an individual then, in various contexts, is to make sure our contribution and impact are positive and add to the effectiveness of the unit. Much of effective leadership is submerging one's ego in service of the mission and overall team effectiveness. There are often powerful egos at work—sometimes in conflict and sometimes in collaboration—but one of the keys to effective leadership is to focus more on mission and not on ego or the need to be right. The heroic leadership style that needs to be dominant, decisive, right, and always win, will be ineffective in the complexity, ambiguity, and uncertainty of the organizational context. Increasingly, the spotlight is focused on the issue of when charisma, for example, becomes confused with narcissism and negatively affects the narcissistic CEO's performance (Chatterjee and Hambrick 2007).

Self-confidence is typically included in a list of traits, values, and competencies for leadership, but self-confidence originates not within a strong ego, but within the awareness that one can deal effectively with a variety of situations and challenges. Humility can be a partner with self-confidence.

One of the quotes included in the set of most effective leadership descriptions by one of the students in Cohort III, was describing the most effective leader they had known with the following qualities: "humility, controlled ego, genuine, transparent, caring, listened, and passion." Another quote added, "removing your ego from the equation, aligning everyone to achieve a common goal, and showing your people you care." Other common reasons are "leading by example, controlling emotions, self-reflective, listening, give credit, and inspire, motivate, and match behavior with values." Among the most ineffective leadership qualities cited were "let ego ruin good people, demanded respect solely on rank, quite a tyrant, manipulated his people, put personal goals ahead of organizational goals, lacked emotional intelligence, and lacked integrity."

So, leadership and influence are constantly engaged in by everyone. This is one of the reasons emergent leadership is an important topic. If leadership (influence and impact) is constantly being expressed, then emergent outcomes become critical for performance as well as planned performance and positional leadership. To totally disengage the concept of leadership from one's presentation and representation of self as a separate topic or issue, is missing the point of influence. We are constantly influencing through our presence and behavior, whether it is professionally, at home, in social or other community situations. We are responsible for the impact of our presence in our daily lives.

There are, of course, specific tools, skills, and mindsets that enable effective leadership performance, but I'm reminded of Daniel Goleman's conclusions that the most effective leaders are distinguished by exceptional expressions of emotional intelligence, such as self-awareness, self-control, motivation, social awareness, and social skills and collaboration skills. These areas of impact are learnable and apply in any situation, and to a large degree they define us as aware, caring, and skillful people working with others in different contexts. Gaining greater emotional intelligence is developing one's better self. There is also an implied ethic involved, that of caring about the impact and effectiveness of one's personal behavior and about others along with the demonstration of respect for differences in situations and people.

To ask someone if they are a good leader is abstract and disconnected from context and self, and probably won't yield any useful answers, except for a range of responses to the question. Leadership is one of the lived experiences that exists only within a context and interaction with others. One of the reasons the Man in the Arena speech is so powerful is that it defines engagement with effort, outcomes, and striving as an active process. A critic can become a thought leader and have an impact, but most of what we address as leadership is active, engaged, ethical, and focused on mission and service. These key concepts will be discussed further and embedded within our discussion and personal stories.

So what makes up our best self? How is our best self related to our character and integrity? Is our best self our powerful self, our humble self, our analytical and decisive self, or our service-to-others self? Is our best self our authentic self or our playing-a-role-to-achieve-certain-outcomes self? Does best self mean "selfish?" Does developing one's best self mean that one's entire focus is on individualism? The concept of self-actualizing can and probably does contain a sensitivity to others, communities, and culture. Self-actualizing means one's growth not just into one's potential, but into one's awareness, service to others, personal maturity, and communal representation. I would conclude that, for one to be truly selfactualized, they must have an awareness of and involvement in common social entities and an overall sense of universal community as well as a sense of service within their communities. This engagement would respond to the question about whether focusing too much on the self creates a sense of selfishness.

These questions will be addressed in the following discussions, but for now, one's best self can probably contribute more to the well-being of the broader community. Self-actualizing, by definition, is achieving a higher expression of one's potential, achievements, and insights, which would include sensitivity and contribution to others' best interests, whether family, professional, or community.

As mentioned earlier, if we look at the army's motto of "Be, Know, Do," the sequence of the three concepts is instructive. "Be" is about character, the nature of integrity, honor, service, humility, and courage. It gives meaning to how one presents oneself to others in service of high-level goals and aspirations. Service to others, or servant leadership, begins with the nature of one's own values and a broad array of conceptions about the external world, including relevant communities. Communities without strong positive values are often cultist, tribal, exclusive, and based on a limited point of view that represents a barrier to other points of view or criteria that are more inclusive and service-based. The military does an effective job of growing positive values that begin with the growth and integrity of the self that then serves communities, whether it is a military unit or actual external communities that may be found in combat zones such as Iraq and Afghanistan. But the beginning is with the individual and their sense of their own integrity and character.

Is the military perfect in this regard? Obviously not, as when I ask the veterans to discuss their least effective leader example, it most often begins with some blemish or failure of personal character. There are other issues: "failure to learn," "limited role conception," "lack of inclusion of others," "goes solely by the book."

Our best self is made up of an almost unlimited set of competencies. A competency has three components for learning and establishing itself. First, an understanding of the competency from a value and knowledge point of view. Why is this competency—for example, goal-setting—so important, and what are the consequences of doing it well or poorly? This is the understanding of the what, why, and how. The second component is an attitude that allows one to pursue the competency positively, with conviction, based on the first component of understanding. The third component is building the skill through practice.

We have to learn the mechanics of the skill and how to do it better as we practice. "Fake it 'til you make it" is usually used derisively, yet that is what we do to learn a skill. Practice is necessary, even when we may be learning how to be more intentional with what we do and the goals we set for ourselves.

And as we learn new skills and we fake it 'til we make it, are we being our authentic self? I would conclude yes, because we have chosen the skill to learn because of component number one, understanding the why and importance of the competency. Authenticity isn't just being congruent with our feelings or current state; it's also expressed during the skill-building component, when we have chosen to move in a particular direction or behave in a particular way to be more effective, always under an umbrella of ethical behavior. (See Mary Gentile, *Giving Voice To Values*.) And, in many cases, similar to learning new skills in sports, we're awkward at the beginning, and this awkwardness may look to someone else as inauthentic behavior. While behaving congruently is matching one's expression with one's feelings and inner state, aligning one's behavior with one's values and intent is also important when discussing authenticity.

To effectively lead, influence, and impact others, gain their respect, have credibility, and be congruent with oneself while doing all of this is a reflection of our own maturity and the best outcome of our growth motivation over extended periods and challenges. The integrity of the individual grows with regular self-reflection, study, experimentation, and analysis of behavior in social contexts. This growth process is embedded within a strong sense of ethical behavior and values. Short-term effectiveness and outcomes can be achieved with less than full integrity, but long-term outcomes with multiple criteria for success—such as transformational growth in not only oneself but those we influence—emanate from strong integrity, character, and self-awareness. In almost all of the veterans' writing about this subject of effective leadership, character and integrity stood out. Mary Gentile's book, *Giving Voice to Values*, is useful in this regard in that being aware of ethical issues and completing a successful analysis on the right thing to do in any ethical dilemma is not sufficient. One must take action, even develop "scripts" for responding to questionable practices, and even practice those scripts (Gentile 2010, xiii).

It's compelling to think about the ramifications, outcomes, and connections of one's best self to other aspects of oneself, but also of others with whom one shares the context of leadership. Leadership as the expression of our best self communicates both hope and focus on the mission or goals and the coordination of efforts to achieve this effectiveness.

Throughout the year, we stress the importance of continuing to work on competencies that are connected to high performance in influence and impact. Each student chooses their own goals to develop, and then works with a goals partner to get feedback, support, and accountability. The set of emotional intelligence competencies is a fertile area for choice, since it begins with self-awareness, which is the beginning place for leadership development. Throughout the year, then, each student continues to add to their various elements of leadership competencies that comprise the makeup of their best self. Both self-referenced competencies such as "becoming more intentional," or "setting stretch goals effectively," or other-referenced competencies such as "understanding and demonstrating empathy with others," or learning how to "influence others more effectively" are selected for development.

One's best self is an aspirational concept, meaning that we are always aspiring to be better, and thus to be better at leadership. This continual improvement focus is ingrained in leadership training and discipline throughout the branches of the military, and is reflected in many of our classroom discussions about leadership and personal growth. Few veterans see this as a new concept in leadership development.

There is another reason for the aspirational nature of this concept. Because leadership operates within a social context and involves the well-being of others within it, operating out of our ethical and caring best self is imperative. Again, this is fairly natural to military leaders and doctrine. "Mission first, people always" is the guide to caring about the people with whom you work or serve, who report to you and depend on you for your intent and guidance. We discuss our students' experience with both most and least effective leaders, and the contrast around personal character, integrity, and care for others will become apparent.

It follows then, from my perspective, that being an effective, caring, and ethical leader of men and women requires an aspiring attitude for self-improvement in terms of our competencies and values. We will always, therefore, be aspiring to leadership. This is an idealized approach to not only leadership but an organization's future. In envisioning the organization's future, it is effective to start with the ideal future, to understand what's imaginable and possible. The ideal may not be achievable, at least in the limited timeframe of our planning and forecasting cycle, but it becomes the nature of an organization's direction, and the best self becomes the metaphorical north star for aspirational leadership.

This notion of aspirational leadership identifies the gaps between ideal, actual, and practical, and then focuses on these gaps. One of the major difficulties linking effective leadership to organizational outcomes is that the leader is only one of the variables related to outcomes, and outcomes measured in financial terms may not be sufficient to capture the nature, scope, and impact of effective and ineffective leadership. However, we do know leadership is critical to effective organizations at every level and in every segment of the economy and government.

Questioning how incentives are aligned with multiple desired organizational outcomes is useful. The narrower the specified outcomes, the less opportunity for overall organizational effectiveness, which may affect leadership style and focus. The recent discussion of using a stakeholder rather than shareholder focus for outcomes may broaden the discussion of both preparation for leadership and measures of performance outcomes.

Early Focus on Leadership Concepts and Issues

In addition to developing a profile of the students' collective understanding of leadership, I introduce several key topics they will build on throughout the course: self-awareness and self-knowledge, the difference between having a growth mindset and a fixed mindset, the emotional intelligence framework, understanding the need for situational analysis and adaptability, and the need to set personal goals for leadership competence and career aspirations while in the program.

I use a number of self-assessments without focusing heavily on any one to assist this first step of awareness and self-knowledge. I want students to develop their own profile for seeing themselves using structured and well-known assessments. This is consistent with establishing the imperative that leadership is about who we are, not just about what we do.

Using the work of Professor Carol Dweck, a Stanford psychologist, we assert that we are not necessarily stuck with where we are, but through focus, goal-setting, effort, and proactivity, we can develop greater competencies in those areas we feel important to our success. We discuss areas in which we feel we can grow and areas in which we feel fixed. We develop an approach to valuing the growth mindset and not just being content with what we feel defines us, holding us back from improving in certain areas of both our work life as well as our personal life. The difference in mindset is simply understanding that our sustained effort for growth and self-improvement is more powerful than merely relying on what we might see as our talent as a fixed trait.

Using the concept of a growth mindset reinforces the notion that personal growth is one of the major outcomes of our time together. Typically, the response by the veterans to the assignment and opportunity of personal growth is very positive, with little observable resistance. The idea of continuous improvement and skill training along with a culture of leadership training that sees to it that everyone could take the job above them creates an openness to challenge and growth. I counted in the resumé of alumna Takiesha Waites-Thierry about twenty schools, workshops, training courses she had taken between 2001 and 2015 in her navy/coast guard career in the field of intelligence. This was in addition to the bachelor's degree she earned along the way in 2009.

On a side note: in my work with veterans, I have been continuously impressed by their concern for family. We will often discuss goals in not just personal terms, but in those of family, and why their effort to improve is tied to their families' well-being. I also hear stories of how relationships improved at home as a result of greater self-awareness, and focus on listening, self-expression, and empathy. Among the benefits of this approach to leadership is the transferability of these skills to home, professional, and social contexts.

In the early discussion of emotional intelligence, the MBV students are quite open to the concepts and competencies expressed in this framework. When I direct the discussion to the concept of empathy early, I find an openness with the veterans to developing this personal competency. While they are willing to discuss the value of empathy, many did not feel very competent in expressing it. This became a common goal for many. Indeed, the most popularly stated goal for improving emotional intelligence competencies was in the area of empathy for others and being able to act on this empathy to achieve organizational goals while maintaining hierarchical relationships. A related competency, effective and active listening, was also often cited by the students as a weakness, at work and at home. Veterans often cite empathy by people who have been deployed in combat zones as a difficult skill and emotion to begin to reuse upon reentry into civilian life.

Most veterans are very situationally aware. They have had to be. In looking at business situations and industries, the key dimensions on which they must focus for differentiation are often unknown to them or ambiguous. Concepts such as structure and hierarchy, leadership and management, organizational history, and organizational uniqueness—including the differences between industries and technologies, even problem-solving approaches, need to be addressed to understand the effects of constant change in the business environment.

They also may not be aware of how to abstract and analyze different case situations. This is where using a variety of actual business situation case studies is important as an awareness and learning strategy. They are used to quickly sizing up a situation and making a quick decision as to action, but may have difficulty when exposed to many other and broader dimensions of different industries' unique organizations, and rapidly changing and complex environments. Experience in one context may not always be transferable to others. The need to be right seems also to be prominent in quick, perceptual decisions about situations, and is often connected to the rightness of hierarchy, which suggests that compliance is the most operative response to troubled situations. We encourage students studying management and leadership to think critically about the responses of those in authority, and to seek responses that satisfy their analysis, emotional responses, critical thinking, and problem-solving abilities.

Through the use of actual cases in different contexts and industries, we introduce the concept of adaptability. When faced with unusual situations, we must abandon trained and reflexive action strategies for problem-solving, innovative ones (see Heifetz's approach to adaptive leadership).

Learning to think strategically and systemically is a key goal at this point, and understanding that separating the familiar from the unique is critical to effectiveness. It's also difficult to learn to look beyond an assumption of a top leader's infallibility, which is attached to the assumption of the rightness of hierarchy. In addition to focusing on situational differences, we introduce the concept of "managing up," where one must take responsibility for their contribution to the effectiveness of the relationships in which they are committed. The most relevant relationship is often their direct boss.

Learning how to overcome passivity and dependence is challenging and rich for aspiring leaders. This acknowledges that the boss must be aware of the needs of the relationships and ask (and demand) contribution from their direct reports, rather than just compliance. Taking initiative, being assertive, taking responsibility, and contributing to the key relationships and networks in which one is embedded is challenging. The awareness of the need to do so, while at the same time understanding and responding to the particular style of one's boss and others within the hierarchy is key to success.

Team Design and "Post-Heroic" Leadership

Within the cohort model, there is a special stress on team or interdependent work in many of the sessions. Projects are often organized by three to six team members, and the projects vary as to the requirements for interdependent work. Typically, students will break the project into parts, with each member doing a part alone, and then someone putting the parts together at the end and calling it a team project. True team projects require interdependent work by the members, where collaboration, support, feedback, and building on contributions are key components. If the idea of mutual accountability takes hold, then we could observe teams interacting interdependently to achieve a mutual result. Real teamwork has a real team product or outcome, not a conglomerate of individual efforts (see Hackman 2002; Katzenbach and Smith 2001). And yet, combining five independent efforts on five different portions of the assignment is often the norm, rather than interdependence and mutual accountability.

It is also often the case that we limit the collective assignment by responding through our personal experience of either being competitive with others or not having experiential referents for consensus or synergy. Achieving consensus and synergy within a team is difficult and time-consuming. It also requires a measure of trust among members, and trust must be earned. If all assignments are viewed as temporary and rotational assignments are the norm, there may be more than a reluctance among team members to engage in trusting relationships. Too, relying on training for role performance may reduce the need for trust and interdependence, except in high-performance teams where members may be required to move into another's role either on request or as a reaction to a crisis.

The concept of "post-heroic" implies that everyone contributes to the mission, not just the lead person. Heroic leadership implies the top person makes all decisions, and they're seen as mostly infallible. Compliance, therefore, is the main operational concept. This principle of the highest-ranking person in a team leading it in decision-making is common in military units. It was also the military, more than fifty years ago, that began looking at the idea that different situations require different decision-making techniques. For example, the consensus-seeking exercise called "NASA's Lost on the Moon" (introduced two years before we actually put a man on the moon), said that in complex and ambiguous situations, it is more effective to use the collective wisdom of the group than that of its highest-ranking person. We do a similar exercise in the MBV program, where the veterans must pool their knowledge in an ambiguous situation to come to the best decision when placing managerial activities into the order in which it would be best to perform them in a project management environment. About nine out of ten teams reach the outcome that the team actually makes better decisions than just the average of team members, and most often, better than the best individual in the team.

The exercise introduces consensus decision-making and the concept of team synergy, where the team outcome is more than the sum of the efforts of the individual parts. One of the activity's goals is to develop skills for managing ambiguity and team decision-making when there is only a peer structure in a group, and members must learn how to work with one another, often relative strangers. Learning how to build on others' ideas and facilitate team effectiveness in an unstructured situation is challenging, especially if one is used to structure, rank, and training.

One of the requirements for post-heroic leadership is a strong team concept of interdependence and contribution. This implies that everyone knows the mission and its requirements thoroughly, along with their own function, while managing their team relationships.

Growth in Personal Power

When discussing personal change and increased influence capability, growth usually implies the increased power of an individual. Increased competencies and capabilities mean that one can be more effective in various areas and endeavors and have greater influence through their capabilities and presence. Power is typically narrowly viewed, in terms of organizational or position power demonstrated through rank, title, and authority. In the veteran group, as in other groups, personal power can be expressed in terms of physical fitness and the ability to express this power.

Power is also often expressed as political or financial power that comes through wealth and control over resources. There's an imbalance of power suggested in concepts such as subordinate or follower. This is one of the reasons, when instructing in leadership, I don't use these concepts. These two basic words within leadership discussion could imply compliance with someone else's wishes or passivity (rather than initiative). When trying to get everyone to experience growth in their own leadership strengths and to understand that influence and impact do not only emanate from hierarchical position, I try to avoid using hierarchical language. The sociological concept of "the power of lower participants" (Etzioni 1961; Mechanic 1963) is a key example of viewing power from a more complex base than merely position, title, and hierarchy. For example, the person who controls access to senior executives, or who has a special talent, or who works for powerful people, or who is consistently helpful and useful within an organization, or who can frustrate others' efforts by withholding service or slowing down the pace of work, or who is in great demand, can exercise power with performance.

I encourage students to view power as more extensive and useful, and to believe they can develop various types of power, including those that they may not have thought about before, which could serve them well. For example, being expressive is more powerful than being withdrawn. Being optimistic is more powerful than being pessimistic. Being proactive is more powerful than being reactive, even though one could argue that an individual who is excellent at reacting to events is strong as well.

I ask the students to brainstorm their multiple sources of personal power, and make it a fun task. "Make your list as long as possible, and keep going, even if you feel limited." I want them to feel the full impact of the multiple sources of power they potentially have and those they could develop. Most of what we do then, in leadership and influence, is to identify and assess various sources of power and how these personal sources might be used more effectively to achieve desired goals, and how one might further develop those sources to be more influential even if one does not occupy a position of organizational power. Most of the actual business cases we analyze involve some sort of passivity and lack of developing and employing various sources of personal power. For example, people who are skilled at developing professional relationships have a strong base of support and mutual benefit to call upon when they need to.

I mentioned that I ask the students to assess themselves against twenty-two dimensions that make up some options for them to develop competencies that have power dimensions embedded in them. Being politically aware and being more persuasive are other examples of the content of the assessment, as well as "expressing myself more powerfully." All represent an attempt to encourage students to view these types of personal competencies as leading to greater personal power. I also encourage them to examine the framework of emotional intelligence that contains a wealth of competencies that add to one's EQ and personal power.

We also look at power within relationships and the power of networks. Networks and networking are important parts of the program, and becoming familiar with the potential value and power of relationships and networks is key to their professional and personal expansion. The concept of managing up within an organization is often foreign to most students, not just military veterans. We couch it in terms of adding value to any relationship and contributing to its effectiveness within its organizational context. This is one of the ways to discuss the difference between compliance and contribution, and how to do both effectively without feeling you've given something away in the process.

The managerial concept of empowerment is often activated within a team environment, where all members of the team must carry their weight, and often fill in for each other under the umbrella concept of mutual accountability. This is one of the most difficult concepts for students to accept: that team accountability means that all members individually and as a team are accountable for the outcomes of the team. We often prefer to stay in our lane rather than contribute to the shared task and responsibilities.

The other set of competencies that relate to personal power is an area titled "influence without authority," where one must continue to perform and influence performance and outcomes, even if they don't have the authority to do so. Some examples of this set of competencies are: being influential through personal credibility; reciprocating around work issues and demands; being seen as available and collaborative; having high emotional intelligence; avoiding manipulative tactics; having strong networking skills; making personal contributions to collaborative efforts; being able to work in diverse environments and with different organizational contexts and membership; avoiding the need to be right; or, seeing interpersonal issues as competitive or zero-sum games. Being seen as easy to work with and a strong work ethic in a collaborative setting, and being generally helpful can positively influence outcomes and performance. These are skill sets available to anyone with awareness of their own behavior.

Later, in Chapter 6, we will talk about transformational versus incremental change. Since the major mission of the program is a successful transition from a military to a civilian career and lifestyle, there are multiple opportunities for transformational change. I will add some stories and personal examples about change to illustrate this experience. This may be in contrast to a more typical business program (e.g., an MBA), where personal goals may be more incremental than transformational (e.g., to become promotable, to learn other business functions and skill sets, or even to change industries). However, there are a number of situations that require transformational change, often mindsets and ways of thinking (e.g., from a medical professional to a business manager, or from a military structure and mindset to a more ambiguous and less structured civilian mindset, or from clear career paths, to "create your own" career paths). So, in most graduate education, and especially if leadership capability is one of the major goals of change, personal change and personal growth should be seen as a major outcome of the education and not just new skills, new principles, and new concepts.

Because this is a transition program, we also encourage the veterans to include in their goal set career ambitions for the program's duration. Our final few hours together, under the banner of our first session, "Leadership and Interpersonal Influence," will hopefully set a positive tone. After everyone shares their well-developed sense of leadership values, traits, and behavior, I encourage a commitment to my five threads: a baseline of self-awareness, adapting a growth mindset, emotional intelligence, situation analysis and adaptability, and setting personal goals for leadership competence development and a career focus for the year.

In many ways, I'm astonished by how easy this first part is to gain acceptance, awareness, and an agreement to move forward in these major directions. The veterans get it. They understand the need for both effective leadership and continuous personal improvement. Some of them have been introduced to emotional intelligence, but all are accepting and even eager to understand more about it. I've mentioned some of the difficulties with empathy, but there is little resistance to the concept. The other big area is the basic one of awareness and self-management and control over emotions and behavior.

More than once, I've worked one-on-one with individuals who are concerned that they only react to their strong emotions, and often feel controlled by them. Usually, these conversations take place outside the classroom, but some are very concerned that they get triggered easily, and have the impulse to respond physically and often violently. The reason they came to me, however, was to learn to control their reactive responses. They are aware of the dysfunctionality of responding this way in the civilian world and being out of control. I can only surmise that not all who feel this way seek me out to discuss this, but the ones who do experience an increased awareness of the issue, the danger of the consequences, and the need to pause before acting when the situation occurs. This discussion usually doesn't take place until the second semester, when we discuss leadership styles and difficult behaviors. The first semester, we work at awareness, understanding one's self-profile, and beginning to set goals. Moving to deeper, stronger behavior will come later, in most cases.

The veterans' commitment to mission first and people always focuses on striving for something outside yourself within the context of the community that needs to work together to achieve this larger purpose, this common mission.

While we fulfilled the need for a unit of membership and camaraderie quite well through a cohort model, where all the participants share a common military background and academic experience in the short run, we depend on a continuing close alumni experience in the future to hold much of that membership together over the longer term.

Given the close dynamics of the community and the commitment to everyone's success ("no man left behind"), it is not much of a stretch to understand the use of family terms—my brothers and sisters—to refer to others in the cohort (as well as to other veterans). For a while, I found it odd that warriors used mostly family concepts to refer to each other and the entire group of veterans within the cohort in such terms, but I grew to understand and respect the underlying feelings. This dynamic reminded me of a paragraph in the book *We Were Soldiers Once . . . and Young*, in which Lt. Gen. Harold Moore (Ret) and Joseph Galloway wrote in much detail about a famous battle in Vietnam in 1965.

> "And in time we came to love each other as brothers. In battle our world shrank to the man on our left and the man on our right and the enemy all around. We held each other's lives in our hands and we learned to share our fears, our hopes, our dreams as readily as we shared what little else good came our way." (Moore and Galloway 1992, xxii)

Experiential training opportunities, such as the outdoor ropes course, described in Chapter 3, also focused on binding members to the community through a combination of individual challenges, collaborative achievements, and group support, along with other lessons from low ropes activities on the ground. We had begun this type of training during orientation in our ELC using the activity named "Meta-4," which drew on their experience of "no man left behind." The point of the game is survival, but it is not clear whether it's competitive for individual survival or collective effort. Groups engaging in this exercise do multiple trials to reduce the number of non-survivors to zero. In my regular undergraduate and MBA classes, it takes about twelve to fifteen trials to complete, on average. With the MBV students, it takes between six and eight. During the most recent engagement with the veterans, one group achieved the goal of everyone surviving within three trials, an unheard-of record. The veterans discovered early that it is about organizing for collaborative action for everyone's survival, rather than immediately falling into the assumption that it is about individual effort and potentially individual competition. This value was very strong in each cohort and was represented in Cohort I's motto, "thirty-eight in, thirty-eight out." It was also manifested in helping each other in academic content areas. For example, in Cohorts I, V, and VI, an accountant in each class put on rather extensive workshops in accounting prior to exams or other formal assignments for the students who felt they needed extra help.

> "This showed me a tight group within. . . . The feeling of the person next to you would do anything in their power to help the other succeed is evident in the program." (Irv Dingle, Cohort VI)

> "By far, however, I feel the greatest change we have made is how we all take on the challenge of a program like this and make our way together as a team to the finish line." (Mark Hymanson, Cohort VI)

The focus beyond self, beyond one's own ego and need satisfaction, was also unusual to me within the graduate business school context. That is not to infer that ego-based strivings occupied 100 percent of every student's effort, because there were always those who expressed a service-based orientation, including professional goals. It was unusual, however, as a major theme in my classes and with the student experience. There were activities that were charity focused, but I didn't hear much discussion beyond a fairly narrowly defined concept of success. In the case of the veterans, the issue of submerging one's ego in service of the collective is part of the culture, beginning with the act of volunteering for service and taking an oath to protect the citizens and constitution of the country, followed by basic training, which further reduces the salience of the individual, and then rebuilding character to contribute to the well-being of the collective unit and organization.

In trying to integrate these concepts of best self, serving a higher purpose, caring for your people who report to you, using family names to refer to your colleagues, and expressing a deep sense of membership and integrity in service to each other and your country, it became easier to conclude that this integration of virtues and intent became a higher calling.

Being with the veterans in their search for their best selves, setting aside the barriers, resistance, and denials to that concept and being comfortable in integrating love, camaraderie, mission, and service became a discussion about our humanity in context with each other and our commitment to achievement, personal growth, and family.

There may be another compelling reason for seeking one's unique best self. In the age of artificial intelligence and robotics, with more and more jobs being made obsolete, Dr. Vivienne Ming is one of the major thinkers in this area. A theoretical neuroscientist and self-described serial entrepreneur, Ming wrote *How to Robot-Proof Your Kids*. She posted the following forecast on her blog of April 17, 2019:

> "And the more unique you are, the more valuable you will be. If you are educating a whole new generation of business leaders, then you need to understand the fundamental importance of those leaders being truly themselves, not as a slogan or an issue of personal branding, but simply because if you educate them to anything less than that, I will build a robot to replace them."

Michael A. Crespo—Cohort I

When I saw an advertisement in the *Army Times* about the MBV program, I thought it would be a perfect program for my wife, Jhoana, who was just starting off in her civilian career. We went online to check it out and decided we would go to an information session on campus. I was just planning on being a tag-along, but Jhoana ended up having an army obligation, so I attended by myself to get her the information. At the information session I spoke with Karla Wiseman, who was the program director at the time, and she tried to convince me to apply. I laughed it off and took the info home to my wife. When I told her what Karla said, she encouraged me to apply. Jhoana didn't apply because she had a conflict with drill sergeant school but ended up applying and getting accepted for Cohort II.

In April 2013, I wrote my application essay and was accepted into Cohort I of the MBV program. I was pretty proud and I still remember walking on campus that first Friday of August—I couldn't believe I was a Trojan. I also remember my first interaction with Professor Turrill that weekend at the Lab (a bar across the street). I remember thinking I didn't think I would get much from the leadership portion of the instruction. I felt I was an expert in leadership, being a command sergeant major who had attended every leadership course the army offered. Boy, was I wrong. Professor Turrill made me think and assess myself—something I wasn't comfortable with. Leadership ended up being my favorite class and has made me a better leader.

Immediately after graduating, I deployed to the Middle East and ended up being there when ISIS took over northern Iraq. It was a challenging time, and I remember using what I had learned, specifically the discussion we had on managing up. It was something I really hadn't considered before, and I also realized I needed to communicate to the leaders frequently. After my deployment, I went back to work and was immediately promoted. I was now the senior director at my company, and it had a lot to do with me getting my MBV. This position included the responsibility of sales, which was completely out of my comfort zone, something we were told time and again in the course to embrace.

I recently decided to change jobs, and I am surprised at the quick response I received from my resumé. When interviewing for my new job as a vice president of operations, I asked the CEO why my resumé was singled out, and the answer was, "You're a command sergeant major in the US Army and a USC graduate—we had to meet you."

I met some pretty awesome people and still maintain many relationships from that class. We check up on each other and reach out for help with various things. I recently asked my classmate Patrick Trainor for help with a commission structure I was working on for my employees. Patrick has a lot of experience in sales and was also promoted after getting his MBV. During my deployment, the commanding general needed a secretary to the general's staff to run his office. This is a key position, and I referred my classmate Annette Leija. She was a newly promoted captain, and the position was for a seasoned major. After interviewing Annette, the commanding general wasn't concerned about her lower rank, and she ended up staying on after I left.

Jhoana was still interested in the MBV. She saw what I was doing and how excited I was about the program that she applied to the second cohort and was accepted. I told James Bogle the new program director that she was much smarter than I was. Our daughter was born a month before I graduated, and she attended both graduations! That makes us not only a Trojan family, but an MBV family. I am extremely grateful for having the opportunity to be part of this unique program.

Jengi Martinez—Cohort II

I am Jengi Martinez, a twenty-four-year veteran and active air force reservist, presently serving as a Lt. Colonel and a C-17 instructor aircraft commander. I have over nineteen years' experience leading small to large teams with complex backgrounds and diverse disciplines. Having traveled to over eighty countries, this international and diplomatic experience with multiple agencies has taught me the importance of knowing the customer's needs and culture to better communicate and reach a common goal. This knowledge and experience have made me a better contributing member to my community. The MBV program at USC helped me to apply my skills, business acumen, and confidence to founding my own real estate development firm, DRM Properties. I currently have two real estate development projects with the potential to revitalize neighborhoods and two veteran housing projects under development in partnership with a few of my USC mentors.

I was born into a Mexican-American family, the eldest of two. My maternal side were business owners. My grandfather was a former navy UDT. My grandmother started working at thirteen during the Depression and didn't get a high school diploma until her seventh child was in high school. My mom and her siblings have master's degrees and above. On my paternal side, I was the first to go to college. My dad's father served in the navy during WWII, and my dad was the only one of his siblings who graduated high school.

Growing up, I always looked up in the air in awe. I loved the idea of heights, speed, and adventure. I climbed any tree I could find. I attempted to ride my tricycle down the stairs. If someone told me I couldn't do something, I immediately fixated on doing it. My dad was in the defense industry and built parts for aircraft and was also a huge history buff, which took us to museums and airshows. My parents talked about getting their private pilot's license, but if they had the time, they didn't have the money and if they had the money, they didn't have the time. My wanderlust came from my maternal grandparents, who were avid world travelers, and I was enamored with the stories of their travels, the beauty, the people, the food, the gifts, LOL.

My desire to fly never changed. My parents encouraged my brother and me to do anything we wanted. I never thought anything would stand in my way, because I wasn't taught that it would. Mom would say if you can see it, you can be it—the power of visualization. In early high school, I found out about Embry-Riddle Aeronautical University (ERAU) in Prescott, Arizona. I was determined to attend the "Harvard of the Sky," as it was known. My mom bought me a school pendant, and I hung it on my wall (more visualization). It was one of the colleges we visited my junior year. I knew that was where I belonged. ERAU was expensive, and my dad didn't want to spend the money and find out that I didn't like to fly in little airplanes, so my parents decided I should get some flying lessons. I soloed at sixteen and earned my private pilot's license at seventeen. The picture and caption my parents put in my senior yearbook was of me in a car seat less than two years old. The caption read "From the car seat to ejection seat, we are with you all the way." And they have never left my side! No family member ever told me I couldn't. Both sides of my family were always encouraging and supportive. I was raised to believe that the barriers people spoke of didn't apply to me. I believed that if I couldn't do something, it was because I was holding myself back, not because someone or something was holding me back.

I exposed myself to every aspect of aviation, with the idea that the more I knew, the better I would be. I worked summer jobs in college as a ramp agent, throwing bags for an airline. I worked customer service for a fixed base operator, flew corporate charters, studied aviation safety, accident investigation, and human factors. My education and the people I met took me to the military, where I enlisted and was a mechanic on KC-135R, later becoming a commissioned officer and pilot, having flown T-37, T-1, C-141C, and the C-17A.

The military has been an amazing experience. I have traveled, and met and made friends all over the world. I learned to be a part of something bigger than myself, and about attention to detail, accountability. I have developed an appreciation for people and how small our world truly is. The camaraderie is a part of the military that can be indescribable at times. These men and women sat next to me, taught me, assisted me, and supported me as I trained and later flew into and out of combat zones. Together, we transported much-needed supplies throughout the world, flew our injured military brethren out of harm's way to hospitals in Germany and stateside. That knowledge that you are part of the bigger picture that could save someone is humbling. Returning our fallen back to the States to their families is one of the hardest things to do. I was always appreciative of what they gave and sacrificed. Feeling less because I selfishly was grateful it wasn't me and grateful that I didn't have to be the one on the ground in horrible conditions. I have an appreciation for life, people, and cultures that I know I would never have gained had I not served my country.

In response to having flown over 600 combat sorties, the majority of which were medical evacuations, I felt a need to reduce the effects of war on our service members and their families. My entrepreneurial spirit and sense of social responsibility led to the initiation of the March Aviation Society (MAS), in 2011. For six years, this non-profit organization provided relief funds for southern California's largest military air base and its military members.

In 2009, I was diagnosed with a pituitary tumor, the most common type of brain tumor. I was faced with illness, fear, potential loss of career, and the idea I would never fly again. Flying is my first love; it was all I had worked for as long as I could remember. In many ways, it felt like it was the only thing I had known. After a long battle with the military doctors and the medical processes, I had surgery in 2012 and the tumor was completely removed. One week shy of my first anniversary tumor-free, the air force surgeon general changed the medical regulations to allow me to return to full-flight status. This experience taught me several things, one of which was that I needed to diversify myself. I had no idea where to start, no idea what

I wanted to do, if not fly. School seemed to be the best place to start. Like everything in my life, everything happens for a reason, and I was told about the MBV program at USC.

When I applied to the Marshall MBV program, I was an accomplished fundraiser with an extensive network, a major in the air force, serving as C-17A instructor pilot, and highly skilled in operations management. I had transported personnel and cargo in support of the Department of Defense, medical evacuation, and humanitarian operations around the globe. I had logged over 6,000 flight hours, commanded over 600 combat sorties in Iraq and Afghanistan, and traveled to over eighty countries. Intrinsically, I felt the need to do more. However, I didn't know what or how to go about it. My personal trials, experiences, and witnessing the great sacrifices of my fellow service members along my journey inspire me to positively impact the community around me and, as stated in my admissions essay, my long-term goal was to "further my non-profit work, employ and mentor fellow veterans through my own profitable business(s)."

The Marshall School of Business and MBV program gave me business acumen, along with the connectivity and confidence to pursue my goals. It was while in the MBV program that I immersed myself in USC organizations and clubs. I took advantage of every networking and mentoring program available—specifically, the MBV board of councilors and the Marshall Partners. I was able to draw upon several alumni's expertise and mentorship. With the assistance of faculty and mentors, I found my passion for real estate development with a social cause.

Following completion of the MBV program, I completed the Ross Program at USC's Price School of Public Policy, where I received the USC Lusk Center for Real Estate—2015 Best Developer's Proposal Award, as the principal of DRM Properties LLC.

My time at USC helped me to translate my military skills and apply the entrepreneurial strategies and financial modeling to profitable real estate ventures and business(s) of my own while giving back to local communities. I learned exciting new business platforms while maintaining USC's long-standing tradition of social responsibility. At DRM Properties, I focus on innovative development projects with a social mission: providing below-market housing rates for veterans and their families. I am able to do this with a unique blend of real estate experience, business and community relationships, education, and military service. DRM Properties provides quality, creative financing structures and responsible development that often involves local government and neighborhood participation.

On a personal level, I gained confidence in myself outside my world of aviation. When I started the program, if asked what I did, my answer would be, "I am a pilot, I take things from point A to point B." Within the first few months, that answer evolved, and I would tell you, "I am a leader, a logistics expert." That answer continues to grow, and today I would tell you I am, "A community leader, business owner, veteran advocate, mentor, mentee, motivational speaker, and a Trojan!!"

In 2015, I co-founded and served on the executive board of Carry On! Alliance, a non-profit organization focused on assisting the navigation, education, and integration of the transitioning veteran. I have fully embraced my responsibility as a role model for young women and children. I have been a founder of, a motivational speaker for, and an active participant in several advocacy groups, mentorship programs, and non-profit organizations across the United States. For the past seventeen years, I have been a motivational speaker at several southern California elementary schools, high schools, and colleges, leveraging my military experience, education, and aviation career to motivate young women and children and to teach the importance of science, technology, engineering, and math (STEM) skills. I am a two-time nominee for the Katharine Wright Trophy, which recognizes women who have given back to their community in the areas of aviation and STEM. I am dedicated to encouraging, exposing, and providing opportunities to children and fellow military veterans. I live in Carlsbad, California, and serve my local community as city commissioner on the Carlsbad Parks and Recreation Commission. I joined United Airlines in 2018 as a first officer on the A320 based in Los Angeles.

I had a lot of inspiration, support, and mentorship along the way. I embrace a growth mindset, and I continue to try to give back. I have an amazingly supportive family, an incredible military family, and a strong Trojan family. All of whom I know I can call on anytime.

Takiesha Waites-Thierry—Cohort IV

I dropped out of college in my last semester and joined the navy when I was twenty. At that time, I simply couldn't envision what my next step in life would be—how would this degree I spent so long working toward (which had made my family incredibly proud as I'm a first-generation college student) ensure that I would leave my hometown of Toledo? I'd grown up with a great-grandfather, a WWII veteran, who spoke highly of his time in the navy and told stories of his travels and experiences throughout his thirty-two-year tenure. With that in mind, I went to the recruiting center in April 2001, and signed up. I'd started my next chapter, and my career progression for the next fifteen-plus years, with one seemingly impulsive choice. If you were to meet me now, you would never think I would make such a spontaneous decision; even *I* can't believe I did that. However, when I look back on it, I am unbelievably proud of that young woman because she didn't wait around for anything to happen—she made it happen for herself.

I am so grateful for the five years I spent in the navy. The lifelong friendships I made and incredible experiences made me who I am today. I am mainly grateful for the opportunity to leave home, stand on my own feet, and develop into an intelligence professional.

After transitioning off active duty, a few years in the reserves, and a year stint as a government contractor, I found myself in a federal government agency where I was one of four females in the entire organization, and one of two women of color. Coworkers felt I was given preferential treatment, and that the accomplishments I earned were a result of favoritism rather than the hard work that went behind every assignment I was given. I felt like I was making a meaningful impact in the organization and even within the greater intelligence community, but I also felt undervalued and burnt-out. After a leadership change, I began to question my place and future in the organization.

At that time I came to another crossroad, similar to the one that had drawn me to enlist in the first place: *what was next for me, and what action did I need to take to ensure it happened?* My family relocated from the Washington, DC, area to San Diego for my husband's active-duty navy orders. I was given the opportunity to complete a joint duty assignment in San Diego, but even with that, I knew that I wanted to eventually leave federal government service and try something different; I just didn't know what. I knew that pursuing some sort of business degree would be beneficial, and I was ultimately led to the MBV program at USC.

My experience at USC changed my life and my perspective! While I'd always been interested in pursuing a business degree, I wasn't quite sure how I'd do that, since my life without school was already so hectic. I didn't think I would be able to go to school nearly every weekend, two hours away, while maintaining a full-time job and two kids while my husband was deployed. However, I realized that whenever I was ready to leave the federal government, I wanted to pursue a degree that would assist in my transition to the private sector. While the work was certainly difficult and challenged me in many ways, it was really the people I met in school who changed my life. I didn't know my own strengths or full capabilities until I started at USC. My cohort motivated me, and we held each other accountable. There was a core group of people with whom I became extremely close. To this day, I maintain a tight-knit relationship with Antonio, Brenda, Sean, and Tracy. They are my personal board of governors, and I rely on them for advice, to keep me honest and humble, and, most importantly, to call me out on my crap.

The leadership lessons and core competencies really helped me to transition in my career, and I was challenged to conduct several self-assessments. During that process, I really learned who Takiesha is, what I am capable of, and areas in which I hadn't previously been totally honest with myself. I developed an almost scary level of self-awareness. I now always look inward when I am experiencing a hurdle instead of immediately passing blame on others. In that process of self-awareness and growth, I also decided to leave behind something: self-doubt. Prior to MBV, I always presented myself with a lot of confidence, but internally, I was doubtful of my skill and knowledge. I was just doing a fake it 'til you make it act. Shedding self-doubt has allowed me to grow, trust my education and experience, and even guide others who come to me for counsel.

Lessons in self-regulation specifically and being more receptive to change are why I was able to take the big leap of faith and resign from the federal government. I always thought about resigning, even spoke of leaving, but I wasn't convinced I'd ever make the jump because of fear of change and self-doubt.

I am so happy all of those leadership lessons helped my confidence and enabled me to start a new career at Bank of America, leading the US intelligence and analysis team within global corporate security. It's incredibly important to be true to yourself about where you are in your career, and where you want to go next—even if it's just the acknowledgment that where you are now isn't where you want to stay. It's equally important to dig deep and do the difficult work to identify your strengths, opportunities, and plans for improvement. I believe that way of thinking has served me incredibly well over the years. However, it's certainly not without the help of amazing family, friends, classmates, and coworkers who went the extra mile to challenge and support me in my journey. As I write this, I am preparing for another transition: I've recently been promoted to director of global intelligence and travel security analytics at Bank of America. I'm incredibly proud of the work my team has accomplished during my time as the US intelligence manager. But I can't wait to get started on this new chapter of my journey.

Bruce Voelker—Cohort V

Growing up in a military family had a profound impact on my early development, splitting my first eighteen years between Missouri and South Korea. The latter ended up being the most impactful for me, contributing the influential social backdrop to my formidable years.

Following graduation from high school in Seoul, I made my way to Minnesota State University, where I attended on an ROTC scholarship. It was there that I pursued and explored my interest in health care, which eventually led to my career as a medical service corps officer in the army.

I had what I can only describe as an opportune and fortunate military career, with assignments in South Korea, Germany, and Afghanistan, spanning across six wonderful years. My service afforded me a mixture of clinical, front-line, and special-duty assignments that provided me with a unique portfolio of experiences that led to my transition to Kaiser Permanente in Los Angeles as a special projects consultant.

Part of my long-term goals as a civilian was to pursue some type of postsecondary education. I meticulously searched for the right program, and after considering various MPH, MHA, and MBA programs from UCLA and Pepperdine, I still felt uncomfortable committing my time, energy, and money to any of them; something was missing from what they were offering, but I couldn't place what it was. I eventually came across the MBV program at USC, where the fog of grad school searching began to slowly clear for me.

Through research of the program and learning what it had to offer, I started to prioritize my desire for recapturing that team environment I missed from the army. I wanted to embark on this next phase in my life with a diverse group of individuals from whom I could learn and grow, but who also possessed the core set of values and beliefs I experienced in the military. I had been out for over a year when I came across the program, and it wasn't until I went to an orientation in person that I realized how much I had truly missed that camaraderie. My time in the military is a chapter that was heavily shaped by the brother- and sisterhood-like bond forged through shared adversity, trials, and growth. After learning about the unique cohort experience where we would have the opportunity to leverage the skills and experiences we gained while serving in an environment with fellow veterans of all walks of life, I knew I had found the right vehicle for not only academic but more importantly, personal growth.

The program's greatest strength and the attribute I hope it continues to develop is its ability to promote introspective growth and change in its cohort members. This program is at its best when it acts as the facilitator/catalyst/vehicle for helping veterans through their respective transitions. For me, this transformative change came in the form of perspective; more specifically, the impact that understanding and leveraging power can have in finding success as a civilian.

The idea of power was one with which I wasn't particularly comfortable when entering this program. There was a certain stigma associated with wanting to obtain power; one that prior to this course I did not want associated with me. Why did I have this hesitancy to openly embrace power? Societal norms certainly played a significant role, but more than anything it was my naiveté when it came to know how to use power, or why one would want it. I now know the pivotal role power can have on my professional and personal life, and have recognized that my path to power is fueled by developing a sense of purpose and isolating three key components: who do I want to be, what do I want to achieve, and most importantly, why do I want to achieve it? I believe my true north is cemented in my desire to capture and maintain some level of impact in health care by helping to mold and develop future leaders within the industry, which is a realization I would have never achieved without the teachings, development, and experience of the MBV program.

Finding this course could not have come at a better time for me. Having ridden a wave of professional clarity coming out of the military, to confusion as to what I wanted to do when I "grew up," then back toward my internal means as a direct result of this program, I needed something to focus my efforts in a direction I could start taking my career. The exposure and lessons the MBV program provided opened my eyes to my deficiencies as a professional, and what path to potentially embark on in order to improve upon them. Since graduating from Cohort V, in May 2018, I accepted a new role within my current organization, Kaiser Permanente, as a senior consultant, but in a completely new area for my wife and me: Washington, DC. Although my more granular purpose is yet to be defined, what I do know for certain is that I have an earnest desire to make an impact within my career field as a health-care consultant.

My time with the program and the guidance and tutelage of Professor Turrill and the MBV faculty have shaped my professional trajectory into a more leadership-development-focused space, which I intend to continue to cultivate through stretch assignments as a coach and facilitator for my organization's leadership development department (partnering to deliver courses such as change leadership, leading innovation, and executive presence). My journey out east has also inspired me to pursue an executive leadership coaching certification from Georgetown, which will prove valuable for when I transition into a full-time role as a leadership development consultant; a culmination for which my time with Cohort V was truly the catalyst. Without my experience at USC, I most certainly would not have discovered the insight or courage to allow me to be in the position I am today, and for that I am truly grateful for having found the MBV program. Fight on!

Robert Graves—Cohort VI

What would you do with a second chance?

Me, when I die, I will have built a school for the less-than-privileged for kids from broken homes and single-parent households.

Since I was a teenager, I knew in my bones I wanted to be a high school guidance counselor. Later, as a non-commissioned officer, this passion to change the lives of individuals in the transition from adolescence to adulthood strengthened, and the reason developed and became clearer. Why, at that age, was it important for me to have this *need* to throw myself into the lives of the individuals who would come into my life, and care enough to help set them on paths that would help them flourish in life—and not even think twice about the WIFM, or *What's in it for me?*

Every single person who stepped foot into my shop was asked, "Why did you join the Marine Corps?" A large percentage of them responded with something close to: "Because I didn't have any other options."

What's it like to be an individual who doesn't know that there are unlimited options available in the world to try anything, and become something? I know all too well what that is like. Those marines walking through my door, answering my question—reflected my reality. They were me! *I* didn't know of the plethora of possibilities, because nobody was there to guide me! All I knew was I didn't want to go to the thirteenth grade and sit in the halls of Santa Monica College with all the rest of the "losers who could not get in to, or afford a *real* college." (This was a real thought of mine because I didn't know any better at the time). I knew I didn't want to stay in the home of my mother; a woman to whom I give credit to this day for raising me with the strict discipline that made what were the most mentally and emotionally demanding times for most of the recruits in Marine Corps boot camp a cakewalk for me. And I had already grown up jumping from city to city, and wasn't tied to this concept of family, so why not have another fresh start?

When these marines who would walk through *my* door, and answer the question of why they joined the Marine Corps with an answer such as, "I didn't have any other options." I was looking into a mirror, and I knew that once I separated from the service—I would work hard to break the cycle of these young men and women, not knowing they had options and that they were *just* as special as—if not more special than—their counterparts, coming from nuclear families, who received copious amounts of love, support, care, affection, discipline, and guidance. I knew then that I wanted to be the catalyst of change, but as life will ultimately teach you, your plan, your road map to comfort and happiness, is not worth the two cents you have.

Learning must occur.

Currently, I am the director of operations of the Department of California DAV. DAV stands for Disabled American Veterans, which instantly creates a barrier against building rapport with the veterans I work to serve, because nobody wants to consider themselves disabled; where I must explain that if a veteran has been gassed, injured, or ill at all while in service—they are eligible to be a member. This was a blessing that seemingly landed in my lap . . . but I'm a firm believer in the cliché, "Luck is when preparation meets opportunity," which gives the hard-working individual who has only heard about this myth of work-life balance some solitude with working all those late lonely nights.

This opportunity was given to me as I was contacting everyone (literally *everyone*) in my "Rolodex" during my very brief involvement as the COO for a virtual-reality-meets-military mindfulness startup, into which I had been fortunate to be invited from an individual I'd met via LinkedIn. He saw that I was heavily involved in a lot of what he was moving into in the mindfulness world, as I had just worked on these programs and concepts over the summer at West Point.

Oh, yeah, that's right, I interned at West Point—days after finishing my first master's in sport and performance psychology at California State University, Northridge.

I graduated on a Friday—and left on a Tuesday. I got a speeding ticket in Pennsylvania on my birthday, and I spent Memorial Day at Ground Zero in New York. I drove across the country because I planned on sleeping in my truck that whole summer during the internship. Again, I was blessed for being selected, as well as for the opportunity, but this internship was unpaid along with no room and board, and I have a family as well as a mortgage. I was hungry to learn, and ready to do what it took to have that opportunity. And, frankly, I wanted to see if I had the grit to go through it. My (now) dear friend, and supervisor at the time made sure that wasn't how I would spend the summer, and their belief in my abilities solidified a level of confidence in myself that one can never take away.

I learned a lot at West Point.

I learned a lot about myself. I learned a lot about expectations. I learned a lot about vulnerability, and I learned a lot about humility and gratitude. For instance, I hadn't been aware at the time, but every student at West Point comes to the academy with some form of approval from a legislative power-house—a senator, governor, secretary of defense. Every cadet there outshone however many other fish in their small ponds, and showed up to the United States Military Academy only to quickly learn that once they were special, but now they were simply average. What they don't understand off the bat is that average at West Point goes far in life; and if you have what it takes to get in, all you have to do to succeed is get out of your own way and trust the process. These feelings of inadequacy and not being good enough were common in this group of future leaders. They were taken out of their arenas of glory and thrown into an organization that would pull out the best of their characteristics and mold them into what the Big Army would need them to be. This was a hard transition for a lot, and I was fortunate to be in a position to hear the beginning stages of heroism.

The most important lesson I learned at West Point I learned by accident.

I'd been given the freedom to go through all of the files that were associated with this section of the academy, and I took full advantage of that opportunity. This autonomy eventually led me to learn that I wasn't the first or second choice for the internship. In fact, I was only there because someone else had had to pass up on this opportunity. Initially taken aback, I recovered from my ability to reframe non-ideal situations and found humor in that I was the first runner-up; because I knew what I brought to the table. I learned then that it doesn't matter the circumstances that led up to the moment— what matters is the moment, and if you can show up when luck strikes again.

Before West Point, I ran away from a six-figure job to go back to school. I've written a book about my personal transition for which veterans reach out to me and thank me. I've hosted the #YearOfTheVet podcast to have other veterans come talk about their lessons learned in transition, which people have reached out to and thanked me for, and I've been very blessed. But there is darkness on this path. Working in the veteran space was never my plan, but I've been given this second chance at life. And this is where it has ended up so far.

I have a very public story, so I don't need to explain all the broken moments that created who I am today. However, to sum it up in one important sentence: I opted to stand up for myself in military court of law, and was found guilty in a general court-martial—but was allowed to finish my service obligations and leave the Marine Corps honorably . . . as I had served.

I was facing seven years in the brig, yet I had been given a second chance at life (for the nth time). I often talk about this with members of my cohort and some of my fraternity brothers who made it into Cohort VII (shout out Sigma Tau Alpha Veteran Fraternity based out of CSUN) . . . but where we started . . . we weren't supposed to be here.

We grew up in broken homes. We came from single-parent families. We played sports. We played hooky. We played with the law, and our lives. We made dumb decisions that made us more apt to survive in our environments, and we took advantage of opportunities that would improve our current situations, because we knew that those opportunities were not flowing in a never-ending stream of availability for us. We were hardened by our environment; and similar to the end of each day of God's creations in the Book of Genesis . . . it was good.

What we all agree on is that the military gave us a life—and USC gave us all a second chance at life.

My court-martial ultimately tied my hands, and limited me from working inside the education system, which was odd since I'd had an honorable discharge and a renewed secret clearance. A specific school system somewhere in Los Angeles kindly denied my ability to work for it. My dreams ripped from underneath, and for me . . . that's when I died.

Forced to pivot, before that was a widely used term in my vocabulary, that door—which closed so swiftly and abruptly in my face, that door closing, was the whole world opening up for me—and I just had to trust the process, and focus on my why.

My why?

To be of service.

The one thing I've continually done naturally since as far as I can remember. My why is to be available to those who walk behind me, to help others on their paths to their destinations in life. My why is to provide strength, guidance, and optimism on these hard roads, and rough patches—because I have the strength and the courage to continually do it myself. My why is to pick myself up, because I know that this too shall pass. But more importantly, I know there are those behind me who are watching, so that they too know that they can succeed at the challenges ahead.

I hope you know I didn't write to gloat about my accomplishments. I don't even see them as accomplishments more than I do a strange route to finally opening my school. No, instead I am grateful to have the opportunity to have shared this process with an amazing lineage of veterans. I'm grateful to have the opportunity to be involved with this phenomenal project that Professor Turrill has created to memorialize the program that will soon be the reason America really is great again. The USC Marshall MBV program is helping place some of the greatest leaders in the world on the path of running the United States, period. And to the USC Marshall School of Business, I thank you for truly being a selfless organization, and literally changing the lives of every single one of us, whether we were aware of the change or not. I often say that we were spoiled at USC; but from the moment we were given a lesson in finance—explained utilizing concepts we understood (chaos), via dominoes and poker chips—I believed in USC.

One of my favorite stories to share takes place in one of the training environments, simulating life on Mars. Vegetation was taking. Life was flourishing. But at some point, over time, the taller trees were breaking after growing too tall. The research determined that because the trees had grown without the stress of the elements (such as wind) around to constantly create the small micro-tears in the tree-trunk that naturally occur in order for the tree to repair themselves and become stronger (similar to muscle), their structure was not sturdy. For it is the stress that we endure that makes us able to be on the road that leads to this moment right now.

So much has led up to this moment for me, and many of you have your own stories. But the one thing that I know is that if you are reading this, you are a person who knows the power of resilience, and the reward of resourcefulness and persistence. At some point, life stood still—and things went dark. So many questions unanswerable, so many opportunities to quit, to give in, to give up. So many variables stacked against you.

When you are given a second chance, what will you do with it?

I love where I am today—in the veteran space. However, I ultimately know that it is my place in the world to provide to our youth the lessons and opportunities that could open their worlds to endless possibilities. I mean, if they want to join the military, so be it, but they will have the proper mindset, that they have options and can walk among giants.

Lawrence Abee—Cohort VI

> "Between stimulus and response there is a space. In that space is our power to choose our response. In our response lies our growth and our freedom." – Viktor Frankl

A liminal space is known as a state of being in between. They can be places and times of uncertainty, adversity, and progress. I want to tell you a story—one that highlights my childhood briefly and the journey of who I choose to be.

At an early age, I valued the notion of the patriot. I often heard stories about my father, Larry, a Vietnam generation marine, son of a World War II Army veteran, whose family was established in the Carolinas and had an illustrious history of military service. I knew after service he was a machinist, an engineer, and a real estate private equity funder that started our family business, LA Financial Management & Realty Services (LA Financial) in 1979—a full-service real estate and multifamily office out of Chino, California. The stories were very important to me as I grew up without my father. My mother never spoke about him because he died from glioblastoma, terminal brain cancer, when I was two years old. My mother, Lilia Lacson, was a mortgage broker and met my father after she immigrated to California from the Philippines following Ferdinand Marcos's attacks on political families during the 1980s. The Lacson family was prominent with ancestral roots to and from the president of former Republic of Negros; survivors and guerillas of the Bataan Death March; senators; Mr. Philippines; mayors of Manila; and to date, operates one of the largest private security contractor firms in the Philippines, employing over 4,000 people.

After my father died, I was sent to live with my grandparents in Tondo, Manila, until age seven. Despite family prominence, we were by all means not endowed, and our family lost wealth during the reign of Marcos's dictatorship. During my upbringing in Manila, I experienced the embodiment of a Third World country, where people lived in shanty villages rampant with hunger, murder, and a dearth of utility infrastructure. I ate one and a half times a day and pumped water from wells to shower. I vividly remember the sights and smells of the Smoky Mountain garbage dump where people worked, slept, ate, and bathed all around burning heaps of filth. What stuck with me more fondly, however, was the amazing resilience of the Filipino people—most were always smiling and happy despite the economic conditions, and it made growing up without a paternal figure easier because others were genuinely suffering worse. From there on, I developed an affinity for upward mobility, appreciation of space, resourcefulness, and problem-solving to make the world a better place.

I returned to America when my mother regained stability, and she remarried in 1997 to my stepfather, David. David was a police officer for a southern California agency, had a real estate hobby, and happened to also be a marine. David was the father I never had—David *is* my dad. Immediately following the 9/11 terrorist attacks, David was involuntarily deployed numerous times back to back as a counter-intelligence chief until 2012. I saw my dad for approximately eight months cumulatively the entire time I was in high school. After the Battle of Fallujah in 2004, I knew I wanted to be a marine. I enlisted in 2006 and earned my eagle, globe, and anchor at seventeen. I entered the intelligence field and deployed in support of Operations Enduring Freedom, Iraqi Freedom, and New Dawn; most notoriously, having operated in the Al Anbar capital, Ramadi, Iraq. By 2009, my younger brother followed and enlisted in the Marine Corps. It was apparent the men in my household all wanted the same thing: to bring back those who were over-deploying, contribute to a calling to those who answered before us, and fight for a country worth fighting for. At the peak of the surge strategy—all the men in the five-person household were absent from the home serving the country, and it came with great cost on many different levels. We lost a lot financially, but more importantly, we lost time we could have spent building our family or growing professionally.

When I got off active duty and entered the Marine Corps reserve, I immediately took advantage of my educational opportunities and declined an offer from UCLA to study at UC Riverside to remain close to my business endeavors. While in undergrad, I was flipping vintage Harley Davidsons, took on a limited partnership in a natural foods product company, and learned how to grow a farmers' market/retail business from the ground up—which eventually sold and remains in strong business to date. Concurrently, I worked on real estate acquisition and disposition of our portfolio in small multifamily, single-family residence, and land. Although I had an "in" to get ahead in real estate, my family had restructured years prior under the leadership of my aunt, Loida Atienza—who grew the firm as its current principal after Larry's death. There came a point in time where I realized that my family firm was only going to benefit my cousins: an inconvenient truth I still struggle with today. Accordingly, I moved on and began managing commercial real estate for a large public agency and represented tenants of sixty-six facilities encompassing 1.2 million square feet of gross leasable area. The experience was worthwhile; however, I wanted to position myself to seize my family business one day, as if my aunt had never taken over. While growing up in Chino, I saw companies like Majestic Realty turn cow and crop fields into prime real estate, and I dreamed of someday doing the same. I often wondered if my father never passed, could we have done that? The only way I thought I could have a chance at the family business was to distance myself and become my own principal by getting gainfully employed as a peace officer, doing my own real estate deals and creating value on the side, and searching for the right turning point.

When I learned of USC Marshall's MBV program, I was exploring what could be next for me outside of a long political career in law enforcement, considering I had admirable professional and personal goals. Prior to MBV, I had attempted two separate master's programs at different times in life and left within weeks of discovering the perceived value was not realized when I was there physically or through distance. What was appealing to me about MBV was the average age and leadership experience of its students and emphasis on value creation through entrepreneurship. And joining the Trojan family. I entered the MBV program by grace of the selection committee's belief that my military role as a marine platoon sergeant coupled with my other experiences would enable me for high potential. And rightfully so.

Although I had to take student loans to be at USC, you cannot put a dollar amount to the value realized at MBV. MBV is about large social impact, transformation, and innovation in an era of change. My education was very personalized and specific to my interests. The pedagogy was finely crafted and designed by one of my mentors, Professor Emeritus Bob Turrill. Most, if not all, of the curriculum was taught by senior faculty and gave me access to a world-class education. The time, resources, and scale we engaged were intentionally executed with purpose from the first to last days. My cohort mates significantly added value to my education by multiplicity of their leveraged experiences, or having attended the Naval Academy, West Point, and so forth. What I cherished most about my MBV experiences were: the meaningful and authentic relationships I developed; gaining a social board of directors; being part of a program focused on problem-solving rather than just profits; embracing vulnerability; and fine-tuning my career trajectory and growth mindset with my mentor.

Ultimately, post-MBV, I would like to spend the majority of my life making meaningful social impacts on a large scale and to primarily work in real estate development across the world. My most recent endeavor involves founding the Swinkle Group LLC. Swinkle is an opportunity zone-based venture that provides autonomous drones and other technologies for public safety to save lives and reduce the pain that is costing taxpayers and insurance premium pools billions of dollars on an annual basis due to less than favorable interactions between citizens, criminals, and law enforcement officers.

When I'm not working, I enjoy participating in good causes, riding motorcycles, racing go-karts with my two boys, Forrest and Atlas, building things, adding more spoons to my collection from Yogurtland, and singing and playing the piano. Attending the MBV program at USC Marshall is a humbling privilege. I would have never imagined being at one of the best institutions for a world-class education and alumni network given such a unique life path. The history of the school has had strong military support, and I hope my story can contribute to make an impact on the MBV program. I am a committed shareholder of the Marshall Partners and encourage those within the Trojan family to help continue moving forward.

CHAPTER 5

LEADERSHIP—THE VETERAN VOICE

Cohort IV in the lobby of Popovich Hall

In Chapter 4, I discussed my approach to understanding leadership and encouraging the veterans to grow beyond their state of leadership competence. In this chapter, I discuss their contributions to the discussion of their background, including a focus on what they have concluded about what creates the most and least effective leadership behavior. We share these responses, and I conclude each year that these two lists generated by the cohort are the essence of positive and effective leadership. The fact that they are so astute on both sides of the question informs us that even with all the positive leadership training in the military, there are still leaders who exhibit *least* effective traits, values, and behavior.

We begin with a discussion about cohort members' beliefs, knowledge, and skills before doing any further discussion of leadership. I'm both interested in how they view leadership and how they have been trained as well as wanting to authenticate their knowledge starting point without any assumption of changing what they already know and believe. Discussing leadership with well-trained and indoctrinated military leadership is humbling at best, but in many respects much easier than trying to persuade other groups of students of the importance and even the existence of leadership as a real thing.

Currently, there is much debate about both the effectiveness of leadership training and the lack of professional standards within leadership education and training. In fact, criticizing leadership development programs and approaches is almost becoming an entire field of discussion by itself (see Jeffrey Pfeffer's *Leadership BS*, Barbara Kellerman's *The End of Leadership*, and a new book, *What's Wrong with Leadership?* as examples of this current sensitivity and debate). There is no such barrier with military veterans. They know leadership. They easily discuss effective and ineffective leadership and reasons for both.

In another book by Barbara Kellerman, *Professionalizing Leadership*, she discusses the various programs and approaches to teaching and learning leadership, and makes a strong statement about the military's effectiveness with developing leadership and leaders. She writes:

> "Let me state this as plainly as I can: Learning to lead in the American military is unlike learning to lead anywhere else in America. Learning to lead in the American military is better. Learning to lead in the American

military is harder, broader, deeper, and richer. And it is longer. In the American military, learning to lead lasts a lifetime." (2012, 54–55)

And, as I mentioned earlier, many books and discussions of leadership don't include descriptions and discussions of military leadership, which I conclude is a major oversight of relevant thinking and approaches to leadership.

So, while there is much debate about leadership education and training in universities, including MBA programs, and corporations, the debate hasn't included the military. Thus, the background with which our students enter the MBV program is taken as foundational, the starting point on which we ask the students to continue to develop their competencies and values, strengths, and intentionality.

Before we begin our first activity where the students share their background in leadership, I offer only that I use the concept of leadership, and provide very little focus on the leader. In a class on leadership, I avoid using the concept of either *leader* or *follower*, as I want to focus on the process of influence and impact and how to develop the competencies that lead to greater influence. When focusing on the leader, we tend to focus up the hierarchy. However, when discussing leadership as a process of influence, we can focus on our behavior and day-to-day relationships in accomplishing work goals. How to be more effective, and use influence as part of our effectiveness, not just performing either job tasks or our formal role. When we discuss cases or role-based activities, I want them to notice everyone's behavior and influence when contributing to the work of the organization. Everyone has a responsibility to contribute to the goal to the best of their ability, and this may actually take them outside the description of their role. In many discussions, I hear students talk in terms of "who's in charge?" or "who's the leader?" ignoring the contribution of those lower in the hierarchy to the overall success. Also, by seeing someone else as the leader, it's tempting to deny the consequences of our behavior and the meaning of our presence. The idea of using our presence more powerfully to achieve greater effectiveness puts everyone in the responsible role of contributing and carrying their share of the load, rather than to offload the responsibility to the leader. Without this idea of being present and contributing one's influence, we fall into the pattern of merely complying with the leader, but not contributing.

The goal is to sharpen one's awareness of how to use their presence to have greater influence and impact. The concept of influence and presence means that we're always "on." We are always representing not just ourselves but the organization for which we work and other groups in which we may have membership. There are many stories of people thinking they are on their own time, behaving in a way that doesn't positively represent them as a person, nor their organization. If one takes the concept of presence seriously, one can understand the issue of constant responsibility for one's influence. That places the individual in a greater position for influence, regardless of rank.

I'm reminded of an example of a university president who wasn't seen much on campus, and after a while a "president sighting" became almost a game. Even in such a large place as a university, the leader's presence was monitored. This was in contrast to the next president, who slept in his office early in his presidency as the community was going through racial violence, and his presence on campus, while mostly symbolic, was noticed and applauded. As a new leader, he made an immediate impact through his presence, not a speech or action, just by showing up and being in a particular place in a timely hour of crisis—being present.

Another example I use is a particular case example where a CEO takes his executive team off-site for a team-building retreat. Poor morale, bickering, and open competition and conflict were the symptoms, and he wanted to bring them together to discuss both the content of their strategy, but also the process dynamics of how they would work together. It was a two-day retreat, and it was going fairly well, so that on Friday night, the CEO called for an early cocktail hour followed by a special banquet-style dinner for the participants. It was a nice event, and a nice gesture on the part of the CEO, positive recognition of two days of hard, sometimes contentious, discussion and planning and problem-solving. He excused himself from the dinner because he had to return to the city as he had concert tickets for that evening. Most of the work had been accomplished successfully, and a more positive mood had grown, so he was fairly satisfied with this progress.

Students are often mixed on this behavior being important. I would always conclude with the question as to what his leaving his team at that point signaled to the team? What example is he setting, and what is his commitment to the continuing growth of the team? Did he see his presence as important? If not, why not? Did he signal that his prior commitment to going to the concert was more important than his team and their continued development as a team?

Working with veterans, it was quite clear to me that presence mattered. Discussions around "leading from the front" rather than the rear were common. I also was aware that they tracked my behavior and that of my partner, the program director. "Leading by example" was a frequently cited behavior included under the positive and effective leadership characteristics. "Leaders eat last" is another common norm that has a powerful message of presence. Take care of your people first. Where you are and what you do matters, and everyone is watching. How and where one shows up are important when discussing leadership and leader behavior. *Where* one shows up signals presence, and *how* one shows up represents leading by example. One of the most powerful pictures representing the use of presence in leadership is the picture of General Dwight Eisenhower talking face-to-face to paratroopers getting ready to board their planes to fly into France on D-Day, 1944. In 2019, the seventy-fifth anniversary of the D-Day invasion, the picture was published again in the major papers, a four-star general being present with a group of men, many of whom he knew would not return from the battle. While he couldn't be everywhere that day, this picture gave a sense of his intent and the use of his presence with the actual soldiers going to battle that day. We don't know what words were shared, but we don't need to. The picture tells the story of a leader being present with his troops at the moment of the beginning of this most critical battle. I remember the impact this picture had on me when I first saw it. It still has that impact seventy-five years later.

This awareness and implications for the behavior itself, as well as the impact and consequences of the behavior, is where we begin. This early message has been to be aware, value your presence, be intentional, understand the choices you are making, think through alternative responses, own your behavior, assess the consequences of your behavior, and take responsibility for your part of the relationship, process, and outcomes. Symbolically as well as actually, the presence of the leader is critical. The concept or management approach, called "management by walking around," is based on the assumption that the presence of a leader is important and can lead to stronger commitment by those who work for and with them. In the virtual world in which we live much of the time, this concept of presence is still important, just more difficult to demonstrate.

Another reason I don't discuss the leader and don't ask students to read about famous leaders is because it's easy to either be inspired by a positive leader or to be turned off by a negative leader, but it rarely has to do with who we are or what our behavior is. Learning through good and poor leadership examples, or identifying with certain leaders, has some usefulness. My assumption is that reading about leaders is a distancing process. We admire or dislike a leadership or charismatic figure from a distance, but it has little to do with us. We can be temporarily inspired or righteously disgusted, but we are distanced and untouched by the event. We have no stake in their performance or situation. We can pick up tips on effective leadership, be moved by someone's courage, for example, but that will have little effect on changing our behavior, and above all, it's safe. It's not actual work. Actually developing your behavior, using more critical thinking skills, becoming more situationally aware and adaptable, analytical, focused, aware, and then assessing, seeking feedback, and setting new challenges is real work, and it leads to skill-building and change-- by learning in the arena.

The cohort's leadership summary: We start with where each person is, and what they know, value, feel, and express as their understanding of leadership. I ask for their training, experience, and deeply held values. I will include a summary taken directly from Cohort III and add some additional quotes from other summaries of their sharing of their beliefs and values. If we combine both their lists of most and least effective leadership behavior and characteristics, we end up with a fairly comprehensive picture of both effective and ineffective leadership behavior. Both lists were generated from personal experience of all the veterans in Cohort III. The following is the summary developed by the full cohort during our first class session on leadership early in the life of the cohort:

Definition and Characteristics of
Positive Leadership—Cohort III

"A leader leads by example.

A leader sets the tone for the organization.

A leader is confident, genuine, and authentic.

A leader develops the people under them through mentorship.

A leader has strong soft skills.

Leaders know how to adapt and evolve to overcome an obstacle.

All leaders have experienced failure and learned from their mistakes (fail forward).

A leader knows their weaknesses and how to delegate.

A leader encourages open lines of communication and is personable.

A leader picks people up after they fail, preventing them from losing self-confidence.

A leader does not make excuses and is accountable for their actions.

A leader is persuasive and knows how to influence the group to achieve buy-in.

A leader practices servant leadership.

A leader acknowledges/praises both the group and individuals when they have done a good job.

A leader understands the power and responsibilities that are associated with the role."

A quick reading of the list of traits, characteristics, values, and behaviors submitted by Cohort III leads to the awareness of the leader as example, and setting the tone for the unit or organization are primary characteristics. It's more about "my behavior" than my words or instructions. The second thread is the principle of service to those being led, rather than obedience or loyalty to the leader. Also, there is no mention of a strong ego or dominant personality, and little mention of charisma.

Setting the example and seeing leadership as service, I found, are consistent throughout all six cohorts. These threads don't specifically address the task content of any organization or unit, but rather how the influence process and the example set by the leadership affects outcomes and the dynamics of the unit. If leadership wants to have effective influence and power, those in leadership positions need to be seen as modeling appropriate behavior and expressly serving those being led in the organization. The congruence and alignment of one's words with one's principles must be apparent and accepted by others in the unit and must be dependable and consistent. That is holding context, or consistently representing and behaving values, expectations, and norms of behavior. One might argue that being in control and giving accurate feedback of criticism of others' behavior might be less important than congruence of serving and providing resources and assistance necessary for effective performance.

The second activity seeking students' experience of positive and negative leadership experiences and guidance asks all students to share their most effective and least effective leadership experiences and examples with the entire cohort. The following set of experiences is also from Cohort III and has been excerpted from their entire inventory of key observations.

Most Effective Leadership (Leader) Descriptions

(These descriptions were attached to a specific effective leader in the students' experience, mostly from the military, but not completely.)

"Now that my concept of leadership has matured, I see it as not only having the management tools to move people, projects, and things along, but also showing your people that you actually care, removing your ego from the equation, and aligning everyone together to achieve a common goal."

"I have found the core leadership traits of the Marine Corps—justice, judgment, decisiveness, integrity, dependability, tact, initiative, enthusiasm, bearing, unselfishness, courage, knowledge, loyalty, and endurance—to be extremely effective traits that inspire others."

"Leadership is a measure of one's ability to influence others to accomplish their goals."

"Leads by example . . . believes they serve their subordinates rather than the other way around."

" . . . your leadership style has to change not just with your position, but also with those you are leading . . . appropriate for each individual (direct reports) and the organization."

"Listen, be open to suggestions, make yourself available, build trust, delegate, positive attitude."

"Self-reflect, continue to learn . . . tactful communication . . . match language to values."

"Accountability, willingness to take responsibility, control emotions . . . give credit to those who contributed to success."

"Develop a sense of curiosity, time management, empowerment, bear the burden for the group."

"Humility, control ego, genuine, transparent, care, listen, passion."

"Inspire, motivate, and influence . . . work as a team, lead by example (match behavior with values), give before you get."

"Leadership is often assessing, formulating, implementing a course of action and reflecting on results."

"Be able to manage up, persuade superiors, clearly communicate directions."

"Confident, knowledgeable in the task to be accomplished, trustworthy, open minded, diligent."

"A good leader gets their people to buy into their plan, but a great leader does that while presenting an ethically sound plan that promotes the growth of their followers."

"A leader has strong soft skills . . . but knows their weaknesses . . . does not make excuses . . . authentic."

Least Effective Leadership (Leader) Descriptions

(Again, these descriptions were attached to a specific person the veteran used as an example of a least effective leader.)

"Lacked integrity, commitment, selflessness, and did not take responsibility."

"Lacks ability to provide clear expectations and clear sense of purpose."

"No goal or sense of direction."

"Put own goals before organizational goals; abused authority."

"Insecure and lacked confidence . . . bad management stems from insecurities."

"Micromanaged analysts' work and treated them as incompetent."

"Let ego ruin good people's careers."

"Manipulated each member, to secure his position."

"Embarrass people in front of colleagues . . . passive-aggressive."

"Preferred a confrontational posture; asserted his positional authority."

"No intention of developing people under him."

"Didn't establish a supportive work environment or establish unity."

"Not leaders but functional occupants of their titles."

"Demotivated his people through extreme attention to detail and lack of trust in subordinates."

"Led from behind the desk."

"Lacked emotional intelligence."

"Did not want to take risks; inaction becomes the action taken."

"Quite a tyrant: would not tolerate any dissension."

"Not a very good communicator."

"Missing or late to meetings; stories at the expense of people who worked for him."

"Could not connect with employees; discounted subordinates' experience."

"Irrational decisions that would degrade effectiveness."

"Demanded respect based solely on rank."

In both the effective and ineffective leadership lists, the issues of character and integrity are pronounced. Included in the discussion of character are ego and personality strengths and failings. How one presents oneself is an expression of one's character, integrity, and ego. This seems to be somewhat more critical on the negative or ineffective side of leadership; whereas, on the more effective examples of leadership, we find a number of competencies in influence and relationship in addition to the general issue of integrity and strength of character. Character issues and lapses will derail leaders, but character and integrity are foundational in the effective side, and specific competencies stand out. Managing up, expressing confidence, listening, giving credit, and developing caring relationships skills and emotional intelligence become important once the positive foundation of integrity and trustworthiness is established and accepted. Expressing humility, caring, and being transparent and authentic are frequently cited, as is the concept of service to others.

One of the additional threads that stands out relates to those who use rank, position, and role to ensure compliance; whereas, effective leadership is more personal, tied to individual authenticity and integrity, and especially caring for the people as individuals and as a unit, and leads to a sense of trust of leadership by those subject to that leadership. I find that is especially notable in a highly structured organization built around rank, hierarchy, conformity to rules and compliance, and where training to the point of automatic responses is required and achieved.

For some, these ideas, competencies, and ways of being may feel antithetical to the notion of bosses being strong, dominant, and decisive. In the veterans' case, leadership respect is earned, not demanded. The word "compliance" is not mentioned, and my assumption is that in a structured rank environment, compliance may be seen as a given, but effective leadership is developed through personal example, overall competence, and caring presence.

This is not exactly the popular image of the heroic leader, the person who is in charge, makes all the decisions, wins all battles, and expects others to effectively carry out their duties. The more post-heroic leader creates a service orientation and encourages others to share a common vision and share in the responsibility of contributing to a high-performance orientation and a sense of more of a partnership. In transitioning from a compliance mentality to a more contribution mentality, we might think that business, in general, would have a greater sense of contribution versus the military, but that has become less clear to me. Reading a file of an applicant who was a medic in Afghanistan, and while evacuating wounded soldiers, was wounded himself, brought this concept to reality.

> "During my 2007 rotation in Afghanistan, enemy forces ambushed my unit outside the Saret Koleh village of the Nuristan Province's Landay Sin Valley. The numerical superior force pinned us down for seven hours while we fought foot-by-foot and inch-by-inch to move to a more defensible position. In the first hour of the firefight, I, along with several other soldiers, was wounded. I was shot moving from one casualty's position to another in order to provide medical treatment. A small quick reaction force came to evacuate the wounded. I was instructed to load up with the rest of the wounded. I refused. The fight was not over, and I was not leaving my brothers until we all got out. The fight continued for several more hours until my unit gained a foothold on a defensible position. Several more soldiers were hit, and I went to all of them to provide care. I was awarded the Silver Star for gallantry in action that day. The overwhelming incoming fire and mounting danger was not enough to keep me from my goal that day."
> (Rob Fortner, Cohort IV)

His commitment to the wounded soldiers, his caring about his role and challenge as well as the individuals who were with him that day, created the conditions for his extreme contribution, leaving the concept of compliance on the field.

A transition example carried a similar message (and will be presented and discussed further in the final chapter). One of our marine officer alums took a managerial job out of state in an order fulfillment center. He took over a large group of associates who were constantly under immense pressure to perform, but whose morale was slipping and whose behavior appeared stressed and challenged. He shared the slogan, "mission first, people always" and explained its meaning to the group. While high performance and accomplishing their mission was expected, his role was to serve them, provide a role model for them, and monitor and enhance their well-being. He held himself to a high standard of performance and care and would model that behavior along with them, but he would also be there for them, to make sure they were cared for. The response from his associates was that no one had ever expressed anything like that before, that their well-being was also important in this high-performance culture. In my time with military veterans/leaders, it was not unusual for them to express this dual approach.

This awareness led me to share with them early in our time together that we had no intention of diminishing their leadership background or training, but to build on it. Their dual approach to performance and people with whom you worked and led created a dual focus and responsibility. Performance, yes, always, but also caring for the well-being of the people working with and for you. It was impressive to me that, for the most part, the veterans understood that to be effective in their leadership role/function, they needed to have not only high integrity and competence, but must also demonstrate caring about those who worked alongside them.

When asked about how we should bring people along with the mission, direction, and goals, I would reply that you need to enroll others into the vision and direction. Enrolling others in a particular direction and way of thinking can be quite a different process than ordering people to comply. Enrolling others, then, can become a powerful transition competency for military veterans who are very used to being very direct about what they want. The outcomes may be the same behavior and performance, but the process is more inclusive, and involves the others' acceptance and buy-in of the direction rather than merely a conforming compliance to the direction.

I have found the following ten actions to be useful to achieve this enrollment, and I credit many of these ideas and principles to my time with the veterans.

The Art of Enrolling Others

"The art of enrolling others in your ideas, goals, and direction to increase engagement and commitment versus merely asking for and demanding compliance. Ten principles:

1. **Have a clear sense of direction and goals.** A compelling direction is highly motivating, versus a vague sense of purpose and goals.

2. **Be positive and optimistic about the future**—it's contagious! Being positive and optimistic also helps communicate self-confidence.

3. **Share and communicate the vision, direction, and goals frequently.** Focusing on and emphasizing clarity of direction leads to everyone "being on the same page," and buying in to the mission's purpose and goals.

4. **Be open to being influenced by others** in terms of how we might achieve our objectives. The openness to "mutual influence" can be powerful in terms of everyone contributing to the accomplishment of the mission, rather than a total top-down approach.

5. **Challenge with high expectations** for individuals and the group (team), and be more encouraging than critical. Similar to having clear and compelling direction, high-performance expectations that are clear and accepted allow individuals to operate more easily. Once expectations are clear and accepted, positive encouragement is more effective than criticism and coercion in achieving positive outcomes. Positive feedback reinforces positive outcomes, and this applies to noticing and celebrating small/large wins along the way.

6. **Understand and build your own personal credibility** with your knowledge, success, and trustworthiness. Credibility is essential when influencing others. Rather than commanding. your knowledge and track record, and being seen as trustworthy over time, which is a measure of consistency and integrity, are important.

Credibility may be established early or may need some positive history on which to base this perception. Credibility is one of those personal perceived characteristics that can be lost easily through lapses of integrity. There are numerous characteristics listed under the *least* effective leadership profiles that relate to this break from strong credibility.

7. **Demonstrate empathy** for those with whom you work. Demonstrate mutual advantage. Understanding the people with whom you work and finding common ground on which to seek win-win outcomes is a strong enrolling competence that begins with a sensitivity to others and being able to demonstrate caring, understanding, and empathy.

8. **Ask for agreement and feedback, and encourage upward communication**. This principle asks that when engaging in "enrolling" others, one should check for that agreement, and make sure that it does exist. This encourages two-way communication rather than relying on one-way communication, top-down.

9. **Be inclusive and invite others to join with you in a team effor**t. To enroll others, stating a clear invitation is often needed, so that it is unambiguous. This inclusion principle also warns of the dangers of either identity social groups or favoritism existing within a team context where the buy-in must be equal with all members of the team or unit.

10. **Hold context: goals, values, operational processes, boundaries; be consistent and persistent**. It is upon the consistency notion that members of a team (as well as student classes) will base their own consistent performance and commitment based upon how leadership stays consistent with both processes and outcomes of performance over time. Can the members of the team, unit, or class trust that leadership will maintain all these agreements over time? In a classroom, for example, if the professor reneges or changes the rules of the game a lot or even sometimes, the students will lose faith in what everyone has agreed to in terms of

values, expectations, goals, directions, and anything else that is important to maintain the integrity of the group or process."*

The difference between holding up barriers between people—whether the barrier is rank and hierarchy, exclusion, criticism, or an authoritarian style—and bringing people in through inclusion, collaboration, encouragement, acknowledgment of capabilities, and listening is large. Often, small moves may lead to big payoffs. Meeting others, including subordinates and peers or others from another unit, in their workspace rather than insisting they come to yours is a simple but positive enrolling technique. Acknowledging the need for someone else's involvement, contribution, and competence is powerful in enrolling another's collaboration and acceptance of one's position and common goal.

I suggested this as an approach to one of the students who had been promoted over another colleague, and the colleague was making it quite difficult on my student. I suggested he spend some time enrolling the individual into sharing the work and commitment, since these unit goals are not achieved solely by the head person in the unit, and they had worked together in the recent past. He did make the plea that he needed the other person, that he could not achieve the unit's goals without the assistance of this colleague's experience, skills, and past commitment. He reported back later that his enrolling the other individual into joining him worked, and he didn't subsequently have the problems that he had experienced.

These techniques may be seen as persuasion, but are more concerned with inclusion and reference to mutual benefit and common goals, while openly recognizing the other's contribution, actual and potential, in achieving performance outcomes. Also, the key skill of listening rather than telling is a great assist. One can call this type of behavior a team approach, mutual influence, or empowerment, but all enrolling techniques and values lead to positive outcomes if all are operating in good faith and best efforts. These final two assumptions underlie trust in a relationship that has operational goals. Feeling uncertain about whether everyone is operating in good faith and best efforts

---

* (Taken from a presentation to University Advancement Managers, January 16, 2015, based on discussions with my veteran students.)

handicaps the authentic enrolling of others in one's goals, strategy, approach, and ways of thinking about processes. I have found these two basic assumptions about others' intent and effort critical to moving ahead with the enrolling process, and probably to all positive social dynamics and team performance.

Another example of our veteran/students approach to leadership is the following outline of the first MBV/GLP (Global Leaders Program) event, held in October 2017, with over two dozen of our veterans and 107 freshmen honors students enrolled in the GLP at Marshall. (The story of the second meeting, in 2018, opens Chapter 1.) In this outline, the students lay out four of the major leadership values they feel are important for the freshmen to understand and experience. While this is not an exhaustive set of values, these four were selected for their importance to the veterans conducting the training. They designed a four-hour, outdoor, experiential activity to demonstrate these four values with personal and group challenges built in to the activity. Each of the four stations were staffed with about six MBV volunteers who gave up an off-weekend Friday to introduce these leadership values to the freshmen students, and who came in from all over southern California, from San Diego to China Lake. The freshmen were used to presentations by business leaders, including CEOs and community leaders, and found the day working with the veterans to be productive, enlightening, and collaborative. The faculty in charge of the GLP, Professor Carl Voigt, indicated that not one of the 107 students disengaged from the activity that morning with the veterans, and found the morning very useful from a leadership point of view, and also for getting to know other Trojan students from a totally different program within Marshall.

Military Professional Leadership

Volunteers from MBV Cohort V structured a series of hands-on, collaborative decision-making activities for the Marshall GLP. The goal of this project was to expose the GLP freshmen to some important aspects of the veterans' diverse experience, knowledge, and philosophies. Over the course of several planning sessions, the MBV volunteers developed a set of four integrated, theme-based practical team activities that were designed to impart valuable lessons about teamwork and leadership. A brief description of the activities follows.

Humility

The world is bigger than all of us. Most things we each do every day are about more than us as individuals. A common malady accompanying success is hubris and if not proactively checked, self-regard will undermine individual and team performance every time. A healthy, even powerful ego is required to be an effective leader, but continuous reflection on the group goals and team stewardship is necessary to couple the strength of ego and passion to the team, and not just one's own performance.

The Humility activity emphasized:

1. Servant leadership.

2. Self-knowledge and reflection.

3. Awareness.

4. Hold yourself accountable.

5. It's about my people, not about me.

Sacrifice

Taking one for the team does not mean going down in flames. Sacrifice is not the road to martyrdom. Sacrifice is doing what must be done to make others around you perform at a higher level. Sacrifice means "we" rather than "me."

1. Ensure the job/mission is accomplished with or without me.

2. In order to accomplish the task, duty, or mission, I will have to choose between myself, my desires, my time, and the mission.

3. In ensuring that my people are performing at their optimal performance, I will need to sacrifice myself for their sustainment or improvement.

4. The ultimate goal is to progress the mission even if it doesn't benefit me directly.

Tactical Competence

We act as individuals and in groups for a purpose. Continuous improvement and refinement are leadership requirements. It is not enough to know what to do today and tomorrow but also and simultaneously to observe and assess trends in order to develop alternative courses of action and to be prepared to act on new and ambiguous information.

1. Agility and adaptability

2. Entrepreneurial mindset

3. Knowledge required to perform

4. Competence translates to your ability to perform

5. Ability to create more competent people

6. Continuous improvement

7. Constant growth

8. Identify others for improvement to raise their competence

Ownership/Accountability

Own your decisions and actions. A leader must be responsible for their decisions and actions and must lead by, and set, the example.

Importantly, there are many unknowns and contingencies included in and associated with every decision and activity. What is decided, what is enacted, what happens is not someone else's responsibility, it is yours. Look first to what you as a leader can, should, and will do.

1. It's about partnership, not you—"we," not "me."

2. Always take personal responsibility and embrace the role you are in.

3. Own your actions.

4. Get the job done one personal encounter at a time.

5. Stand for something/exhibit and own your values.

(Andre Gomez [Cohort V] and Robert B. Turrill, January 2018, email correspondence.)

This workshop combining the MBV leadership experience and values with this large group of freshmen honors students was an excellent example of the veterans taking charge of a developmental and integrative activity, purely voluntarily, and delivering it effectively. We, as program management, made no input or assessment of their content or process. They were offered the opportunity to share with another academic program on campus their insights into leadership, and they delivered an exceptional experience at a time scheduled by the GLP Program that required the veterans to come in on their off week, and their travel distance was not a barrier. In fact, the following year, 2018, one veteran volunteer flew in from out of state to participate.

In the spring of 2019, the MBV program delivered another workshop to Marshall undergraduates enrolled in the Coury Leadership Program, a program designed to provide a common leadership development experience to all Marshall business undergraduates. This program is led by Professor Jody Tolan, another of my good colleagues. The intention at this point is to have the veterans involved in this collaboration each year as well as in the GLP. The goal of these two programs is to have the MBV veterans share with undergraduate students a military approach to leadership as well as some mentoring across the programs.

Leadership and Effective Team Performance

Moving from a focus on individual expression of leadership and influence to the veterans' positive experience with team behavior, I asked them to discuss and provide examples of their best team experiences. Effective teams are a big part of military life, so the veterans are confident of their knowledge about what it takes to make effective teams. In other contexts, the notion of collaboration and team behavior as a design feature of organizations probably took hold in the late '70s, early '80s, and now the discussion of effective teams is a common topic in both for-profit and not-for-profit organizations as well. Post-World War II, organizational design thinking began to move away from command and control thinking and strict hierarchical and bureaucratic management into more open systems thinking and less mechanistic thinking about organizations to more of an organic approach to process and design. Work teams, cross-functional teams, and matrix design thinking began to become a more effective way to organize work. As "time to market" and innovation became increasingly important for organizational viability and growth, collaborative structures such as cross-functional integrated product design teams began replacing linear, sequential, hierarchical designs. Much of this development was funded by the Department of Defense with their clients developing new technology that coincided with the Cold War era. The military in its own needs to become quicker and more effective in multiple contexts both participated in this move and in this research. As a result, the branches of the military have been big contributors, innovators, and users of more advanced organizational design techniques for about sixty years.

When I asked Cohort IV to share their best team experience, I received an avalanche of positive stories about the quality and maturity of collaborative team performance. Here are some examples of their comments and stories:

> "As their leader, I needed to change their beliefs, values, and attitudes. I started mentoring, coaching, and modeling different techniques. . . .

It was a total team effort and we crossed the line together. Motivation is infectious, and believing in someone was the difference between success and failure."

"Everyone understood their roles and executed them to perfection. . . . I attribute it to three things: maturity, hard work, and mutual respect."

"The navy has a capability to turn young kids into participants of an elite team capable, self-confident, life-saving actions during impossible stress and severe environmental conditions. . . . They also knew their job—stay out of the way, keep quiet, and allow those they trained and entrusted do what they did best. . . . Our success required effective communication, stress management, proper leadership, trust, and conflict resolution."

"The entire platoon began to function more efficiently with a constant focus on the end goal."

"Some of the principles/characteristics that stood out with this team were adaptability, courage, and empathy."

"When people with the same perspective of a common goal move pride out of the way, then teamwork starts. Work hard, play hard!"

"The successful factor was rehearsed, precise communication, leadership, calmness, flawless communication methods and channels, training, risk assessments, contingency planning, collaborative problem-solving, surgical execution, quick response, courage, and debriefs (lessons learned)!"

"Teamwork is not about individual glory. It's about ensuring the mission is complete. Decision-making, responsibility, engagement, ownership, and focus helped our team get through the chaos and ensured the safety of our patients."

"The success of the team was attributed to the training and getting to know how each other thought and reacted to different situations, and then creating SOPs that played to everyone's strengths and weaknesses."

"The main team tenets I employed were: nested goals, support to subordinates, communication up and down the chain of command, recognizing the achievement of all my soldiers and candor."

"Lessons learned: treat your team like they make a difference and they will. Take care of your team, and they will take care of you."

"We operated above the watch-standing rules, selflessly caring for one another as we tend to our shipmates and perform all duties assigned and thrown at us."

"This was all made possible because everyone on our team put others before themselves. We were all fighting for our brother next to us. We were all fighting so that the man next to us would be able to go home to his family. We were all able to come home safely because everyone did their job and everyone trusted that we were doing our job properly. We always had each other's best interest at heart. We always had each other's back."

"Removing our job biases, the unit began to form into its own community, not associating with any one job type, but falling into our own sub-section referred to as 'Alpha Boys,' due to our company designation and our aggressive mentality. . . . Each member of the team knew every job of each specific team member and trusted that everyone within our team would execute their roles when needed."

"My team was newly formed, and by this time we had only been together for eight days and had yet to have the time to get to know each other or to even learn each other's names. . . . Building the team emphasized activities that involved the whole team. Although we hardly knew each other, we all got a clear understanding of the mission, focused on the goal and realized we needed to work together. . . . Team effort—working as a collaborative team. . . . Trust—we quickly learned to rely on each other and respected each other's opinions, ideas, and experience. Openness—they could argue for no more than five minutes and later, amazingly, whether they came to an agreement or not, they always backed each other up! Building confidence—I empowered them to develop their own training plans, allowed a modest budget, gave room to be creative, and challenged them."

Reading these stories, it's clear there are multiple dimensions the students see as important for effective teams: attitudes, demanding or dangerous situations, training, trust, depending on one another, focus on mission and goals, communication and openness, collaboration and interdependence, not letting your teammates down, creating high expectations, knowing each other's jobs and roles, empathy, adaptability, taking care of your people and each other, and courage.

The veterans have difficulty translating their military team experience to a civilian context because teams may not be as structured or highly trained as in the military context. So uncertainty and ambiguity often become a block to progress. So too do old views of rank and classical views of assertiveness. In an unstructured setting where both goals and means need to be shaped by team members, there is hesitation, and often the loudest voices take over rather than a lengthy discussion and analysis by all team members giving and receiving influence almost equally.

Motivation: Important Drivers of Work Performance

In addition to their understanding of leadership and what goes into effective leadership, I wanted to know about some of their current motivations, or what they were hoping to achieve. Motivation can often be seen as the opposite but complementary side of leadership, and an important topic for those in leadership roles to understand about others. This is not an exhaustive list of motivating factors, but a segment of possible motivators that would be appropriate for this group of veterans.

I asked Cohort IV to rank order the top five or ten of the following list of attributes they were looking for in work as they transitioned from the military to civilian careers, or if they were already in civilian work.

1. Increasing responsibility

2. Job security

3. Work/life balance/flexibility

4. Opportunity for advancement

5. Opportunity for self-development/growth

6. Working for self/autonomy/ownership

7. Making an impact

8. Challenging work

9. Feeling recognized and appreciated

10. Meaningful work

11. Good coworkers/team

12. Trustworthy leadership

13. Pay including benefits

14. Working for a higher purpose

15. Feeling fully engaged at work

When asked to rank potential motivating forces in their work, "making an impact," "meaningful work," and "higher purpose" all received high marks, but they were often on par or subordinate to caring for family, which wasn't on the list. Several veterans knew exactly what financial resources they needed on a regular basis to take care of their family, so money, job security, and work-life balance became the additional concept group that had a high ranking, as well. One other dimension needs to be noted: "working for self/autonomy/ownership" was fostered and nurtured through our focus on entrepreneurship throughout the program. While many of our students hadn't considered entrepreneurship before coming in, this dimension tended to pick up momentum during the year as new career possibilities began to take shape. More than once a more senior veteran would mention to me that they felt having their own business might make more sense than trying to fit into a civilian environment where authority and response to authority were not as traditional as they had been used to in their military career.

The combination of being motivated by higher purpose, meaningful work, and making an impact with a strong focus on the well-being of family was understandable, even with this brief glimpse into motivation. We will address the veterans' interest and activity in volunteering and community service later, but I suspect it will look significant compared with an average person's engagement within the community. The drive for meaningful service, and for a higher purpose while being grounded in one's family's well-being was apparent throughout my time with the veterans.

In Summary

Being within this context of the veterans, their values, affect, and service orientation had a profound effect on me and my sense of myself, congruence, commitment, and contribution. It was easy to work with them, to focus on their needs for growth and their resistance when it became apparent. It wasn't all positive outcomes, but it was a caring place to be. Members of the cohort were concerned when others were depressed or ill, or when someone had lost a family member. The cohort acted as a community for support and attentiveness, and the concept of brothers and sisters took on a realistic feel.

During the fires in Los Angeles (December 2017), a student emailed the management team and asked if we were safe, and when we replied that we were and returned the question, we found out they had already organized into a first responder mode in case any member of the community needed assistance. I suspect that would be extended to others who were not also members of the community. They were trained to act and respond, and they cared deeply in this concern and willingness to help, as well as a willingness to risk their own safety to help others. The idea of leadership focused on service and one's best efforts to contribute and care about others was already ingrained in the veterans before they set foot inside the university. Now it was our opportunity to serve and engage professionally with their personal efforts to successfully transition and assist in whatever ways we could to encourage their career aspirations and deeply personal goals.

I mentioned earlier all the effort that is going into criticizing the leadership development field for not having a very good track record of producing effective leaders, with the question left unanswered as to why as an industry we are lacking in success as measured by organizational outcomes, as a result of current or past leaders. And, at the same time, Professor Kellerman's statement about this lack does not include military leadership, which is better, deeper, harder, and lifelong. My experience with almost 400 veterans of all ranks and branches made me aware that all of them had been trained multiple times in leadership values and techniques in order to have almost 100-percent effective succession planning. Should you as a squad member need to step up and take a leadership role with your team, you are prepared—as is every other member. Everyone gets the same message, drill, and challenges, even though there will be obvious differences based on rank and context. With the overarching concept of "mission first; people always," it is clear to me that leadership is a call to service. The fourth quote under "Most Effective Leadership," "leads by example . . . believes they serve their subordinates rather than the other way around," is an approach specifically included in Alex Urankar's story in Chapter 8. Leadership as service puts a different emphasis on alignment of mission, role, and people rather than on outcome metrics and ownership value.

In a reflective column in *The Wall Street Journal,* journalist John D. Stoll discusses the death of one of his mentors and makes a statement that might help explain at least some of the problems with leadership training for organizational effectiveness in other segments of the economy.

"I've chased CEOs, heads of state, and even the Pope around the US and Europe, and **it is a rare bird who cares as much about the success of others as they do about their own.**" (September 20, 2019)

This might be at least a partial explanation for the difference between military leadership effectiveness and leadership for profit and non-profit organizations, the expression of caring both about the people in one's unit and how to help them be more successful, so that the total unit is successful. I think it is also a clear expression of difference in focus and use of presence to influence and lead, and to both support and give credit to those doing the work who are part of one's team.

In Chapter 6, we will discuss change and use the concept of transformational change to look at major changes in both careers and worldviews, and especially the veterans' view of themselves. Also, it becomes more apparent that there is a greater openness to a range of opportunities in careers and activities that in the past the veterans did not know existed or that might be reachable. Now here are more personal stories from alums.

Natalya Turner—Cohort III

I graduated from the MBV program in 2016. Before that, I received a bachelor of science degree in business with a concentration in small business management and entrepreneurship from the University of Phoenix in 2013.

An air force veteran, I served nine years. I currently work as a government contractor on the Los Angeles Air Force base as a technology analyst. I find small businesses that make technology the air force can use to support the war fighters.

I have a small home-based jewelry business called "Rock Fabulous Finds." My line was featured in the USC bookstore in September 2016, featuring a "USC-inspired" collection of earrings made with USC cardinal and gold colors.

I also volunteer part-time for a non-profit called Space Innovation Academy (SIA), which teaches space STEM Education to high school students. And I serve as an advisor on the board of the LA Military Charity Fund (LAMCF), where we provide scholarships to children of veterans who want to go to college.

I graduated from high school in 1997 and was accepted to California State Northridge University. I would be the first member of my immediate family to attend college. Attending college is something my grandmother always wanted for her five children and me, her only grandchild. As a single mother, my grandmother worked two jobs, sometimes three, to make sure we would have the opportunity to go to college. It was something that was extremely important to her since she was never able to go herself. My mother and her siblings decided not to complete their college education, so it was up to me to take on that challenge to make my grandmother proud. I entered college excited but undecided about a major and, after a year of classes, felt lost and unsure about what I really wanted to do. So I decided to leave.

I approach leadership as a leader who is good at working with and through other people. I can understand people and how to motivate them. I am a good team member, as well as team leader. I'm able to make decisions in difficult situations and can be both objective and flexible in generating and evaluating ideas. I can see things from other people's point of view and inspire other people's trust. In the area of analysis and strategic decision-making, as a leader, I can provide creative thinking, flexibility, strategic thinking, and decisiveness. I can generate new ideas and approaches to situations. I can easily adapt to changing situations and have the flexibility to adopt new approaches when necessary. I can grasp the big picture and think long term. In the area of bringing management structure, my leadership skills showed that I have resiliency, am action-oriented, good with day-to-day responsibility, have a good work ethic, and am good with organizational priority. I learned my leadership skills during my time in the air force and working as a government contractor. During my career, I had the pleasure of working for and with some amazing leaders. I believe I naturally adopted some of their methods, which led me to selecting the styles I did, and also because those styles are more in line with my personality.

During my time in the air force, I learned a few key lessons that also helped to shape my leadership skills: "mission first and people always" and "lead by example." I learned that if you make the goals and expectations of your people and organization clear and people know where they fit in the big picture of things, that their work matters and their certain gifts, skills, and talents are needed, it creates a more productive work environment. Realize that you have a greater influence on others than you know. Whether you are at school, work, or in a group setting, your words and actions have the potential to impact how people view the total organization, so you cannot overlook your involvement in its success. Being a leader is only partially dependent upon your skills and intelligence. The true character of a leader is demonstrated in their morals, commitment to truth and fairness, and ability to communicate direction. I learned and believe that all good leaders need to have a clear vision, to work hard, to have perseverance, to provide humble service, to show empathy, and to have discipline.

"Life-changing" are the words that would describe my feelings and experience in the MBV program. The year in the MBV program made me take a look at my life and helped me to figure out who I really am and what I want out of life. It was also a different type of educational experience for me and exceeded my expectations. Although the program is intense because we learn a lot of valuable information in a short time, if I had to choose again, I would still choose the MBV program over a traditional MBA program. I loved the emphasis on leadership, entrepreneurship, and self-development. The MBV program and USC Trojan family/network provided the sense of community and camaraderie I had in the military. Also, the numerous resources we were provided from the MBV board of counselors, career counseling, and networking events with different industry partners helped significantly.

As this semester and year come to an end, I feel that given all the things I've had to endure in my personal life, I have done a good job. But I feel I could have done better. This whole year I have had the "fight on" mentality. I got knocked a lot, but I have always mustered the strength to pick myself up and keep going. My faith is the biggest part of my will to keep going. Also, the people with whom I surround myself help me to stay focused and motivated. This year has taught me that life is short, and that all we have is today. The passing of my mother and aunt (my mom's sister), losing my job, and other things I endured this year forced me to change and pushed me beyond my comfort zone in all areas of my life. I always considered myself a strong person, but I learned I was more resilient, capable, and courageous than I ever thought I could be.

This year has made me take a look at my life and try to figure out who I really am and what I want. I realized that the biggest thing holding me back is myself. I am beginning to break free of limitations I placed on myself throughout my adult life. At this time, I have the opportunity to shape my life and career exactly the way I want. I know I need to take more risk. The scary thing in taking a risk is the possibility of failure, but also a chance to be great! I have a few barriers to overcome, but I know that continuing to push past those barriers will help me find the joy, life, career, and success for which I have been searching. I know that if I never left my comfort zone and don't continue to "play up," I would be sabotaging my chances to find those things.

This program has changed my life forever. Professor Turrill, I remember during orientation weekend, said, "Yes, you will learn about business in this program, but you will learn a lot more about yourself." He was right! I reflect back to my frame of mind when I first started the program. I was in a very vulnerable space and no longer felt confident in myself, because my whole life had been turned upside down with losing my mother and aunt, getting laid off, and a lot of other things. Everything I thought I knew about life and myself had all changed. Although I'm resilient and continued to press on despite the setbacks, I can honestly say when I started the program, I wasn't quite sure who I was. Over the past year and through this program, I learned the importance of emotional intelligence, and mindfulness. I've come to understand my strengths, weaknesses, behaviors, and to be able to identify my sources of power. Learning those things and so much more in this program empowered me to start embracing the person I am becoming and start making decisions to support my future.

At this point in my life, I'm very committed to my personal growth as I continue reaching for my future goals. I feel like I have the opportunity to create the life I truly want, and I have nothing or no one to hold me back. I look at my life right now as a blank canvas and I can paint the picture any way I want to. What a blessing it is to be in this position!!! I know that as I continue to move forward, I may face some opposition, but I know it takes courage and resiliency to try something new, risk failure, and persevere in the hard times! I'm choosing to maintain a consistency of purpose and remain faithful to the promises I made to myself as I seek to reach my goals. I know that if you want to accomplish a goal, it is important to stay true to your convictions, and although you may face opposition, it does not have to stop you.

So moving forward, I leave behind lack of confidence, fear of the unknown, and fear of failure, and I will continue to "fight on!"

The MBV program means a lot to me. It transformed my life in a lot of ways. I feel so blessed to have graduated from such an amazing, prestigious program. I'm a very spiritual person and believe that God orders your steps. He has an individual plan for each of us if we are willing to step out in faith, do the work, and participate in His plan. He knew that I needed to be a part of this program to help me continue moving forward with life after all the setbacks I had, and for that I am forever grateful.

Sonny Tosco—Cohort V

I was one week removed from being ousted from a startup I cofounded. Confusion, depression, and the angst of failure clouded my mind, making me question whether going to the event would be worth the time. I decided to move past it; there isn't much time to grieve in startup land, and I'm glad I did. It was that night that I met Adam Cohen. After the fireside chat, we left the venue for the obligatory happy hour. I found out Adam was also an academy grad, so we immediately had rapport. Our team recently snapped the fourteen-game losing streak to his school, so naturally I had to mention it.

I soon found out that, one week prior, Adam had graduated from the MBV program at USC. I was intrigued; the possibility of grad school seemed like a distant reality for me. Years of startup debt placed me in a difficult financial situation, the time spent studying for the GMATs could be allocated elsewhere, and being in a two-year program would be at the expense of other opportunities. Adam addressed my objections and, when I went home that night, the first thing I Googled was "USC MBV vets."

I knew that cofounding three startups by that time granted me the wisdom only learned from experience. Much of my business acumen was self-taught, the other from failure. However, I knew where I needed to improve, and the MBV provided me the best platform to obtain the core fundamentals I needed to continue on the journey. Silicon Beach was expanding and was the third-biggest startup ecosystem in the country. Cultivating a network there would be great for my career in the long term. When speaking with James Bogle, he shared some of the programs I could leverage to finance the school, addressing a huge burden.

I became a Trojan two months later.

Being in a room full of vets again for orientation weekend was like in-processing after a PCS. You knew that you were in a room with high-caliber individuals who had the grit and work ethic to get the job done. Professor Turrill and James Bogle laid out the expectations for the program on the same weekend, communicating to us that the outward journey to professionally develop should not overshadow the journey inward, to know yourself and how to authentically create value.

After the first weekend, I found the people in my cohort whose ambitions aligned with mine, a long-term roommate, and a goals buddy. Throughout the year, we continued to work on projects together and develop close relationships. I was fortunate enough to grab coffee with Jim Miller, a business partner of Keith Ferrazzi and a USMA grad. His best piece of advice was to form close relationships with the people in the program. I'm grateful for receiving that advice early enough in the semester to invest the time into my circle. The teachers and mentors with whom I was fortunate enough to interact re-routed the course of my life—more on a personal than a professional level. As obsessed as I became with my work, it was at the expense of spending time with my young family. Hearing the perspectives of people who have navigated those obstacles, like Chris Lord and Professor Turrill, gave me the wisdom they've obtained from years I have not lived. MBV not only made me a better professional, but a better father and husband.

As May neared and the capstone project was submitted, I could not help but feel like the ending was bittersweet. I wouldn't see my friends as frequently anymore, but the journey had come full circle. I came into the program with tireless ambitions and left with a focus only refined through the aperture of wisdom.

Immediately after graduation, I was able to become the general manager of a coding boot camp in the Bay Area. MBV taught me how to understand the financials of a successful company. After seeing more of the operation, I moved on to another opportunity.

It was at this time that an MBV alum shared an opportunity with a data science consulting firm. I knew Dave from class as he and I were among the few who were working in the tech industry. His company was hiring a technical product manager for their Facebook client. The interview was the hardest I've been through, but MBV gave me the tools I needed to excel above other applicants.

Since starting at Facebook, I've been able to make an immediate impact by being the communication broker between the technical and non-technical members of our team. I came into MBV conversant at a technical level, but after MBV, I was able to resonate with the other side of the table, allowing me to ensure our cross-functional team was aligned toward a goal.

My family and I are now in a better place. At a time we were thinking of splitting the family for my wife to pursue an opportunity with Accenture in San Antonio, but we fortunately found a better one that allowed her to work from home with Blue Star Families. The startup experience and MBV taught me how to thoroughly evaluate opportunities and include my family in these decisions. Gone are the paranoia and doubt that underscored these decisions in the past and in their place is a restored confidence MBV provided confirmation that I'm aligning my ambitions with the interests of the only stakeholders that matter, my family.

Jake Williams—Cohort IV

I pursued the MBV at the USC Marshall School of Business for the educational and career opportunities. I spent a little over twelve years in the navy, was a Navy SEAL for ten of them, and am grateful for the experiences during that time. Despite the incredible journey, it was time for me to hang up the uniform so I could be present with my family. It had taken a toll on them: countless days on the road training, five combat deployments. During that time there was a wedding and the birth of two children—today, we have three. When I learned about the MBV program, it struck me as the ideal opportunity to learn the business world as I transitioned out of the navy. Being stationed in Coronado during that time, the close vicinity allowed me to fulfill my obligations at my command while pursuing the MBV.

From a young age, I have sought new opportunities to challenge myself and people around me. When I was seven, I started a local trash can service business with my brother and a friend in our neighborhood. On trash days, we would take our clients' trash cans in and out of their yards and billed them monthly. We grew the business in the neighborhood and our profits supplied us with enough cash to support our youthful hobbies. My brother, friend, and I have all moved on, but twenty-four years later, the business still continues to provide a trash can service from a few local kids who took it over. In high school, I started my own vehicle sales business and obtained my vehicle salesperson license from the state of California. I started selling cars for my family members who needed help with their transactions. Word of mouth spread about my services and I started receiving vehicles on consignment that I would sell for a commission. I started by selling Hondas, Fords, and Toyotas. By the end of my four years running this business, I was selling BMWs, Mercedes, Porsches, Ferraris, and specialty vehicles. The learning experience was invaluable, and ever since I have had the desire to start and run my own business. I wrapped this business up as I enlisted into the navy.

For as long as I can remember, I have wanted to serve our country through the armed services. I am proud of our heritage. I firmly believe we are the hope and light to the world, and I wanted to contribute to keeping freedom's torch lit. I believe there are good and evil in this world, and it takes good men and women to stand up against the evils for life to thrive. For these reasons, I joined the military to serve the nation that has given me and so many others the opportunity of freedom.

Before starting the program, my short-term goals were to become well versed in the world of business. I realized I didn't know what I needed to know to have a successful transition. More specifically, within my short-term goals, I wanted to learn the technical business skills I had not been exposed to yet. A consistent thread that links my short- and long-term goals is time with my family. I chose this path because I want to excel in the areas mentioned so I could be efficient at work in order to be able to spend more time with my family while starting this next chapter in my life. Long term, I want to start my own business and provide an exceptional product or service that would make consumers beat a path to my door. I wanted my business to provide me with the freedom to be with my family and be present as my children grew up.

Having graduated from the MBV, I am equipped with the tools necessary to achieve these goals. I am on the path now—it is a tough path, often ambiguous, but with the lessons I learned from the MBV, I can confidently proceed. Not only do I continue with confidence, but I am surrounded and encouraged on a regular basis by the seventy-seven Trojans with whom I graduated who are in the trenches with me in their own industries.

A brief snapshot of my experience and leadership in my endeavors thus far. Right out of high school I enlisted in the navy. After graduation from boot camp, I was the section leader of my "A" school for basic engineering common core, responsible for 103 other recent boot camp graduates. As the section leader, I was responsible for the daily headcount, uniform inspections, watch bill, and barracks inspections to ensure cleanliness and readiness of all students. Upon completion of "A" school, I checked into Basic Underwater Demolition/SEAL training. In each graduating class, the students vote for one all-around exceptional student among their peers as top of the class, honor man, and the instructor staff confirms the choice. The honor man award is given for top performance in all aspects of training, including leadership. After six months of training my peers, the instructor staff selected me as the class honor man at graduation. Six months later, at SEAL qualification training graduation, I was awarded class honor man again, based on the same merits. At SEAL Team SEVEN, I held several leadership positions. I was the fire team leader for my squad. I was responsible for the safety and tactical employment of my five-man team on the battlefield for over 100 special operations in Iraq and Afghanistan.

While serving as the fire team leader, I was also appointed as SEAL Team SEVEN's lead joint terminal attack controller (JTAC) program administrator (PA). A JTAC is responsible for the direct communication and employment of close air support, artillery, mortars, and other non-organic fire support. As the JTAC PA, I was responsible for all record management, currency training, and deployment readiness for all twenty of SEAL Team SEVEN's JTACs. I was appointed troop department head of intelligence for our forty-man element. As the lead intelligence operator, I led and managed a five-man multi-spectrum intelligence collection and analysis team that interfaced with six government agencies to develop targets that needed to be prosecuted. I was the leading petty officer (LPO) of a thirty-man platoon while deployed to Afghanistan. As an LPO, I was responsible for the daily administration, combat leadership, mentoring, and teamwork of my thirty-man platoon. I was awarded the Admiral Ricketts Inspirational Leadership Award for this deployment. One sailor a year is selected for this award, based on exceptional performance. After my time in a SEAL team, I became a SEAL instructor, where I was a part of the selection process for new SEAL candidates. I was an instructor for the infamous hell week and close quarters combat. During this time, I led hundreds of high-risk live-fire evolutions, mentored students in the core values of a SEAL, and was named instructor of the year.

Without a doubt, the highlight of the MBV program is all the lifelong relationships that were developed. I can honestly say that when entering this program, I had no expectation of making these incredible relationships—my focus was on learning the business curriculum. Of course, the curriculum was incredible, exceeding my expectations, but the power of the Trojan network and culture of USC are amazing, so much more than an education. It was through these relationships that I was able to develop and refine my own leadership competencies. One of the most impacting competencies I developed was managing up. Managing up has been a very effective tool in my professional and personal life. I found this to be a strength of mine in leading others. Prior to learning the term "managing up," I referred to the same action as "expectation management." Managing up opened my eyes to a familiar concept; putting it to practice has proven its effectiveness. Managing up has allowed me to effectively lead and influence those above and below me. At the heart of managing up, one must be willing to view the circumstances from the other party's position. When you are able to view a situation through the lens of someone else, it helps guide the actions and decisions on a particular matter.

I have noticed a very positive reaction from my colleagues—they feel I understand the issues at hand and appreciate the respect that has been given to their stance. The social styles evaluation provided confirmation for the style I was certain would define me. I am a driver. I find satisfaction in accomplishing tasks and crossing them off my to-do list. I thrive in adversity and with strong challenges—the bigger the challenge, the sweeter the victory. With this in mind, I must be aware of the flip-side of this attribute. The managing up mindset kept me focused on my strong drive and the importance of listening to others on the team, which made me a better team player.

During our last semester, I made a conscious effort to balance this difference effectively. Our Northrop Grumman project afforded me a great opportunity to work on this. On our first meeting, our team established its expectations for the project with input from all its members. For our team to increase our process gains, we put in place areas of accountability within the team and into pairs of accountability to accomplish our respective tasks. We outlined the responsibilities of each team member. We established phases of the project whose tasks would require effort and time. At the earliest opportunity, our team went to dinner together to solidify its members' interests and involvement within the project. Our team functioned well—we were very talented individuals who knew how to work as a team. We encouraged input from all members to gain buy-in from the team and create efficient workloads. Taking this approach worked well for me to develop competencies that would allow me to be a driver without steam-rolling others' ideas.

I am fully transitioned out of the military now, and life has been incredible in several ways. It has been incredibly challenging and rewarding. I still have a long road ahead of me to accomplish my goals. The lessons I learned during the MBV continue to have a direct influence on how I approach new situations and solve problems. My experience with the MBV helped me decide my next career path out of the military. At the time of this writing, I am at a phase in life where I am completely restarting—a new city, a new home, a new career, and baby number three all happened within a few months of each other. I have full confidence that I can and will achieve the goals I have set for my family. One of my biggest challenges I face today is building a new team. It's amazing to me how challenging this can be, even with all my time spent in a team environment that dealt with life-and-death circumstances. The difference I have found is simple but not easy, and I would not have discovered this if I were not in my current circumstances. While in the military and at USC, when teamwork/team-building is required, we generally are already surrounded by the right people, it's just a matter of putting them in the right place. Of course, that is an oversimplification of how to create a great team, but it is this key difference. The people with whom we are already surrounded are such a critical piece in building the team. The challenge I face today is how to create a team in a new environment where the availability of resources (people and money) is extremely limited. As I look back, I realize I never anticipated the difficulty in acquiring the right human capital. It's not the lack of talent; it is managing time in such a way to find and teach the right talent. I had always told myself that I knew how to build a great team and was a team player, so this shouldn't be a problem for me. Today, I am faced with the reality that you can't build something with nothing.

To this point in my life, the organizations I've been a part of had such a robust and well-functioning infrastructure (i.e., US Navy and USC) that it is often overlooked. With these robust infrastructures come proven systems and a track record of success. I have come to appreciate the value of these systems that help form the foundation of highly successful teams. Not only am I on the hunt for the right people to create a team, but I am building the systems as we go. It will be with the right people that we build an incredible team that performs in our industry. I am excited to move forward. It will be interesting to reflect in the years ahead on how this journey unfolds, and I will be happy to share the victories and defeats along the way.

Jessica Bradshaw—Cohort IV

For as long as I can remember, the military has always been a huge part of my life. One of my earliest memories was flying over the Pacific Ocean to Japan on a military aircraft, where we were strapped to the walls of the plane and my dad brought me to the cockpit where we could see the aurora borealis. I was two at the time. Growing up with my dad in the military meant that his two daughters would also participate in whatever military training organization he was involved in. My older sister, Melanie, and I spent many summers as cadets in the Pioneer Youth Corps of Oregon (PYCO), learning about military history and rank structure, conducting land navigation, running training exercises on paintball courses, and rappelling out of the local firefighter training towers. By the time we were in high school, my sister and I had been in twelve different schools, lived in four states, and one foreign country. Our childhood experience was unique because we were constantly moving and changing schools, but it also helped us adapt to situations because the one thing that was constant to us was change.

My dad originally enlisted in the air force, was stationed in Japan and Travis Air Force Base, but later joined the Army National Guard. In high school, he was a recruiter for the California Army National Guard and, upon high school graduation, my sister enlisted in it and was sent to basic training. Not knowing what I would do after high school, and with my sister away at basic, I spent my junior and senior years copying what my friends were doing. I started studying and taking PSATs and SATs and preparing for college. I was always a good student, and I graduated from North Torrance High School as one of the valedictorians of the Class of 2003. I was not considering following my dad and sister's footsteps and joining the military. My mom received my acceptance letter as a spring admit into the University of Southern California, and in 2004, I started my college experience.

My senior year of high school, my parents separated, so it was a difficult time for me starting college. As a first-generation college student, finances were also a challenge. No one in my family had attended college before so we had no idea what to expect. I had received scholarships and grants, but they didn't cover tuition, so I applied for financial aid. At that time, my relationship with my dad was rocky, but if it hadn't been for him, I would not have received an army ROTC scholarship. He introduced me to the recruiting officer for the Trojan Battalion and got me a meeting with the battalion commander. That spring, I joined the ROTC program and began training. Between my sophomore and junior year of college, I was sent to North Carolina for the special forces qualification course (SFQC) unconventional warfare exercise called Robin Sage. For two weeks, I conducted training exercises with Special Forces (SF) candidates as a guerilla fighter named "Moxie." I developed strong team-building skills with my fellow guerilla fighters as we learned tactics from the SF trainees, conducted an ambush on an abandoned airfield, engineered hand washing and personal hygiene stations, and performed basic medical treatment. Coming home from Robin Sage energized my love for the military and my decision to stick with the ROTC program. When I graduated from USC in 2007, I also received my commission in the California Army National Guard the same day, and I rendered my first salute as an officer to my dad.

My first overseas assignment was to Seoul, Korea, for Operation Key Resolve Foal Eagle. That summer, I attended a basic officer leadership course and an adjutant general officer basic course. Shortly after graduating, I was notified that my unit was deploying to Camp Bondsteel, Kosovo, and I spent my first mobilization as the deputy G1. With very little experience, I relied heavily on my non-commissioned officers and developed strong relationships with my section. Without a suitable mentor, I was forced to learn quickly and was humble enough to ask for help and learn mostly from my subordinates. Our team managed many human resources aspects, but the thing of which I was most proud was creating a morale program and helping organize comedy shows, concerts, sports tournaments, day trips, and fun runs. I also helped manage the rest and recuperation program for 1,387 soldiers.

One of my responsibilities as the Deputy G1 for Task Force Falcon was to help soldiers complete packets for follow-on assignments and extension orders. By helping thirty soldiers with follow-on assignments, I also was able to volunteer myself for three years on assignment in Kaiserslautern, Germany. On top of my administrative duties, I accumulated over nineteen months of command time and ten months as a logistics officer. While I was working in logistics, I had to manage the support of three investigative detachments with eleven offices spread throughout Germany, Belgium, the Netherlands, and Luxembourg. At times I would travel to these locations to bring equipment, turn in excess equipment, or inventory equipment. During my last year in Germany, I researched all items on a request list and was able to procure the full amount of requested investigative equipment for the investigative agents within the unit. While I was in Germany, I met my husband, Scott, and a little over a month after my change of command and coming off active-duty orders I gave birth to my son, Dillon, and transferred into the Inactive Ready Reserve (IRR).

I was in the IRR for almost a year. When we moved back to the United States when my husband was active duty, I transferred into the reserves. We were stationed in Virginia for his logistics officer captain's career course and soon were stationed in Mustang, Oklahoma. We worked together in the same multi-component (reserve and active duty) unit, and I managed all human resources-related aspects for fourteen active and 102 reservists. A year into living in Oklahoma, I gave birth to our daughter, Mia. When she was a year old, I started looking seriously into pursuing my master's degree, and that is when I found out about the MBV program at USC.

The MBV program gave me a second chance to come back to my alma mater, complete my goal of a master's degree, and graduate top of my class. When I was accepted to the program, I knew it would be difficult for me and my family, having to commute from Oklahoma City to Los Angeles every other weekend, but it was a sacrifice I needed to make to accomplish this goal. It *was* difficult for my young family because my husband and I were pursuing our graduate degrees at the same time (he received his master's in economics from the University of Oklahoma). When I began the program, it was a means to an end, and I never dreamed it would have such a huge impact on me professionally and personally.

On the first day, I was intimidated by the size of our class and the backgrounds and experiences each person had. But I quickly realized how special the MBV program was. I made a subconscious decision to strive for excellence and put my best foot forward in everything I did in the program. Going into it, my main focus was academics, but it was also important for me to feel connected to the program. Since I did not live in California, I knew I had to take on informal leadership roles to help develop relationships with my fellow cohort members. I started team-building within the class by having study sessions between classes. Being part of the MBV program helped me build confidence in myself and reminded me who I am as a person. As with anyone, I have my strengths and my weaknesses, but now I am able to identify them and am more self-aware. I am proud to be part of the MBV program as well as Cohort IV, because I gained more than an education, I gained a family and support group in my peers and confidence in my abilities. The MBV program was the best professional and personal experience. It pushed me out of my comfort zone and helped me become a better individual. I gained a boost of self-confidence, but it was also awe-inspiring to be surrounded by so many amazing individuals who thought so highly of me.

After my husband and I completed our master's programs, he began his transition out of the military, and we started preparing for our move back to California. This transition was not easy. I utilized everything I learned during the program to help me transition into a civilian career. We moved to Monterey, and it was difficult for me because I did not have an established network, and I knew I would have to build one in a new location. It was not easy finding a job either, but I took a temporary position at Macy's during the holidays to help me further develop my skills in human resources. Within a few months, I took a position in sales as an associate account executive at Comcast Spotlight. After a year, I graduated from the program and became an account executive. In the first three months, I won an annual sales competition for the California region and our local office in Monterey for exceeding our sales target and achieving 165.1 percent of the sales target for the first quarter. I'd pushed myself out of my comfort zone by accepting a position in sales, in which I had zero experience, but my perseverance and drive helped me do well.

While I continue to grow my professional skills, I enjoy being in a position where I can challenge myself and utilize my educational background in marketing and business. Being back in California has been extremely humbling because it's easy to think that you can land a six-figure job after graduating from places like USC and OU, but positions like that in the area we live are few and far between unless you want to commute an hour each way. For a year we lived with my father-in-law before we were able to get on our own feet and, on a limited income, bought a duplex that's much closer to our children's schools and where we work. We started running a short-term rental in one of the apartments while we live on the other side. We also took jobs that gave us the flexibility to spend time with our children, and we are still actively pursuing our dream of starting our own business in real estate. It hasn't been easy, but we are making it work the best we can. It has been two years since I graduated from the MBV program, but I am continuing to make tiny strides as I continue down this path of self-discovery and growth.

Carlos Amador—Cohort VI

Attending USC was a long-term goal of mine since I first stepped foot on campus over twenty years ago. The USC was the first major university campus I ever visited, and while the campus was close to the neighborhood I grew up in, I felt we were worlds apart. I was fortunate to visit the campus subsequently on several other occasions for either athletic or academic competitions during my high school years. I learned that its business programs are among the best in the country and its infamous Trojan family network makes students feel like they have a partner in their personal and professional life. Each past visit to either the campus or sporting events made me more determined to be part of the USC family. Today, I can now say that I am a proud Trojan with a master's degree.

Growing up in the Los Angeles community of Boyle Heights, I was raised by a single mother who instilled the importance of a strong work ethic as a way to better one's life. Like many children of her time in Mexico, my mother was pulled out of school at an early age to work and help the family with finances to make ends meet. When she migrated to the United States, she worked long hours, but always made time to help me do my homework, making sure I would not leave the kitchen table until I was finished with my academic responsibilities. My mother always made it a point to say that while we didn't have much, we were given an opportunity to succeed in this country with anything we strived toward.

The foundation provided by my mother has given me an opportunity to excel at various positions I have held, and has allowed me to gain a unique perspective of the world. From being a line cook for a fast-food restaurant, to being a field manager for the United States census, I learned not only how to prioritize my responsibilities, but also to train and manage others in achieving success. Working with people of diverse backgrounds has given me a unique view of various working environments, along with new skill sets. While I am grateful for early career endeavors, the time I spent in our armed forces made the biggest impact on my personal development.

After high school, I enrolled in the United States Army as a signals intelligence analyst. During my military occupation specialty training, I was named squad leader, a role I took on with great pride and determination. As squad leader, I was tasked not only with making sure orders were followed, but also acting as a role model by leading by example those under my leadership. My fellow squad members leaned on me for their academic studies and physical training. For my role as squad leader, I was recognized several times by several ranking officers. After completing both my specialty and airborne training, I was assigned to the 10th Special Force Group-Airborne (SFG-A). While assigned to the 10th SFG(A), I learned the importance of strategy and execution through multiple deployments. Understanding our mission's purposes and strategic objectives was instrumental to the unit's success. These deployments also gave me an appreciation of the diverse world, allowing me to work closely with our allies and civilians in various countries. More importantly, I learned that the world is full of different perspectives and motivations. I was able to assess these perspectives based on facts and not opinions. This allowed me to get to the core issues, and to develop the best course of resolution. My time in the army gave me the tools to achieve my personal goals and the mindset to be a successful part of a team. With help from my sergeants, along with hard work, I was able to skip a rank and get promoted to senior cryptologic analyst. Being part of this elite unit was one of the greatest accomplishments in my life.

After my time in the military, I started my career in finance at Wells Fargo as a teller. I was able to move up the ranks of my organization by leading projects to acquire new customers and providing training to new employees. I have also been given the opportunity to lead pilot programs and manage banking locations with ten to twenty staff members. This skillset allowed me to give back to my community by engaging in programs that focus on providing financial literacy classes to our local schools and non-profit organizations. Because of the work I've done, I was recognized on numerous occasions by senior management and given various awards.

Much of the success I've had throughout my career is due to my work ethic and the values my mother taught me as a young boy. While it's not been an easy road, I've had to work twice as hard as others to achieve my goals. Despite the interesting journey, I have been very fortunate to have peers and mentors who were willing to share their knowledge and resources to assist me in achieving my goals. I am indebted to these mentors and the roles they played in my life, and I plan to make every effort to play a similar role to others. Although I had been very proud of my accomplishments both personally and professionally, after fourteen years at Wells Fargo, I had reached a point where I had to take time to reflect on my past and see where I wanted to be in the future. It was at this point that I started to revisit my dream of attending USC.

Through USC's MBV graduate program, I was able to further develop the skills to progress in my profession. In today's global economic environment, with all its complexities and regulations, an individual must acquire the skill set and knowledge to excel professionally. The program's focus on understanding organizations and their strategies, which was a growth area for me, helped me understand how I could further navigate a corporate environment and accomplish my goals while providing leadership to others. The entrepreneur part of the program not only helped me understand strategy, growth, and implementation to start a business but inspired me to start my own business venture. One of the great things about this program is that it teaches best practices and theories, and challenges students to start their own business venture.

But the best part of the program was the opportunity it afforded us to learn from fellow classmates. Having worked for the same financial institution for the last fourteen years, it was a pleasure to learn from others in different industries. USC's MBV graduate program also allowed me the opportunity to reconnect with fellow veterans to reflect on our shared past experiences and learn from each other as we progress in our separate professions. Furthermore, the program allowed me to expand my circle of mentors and friends and to become part of the Trojan family.

Graduating from the MBV program has been one of the highlights of my life. It has allowed me to start forming a network to expand my career and given me a new skill set to progress in my professional and personal life. Additionally, it has allowed me to expand my military family and gain new friends through the Trojan network. I am blessed to be part of such an academic institution.

Since graduating, I am confident I made the right choice in attending USC. As I type these words, I am currently entertaining several leadership offers from other financial institutions. USC and the Trojan family have encouraged me as my mother did in the past. Thanks to the MBV program, I am confident I will be able to meet any new challenge I face throughout my personal and professional life.

Andrew Vandertoorn—Cohort IV

I was the youngest of three, my sister the oldest and my brother in the middle. We grew up as an average middle-class family in Phoenix. My dad grew up in Holland during WWII and met my mom on an airplane when she was flying out for nursing school at San Francisco General. My dad was in the Dutch navy before becoming a merchant marine. He ended his career as an officer with Sealand Shipping, which is now called Maersk. The family moved from my mom's native St. Louis to Jacksonville, Florida, and then on to Phoenix. My dad was largely absent most of my life because his ship rotations were four months on four months off, but Sealand usually offered him relief trips that paid extra, which he usually took. When I was in first grade, my parents started getting a divorce. The divorce went on for seven years, until I was in eighth grade. We were middle-class kids in wealthy schools and often struggled to keep up with the spending power of our contemporaries. After going through a divorce for seven years, you see a lot of stuff taken away, sold, or thrown away. I give credit to my mom because she fought for us to go to those schools. So I always took the opportunity seriously because I knew how hard she worked to give it to us. I also realized that the education I was getting was mine—meaning what I learned and did in school couldn't be taken away. Education has always been very important to me. I've always tried to be a great student and worked twice as hard to understand something when I didn't get it.

The idea of service to others was always something I naturally wanted, and the Catholic and Jesuit schools reinforced the idea. It's ironic that my mom recently retired as a nurse after over forty years of taking care of patients, my brother is a captain with the Phoenix Fire Department, my sister is an FBI agent, and I am in the USAF, all of which are service/volunteer-based jobs.

I originally wanted to be an engineer because I always enjoyed building things. Then a family friend gave me my first ride in a Cessna when I was probably seven or eight. I liked it, but wasn't hooked until I was sixteen when I took another flight. I knew right then that's what I was going to do. I knew I wanted to fly as a career. In high school, I was introduced to several mentors who were military and airline pilots, and they are my friends to this day. "You can be a regular civilian pilot, but being a military aviator gives you a lot of access to the world, great missions, cool airplanes, and a good experience." That's when I realized I could do something I wanted and serve a big need for my country.

There is five years' difference between me and my brother and eight between me and my sister. My sister jokes that when her friends were playing with Barbie dolls, she had a real one, and it was me! With my mom working full-time, my brother and sister did an excellent job of helping raise me, but the age gap put me out of the range of being together. I was in grade school when they were in high school, and they were in college when I was high school. I was always one segment or life phase behind, and never in it together. I credit this situation for making me independent. I played soccer, baseball, and karate and enjoyed the team environment. I went to Catholic grade school and Jesuit high school, then Arizona State University. I applied to the air force, navy, and merchant marine academies, hoping that would be my ticket to start. Despite being super involved, and having a great GPA, flight experience, and congressional recommendations, the navy and air force denied me. But I was accepted to the merchant marines. I ultimately said no to them because the summers were spent on ships and I wanted to fly instead. My counselor recognized my service and said as a backup, I should apply to ASU's leadership scholarship program. Only one student from each high school could be recommended, and my school recommended me. I was part of that scholarship program all four years. I continued to fly and gain experience, was a full-time student, and had multiple jobs.

I knew I wanted to serve and fly in some capacity, and ultimately it came down to the USMC and the USAF Reserves. The reserves won because I knew it was a better mission, had a better plane, closer base, and nicer people. It took over two and a half years to interview and finally get hired in the reserves because of the level of competition. The military gave more opportunities, challenges, skills, resources, and abilities to do things regular pilots couldn't imagine, but most importantly, I could be part of something bigger than me. Nine-eleven had already happened, so I knew exactly what I was getting into. I went to training for two years, came back, and two weeks later, I was in Iraq. I've been flying to the same places for twelve years. I have over 5,000 hours of flight time, 2,000 of them in combat zones during 324 combat missions. During that time, I flew millions of pounds of cargo, thousands of critically wounded patients, weapons, helicopters, tanks, bombs, billions of dollars in cash, and whatever else you could think of. I was part of a bigger operation and supported a cause higher than myself. I see lots of veterans everywhere, and I wonder if I flew them back, or if they were among the patients on board during one of my flights. Now that I work for Delta, I have seen both types of flying, and I relate it similarly to the military in the sense that it's still a service.

I've always remembered two quotes. The first is: "The journey of 10,000 miles begins with a single step." Nothing I have done has occurred overnight. The road to get hired by the military was eight years long, and the road to Delta nearly twenty. At no point in time was anything ever guaranteed, grandfathered, promised, or issued. I earned everything literally one step at a time, with many, many failures along the way. I was never a legacy in terms of following a fellow family member into the military or airlines; each of those steps was into uncharted territory. But they were *my* steps. Much like my education, I owned every single one of them, fair and square. The second quote is: "Man's flight through life is sustained by the power of his knowledge." This is written on the main statue in the center of the Air Force Academy in Colorado Springs. Despite being upset by not getting accepted, it reinforced my theory that education is the key that unlocks doors and is one of the main pillars of my ethos. It takes a lot of effort to stay on course and defeat the naysayers, and that quote helps me keep things in perspective and adds a realistic, tangible feeling to how knowledge or education can and should be at the core of not only leadership, but individuals.

I had been wanting to go back to school since 2008. I'd been in the squadron for four years flying my tail off and wanted to go back to school. The airlines weren't hiring at the time because of the bankruptcies and mergers, and the military was on the cusp of ordering one of many surges. I explored medical school, graduate schools, real estate appraisal, pharmacy school, and even thought of being a general contractor. In 2009, an experimental flying program was started that flew a secret airplane over the battle space in Afghanistan. I volunteered and flew it for six months and came back in the middle of the surge and went right back to flying the C-17. I used a lot of my time to look at schools and explore different options. I think the big thing I was looking for was just being part of a community with like-minded, driven individuals. The other aspect I wanted was a physical school in a location I could visit and be a part of events. All of the education with the USAF is online now, and you lose so much of the learning experience I couldn't do it. Several of my squadron members came to the MBV program and said they had a great experience, so I looked into it and really liked it. The best highlight for me was the common military background among the students. It provides an opportunity to automatically have something on which to build a relationship. I really enjoyed the executive who spoke about the electronics company after whom Marshall is named. I related more to the speakers who started at the bottom of the company, and diligently worked their way up than the ones who just started a company and got lucky.

I do think the MBV program really allowed me to create a corporate or collegial style of empathy, which allowed me to determine why some individuals were attacking what I viewed as beneficial changes and leadership. So I now work harder to communicate with them and hear their concerns and get their input in an effort to catch them before they make a decision.

Some of the other philosophies I learned during the MBV that I have incorporated into my life post-graduation focus on the fact that life begins once you step outside your comfort zone. Maybe it's a pilot thing, where I have learned to always stay within the airplane's limits, but I have slowly started to try and apply for change and to do things that are outside my comfort zone. The best strategy to deal with change has always been one of my own personal tenets, and that's to never stop learning.

The other strategy of dealing with change that I learned from MBV is to pivot. I imagine the best-trained businessmen know to pivot early and often. While I can say pivoting is something I consider now, gauging when, how often, and in which direction, pivoting is something with which I still experiment, try to learn from, and ultimately refine. I view pivoting as a perishable skill, like public speaking or interviewing, so at the moment I'm still learning and experimenting with it. Normally, when I set my mind to a task, I don't stop until I accomplish it, no matter the cost. I guess you could say the MBV introduced the idea of an efficient pivot. Ultimately, the main focus for me will always be to stay passionate, stay engaged, and never give up during the process. I'm already looking at other educational opportunities for the future. I have a goal of a PhD eventually. When I retire from the military, I would like to teach.

The biggest thing I left behind was the practice of placing barriers on my own success. Complacency, impatience, and self-doubt that was the result of unfamiliarity or inexperience with a position or situation were true hindrances to personal progression. The MBV program helped me realize I had many skills I could use and develop—not just the ones the military taught me.

I definitely grew personally in many ways during the MBV program. First off, I was part-time in the military, full-time with Delta, and going to USC. So it definitely pushed me in terms of capabilities, time, resources, and perseverance. I did the most I could with the time I had, enjoyed it, and learned a great deal about prioritizing and teamwork. I always prioritized the MBV as the highest because I knew the year would go by fast. In terms of decision-making, despite believing that companies follow strategic short- and long-term growth plans, I learned the only constant is change. Personally, I hate change, so I had to realize that no matter how hard I planned, things would change. I learned to stay resilient and to keep a constant stream of effort working toward the objective. It was very important for me to make new relationships while at USC. While at times the group projects were challenging, I liked them because I got to know others and make connections. As a result, I have a great group with whom I still stay in touch, and they are all doing well.

Since I graduated, it has been a whirlwind of activity. In one of my weekly blogs, I wrote that I talked with my supervisor at Delta and my commander in my squadron. I asked how I was doing, what opportunities I had, and what I should put on the horizon. At the time of that conversation, I was the assistant chief pilot and an instructor pilot within the military. Now I have been promoted to chief pilot and upgraded to evaluator pilot. Both are roles I never thought I'd have, but feel incredibly honored to have been selected for, particularly the evaluator pilot because there is no higher level within the squadron in terms of certification. The commander has placed an enormous amount of trust in me to ensure both the standards of the squadron and the USAF. So, as much as it is a reward for hard work, it is also a burden because the buck stops with you in many ways. The chief pilot promotion was also a great one. My main function is hiring future pilots for the squadron, and it's always so rewarding to work with them and see them complete training and come back.

I have also applied for two leadership institutes in Arizona. The first is with the Arizona State University Leadership Institute. Its goal is to empower alumni to help drive the goals of the university, make an impact in the community, and mentor current students. The second is called Arizona Valley Leadership Institute.

Overall, the MBV has pushed me ahead of my peers and set me up for success. The organizations for which I work and volunteer have recognized it and rewarded me. They have given me a great amount of autonomy and rope to either build great things or hang myself. It's actually a good amount of pressure. I'm ready for the challenges and will give it my best. I'm sure there will be failures along the way. Churchill said, "Success is moving from one failure to another with the same level of enthusiasm." I have found the class to be incredibly motivating and supportive. Even if some of the classmates didn't get along in class, socially they are supportive now. People still stay connected, they attend family and school events, and, most importantly, they remain just a phone call away.

The biggest goal I achieved is one I set out from the start, and announced in front of the class: to make new friends and start a new beginning at a physical school. While the USC alumni network is great, the friends and experiences I made are better. I stay in touch with fifteen to twenty classmates; about five of those are great friends now. That wouldn't be possible if I hadn't taken those first steps to get involved with USC or the MBV. It was bringing us together for the group projects, study groups, ropes course, football games, and nights out in Los Angeles that made it a success. The journey was fast, challenging, encouraging, and stimulating, but the success of the group and its relationships will deliver rewards for decades to come. Getting selected was a great honor, one I don't take lightly and look to carry forward for a long time. I hope during the process I made everyone proud to help, teach, and mentor me and hope to deliver and pay forward the values the program taught and instilled in me.

David Foster—Cohort V

I would like to begin by describing my social/educational background germane to the MBV family education environment. Three of my grandparents were college graduates, and my paternal grandmother earned a PhD at Berkeley in 1941. My father had two master's degrees, and my mother did not finish her undergraduate degree. My father was in the computer business based out of the Santa Clara Valley (aka Silicon Valley, though that name was not common in the 1970s), and the greater Boston "Route 128" area. We lived in suburbs where most of the families were nuclear, single-income, and white-collar. Most of my friends' dads worked in high-tech or finance or other types of office work. I went to public high school, and probably over 90 percent of my graduating class went directly to a four-year college. Local industry in the Metro Boston region was generally waning in the 1970s and 1980s—the GM plant in the next town over was in its final years in the 1980s, and the older mill-town industries along the regions' many rivers had been virtually dormant since the middle of the twentieth century.

Other than a few remaining dairies, orchards, and garden shops, agriculture had retracted into mostly private purpose—some residents grew fodder for their handfuls of horses and cows or engaged in some minor family heritage seasonal planting. A few of my classmates lived on farms, although any farming was supplemented by full-time work elsewhere. We mostly lived in the proliferating suburban neighborhoods. In short, the general path of my fellow high schoolers was to go to college then enter some professional or white-collar work.

I went to a state university (the University of Massachusetts) and studied mechanical engineering as an undergraduate. I was interested in the military probably as a quest for adventure and challenge and with the thought that an office job and grad school were always options for later on, but that there was an age window for joining the marines, so this was something I'd have to do after college. For whatever reason, I was only interested in the marines. All I knew about the marines was from what I'd seen in the movies—so I really knew nothing at all. I thought it would be worth trying to see if I could make it through—typical young man type of thinking. My family tree includes soldiers going back to the revolution, but neither my father nor either grandfather had been in the service. I had no particular preparation growing up for the military in general or the marines in particular. Of my high school class of 165, four of us entered the service after college, three into the marines on active duty, one into the air force reserves.

I entered the Marine Corps via the six-weeks-each junior and senior platoon leaders class taken during two undergraduate summers. After graduation, I was commissioned as a second lieutenant, attended the Basic School at Marine Corps Base Quantico, Virginia, then proceeded to Pensacola, Florida, for naval flight school.

Flight school was a seminal experience for my academic outlook, and there is a clear dividing line in my academic performance before and after flight school. In high school and college, I was an episodically serious student, excelling at times in favored subjects, earning many mediocre grades, and sometimes doing rather poorly when indifferent to the subject. As an institution, the navy's flight school was intolerant of mediocre performance. Second chances were rare. Although I had no substantive preparation for the rigors and expectations of the military or flight school, a light bulb went on in my mind within the first few weeks of flight school, and I quickly became a serious and diligent student. This was probably because I started to see friends get kicked out of the program for one deficiency or another—clearly the navy was not messing around with standards and expectations. My run through the curriculum was very successful, and I graduated with distinction, an achievement I did not foresee and no one else would have foreseen in light of my high school and undergraduate academic performance.

I entered the Fleet Marine Force a few months before the Iraqi invasion of Kuwait in 1990, and deployed to Saudi Arabia and Kuwait with my squadron for Operations Desert Shield and Storm. Over the years of my active service, I became a captain (O-3) and held several administrative and tactical instructor positions in my unit.

I left active service after a total of six years and eight months.

My initial thoughts on leaving active duty was to return to the university. I took a semester of undergraduate engineering courses to get back in the academic groove. I enjoyed the academics but became restless with a pace that was more serene than my time as a marine. After a summer working on a geotechnical engineering research project for the university, I left my studies to manage a local farm for a season while considering my future. I was in my early thirties with some time as a junior officer, had an engineering degree, but had no professional engineering experience. A former squadron mate with a similar resumé was in Washington, DC, working for the Department of Defense (DoD) and suggested I might find a similar opportunity where my military experience and technical education could find some professional traction.

With the exception of a few years stationed overseas and traveling with my wife, I have been in the DoD acquisition system since. Work in weapon systems development and analysis has been illuminating, requiring knowledge ranging from technical fundamentals to the historical and geopolitical contexts of military operations.

My first graduate degree, a master of engineering management from George Washington University, was practical and provided knowledge of the principles, practices, and methods of technical management. The curriculum provided a sound foundation for professionalism, continuous learning, and adaptation in a complex technical organization.

A few years later, I pursued and earned a second graduate degree, an MA in history. I wanted to improve on what I considered a deficient liberal arts education (because the undergrad engineering curriculum included few non-technical courses). I did not anticipate this, but soon discovered that the serious academic study of history was exceptionally valuable and surprisingly practical for my work as an operations analyst. To a much greater degree than the physical sciences or the understanding of military operations and tactics, historical study forced me to navigate a greater range of information ambiguity and fidelity within the rich diversity of points of view and cultural contexts.

In 2016, we were living at a remote navy base in the California desert and my wife was looking for a graduate program. She discovered USC's MBV program and enrolled. She was so enthusiastic about the program she urged me to apply for the following cohort. I was hesitant. I didn't really need another graduate degree for any professional reasons and, more practically, I did not have any remaining GI Bill benefits, so tuition and biweekly travel expenses were going to be substantial family expenses. But as I've always thought and have encouraged our kids to think, you have to apply to see if it is even a possibility, so I decided to apply and see how it would pan out.

Although I lacked no confidence in my ability to do well in an academic setting at a premier institution like Marshall, I also had no overconfidence about being accepted into the MBV program. My age (fifty-two when I started) and educational background did not seem to me to be ideal for the program, but I believed I could provide some useful encouragement and class leadership for the cohort. I was and remain very glad—indeed indebted— that the program accepted me. I had a lot of advantages going into it. I was adept with many computer-based analytical concepts and tools; I had academic grounding in data analysis, economics, financial analysis, project planning, and experience with case study analysis from several courses at GWU; I had considerable academic and professional experience conducting research and writing technical and historical papers; and perhaps most importantly, I had decades of experience planning and working on individual and team projects and had good organizational and time-management skills. Yet, even with all of this preparation, I found the MBV program challenging. Since I was coming into it with a useful professional, educational, and intellectual background, I did my best to be a good group project teammate and a good classmate.

The MBV would have been ideal for me when I was coming off active duty at age thirty. The GWU degree was professionally valuable in a technical sense, but I did not come out of it with any useful ideas on how to leverage either the education or the school's alumni network. It was up to me to make the most of what I'd learned, and I did an adequate but suboptimal job with the leveraging. The best aspect of the MBV is the program's comprehensiveness: a broad suite of germane academic subjects and class projects and committed and enthusiastic staff and faculty combined with substantial career-development guidance and assistance.

Modern economies are built on professional specialization. After close to thirty years under the DoD umbrella, I did not think I would be able to find a credible professional opportunity outside of defense work. However, the MBV gave me the tools and vocabulary to communicate my talents and experience in terms of other industries. In retrospect, this does not seem so monumental, but this was a fundamentally important learning point. I would not have figured this out in another program and deeply appreciate what I learned from my experience with the MBV staff, professors, my fellow classmates, and the incomparable Trojan family.

In a follow-up message, Dave wrote: ". . . in July 2018, I took a job outside of the DoD umbrella with a small consulting company, and have since worked on projects in the banking sector, purely private sector. I had appropriate analytical and managerial experience, but it was the MBV experience that enabled me to make such a major industry switch."

CHAPTER 6

TRANSITIONS IN LEADERSHIP
AND PERSONAL GROWTH

"In the midst of winter, I finally found that there was in me an invincible summer." Albert Camus

"One can choose to go back toward safety or forward toward growth. Growth must be chosen again and again; fear must be overcome again and again." Abraham Maslow

"I cannot even fathom how much growth has occurred over the past year. As we leave the MBV program, I know the maximum amount of growth is just about to occur. We were just moving too fast. Once I truly have time to reflect, the MBV program is the platform on which I am going to make the greatest leap ever." (Greg Vincent, Cohort III)

Transitions and Transformation

This chapter is about the concept, nature, and process of transitioning from the military into a civilian professional and business environment. Transitioning is more than just moving from a military to a civilian role, from a uniform to business casual dress. It's about taking on new challenges, moving in new directions, adopting different values and goals, fundamentally changing your orientation to more than just work, and adopting a new mindset about your capabilities.

It's not about maintaining the status quo or your performance equilibrium, but about changing the forces and conditions in your life to change your concept of self to a more capable and adaptable level, opening yourself up to new opportunities, and discovering new possibilities for your career and contribution to your venture, family, and community. It takes a while and a lot of support and self-evaluation to even consider the array of possibilities that may be available. It also takes courage, some risk-taking, and a lot of optimism to take a step into new territory and different behavior.

Education, including graduate education, is based on good theory, research, models, and case examples and the ability to generalize learning to new situations and challenges. It is also about finding strategies to make new discoveries about yourself and the possibilities for your future life and work. And while learning concepts and theory helps to generalize and apply to new situations, the essence of transition is discovering the uniqueness of contexts, organizations, cultures, and individuals, and your own sense of self and your ability to affect outcomes and change.

Transitions in leadership then is more than shifting your approach to fit a new situation. It is increasing your adaptability and confidence in addressing personal challenges to adapt and grow within different contexts. Accepting the veterans' capability in leadership from their military background is the jumping-off point for growth into new competencies and capabilities, including the ability to read new contexts accurately, and to develop greater capabilities to be successful in them.

The transformational character then of leadership transitioning is that the veterans will learn to see themselves differently and discover new possibilities for their career and for presenting themselves to be more influential. The confidence most veterans gain in this short program is significantly based on the social support generated by the strong dynamic of the cohort structure, where all members share a common background fact that has been instrumental in their development, responsibilities, and commitments over a significant amount of time.

They also develop a strong commitment to the success of the entire cohort, which differentiates the MBV program from many other business programs. Transformation takes place in the present, not in the future, so one must seize the opportunity while in the context of a learning environment that advocates the adoption of a growth mindset. This opportunity typically begins with increased self-awareness and reflection on one's efficacy, as well as engaging one's imagination of new possibilities. The number of students in Cohort VI who decided to leave certainty and security behind to aspire to endeavors more challenging and potentially fulfilling is testimony to the unfolding awareness of new possibilities and opportunities.

> "This is why I talk about the MBV program as a 'personal transformation program,' as opposed to a 'personal transition program.' The program focuses on personal and professional growth far beyond what a traditional graduate business degree program or military transition program could ever hope to . . . that ultimately delivers only incremental changes at the margins." (Troy Baisch, Cohort VI)

Transformational change is not foreign to many of the veterans as they enter the program. Their personal stories often involve the change they experienced by volunteering for the military. Many discuss how their military experience transformed their lives. Many stories are about eighteen-year-olds escaping a drug and gang environment or a less-than-optimal home life or school experience.

Accepting a purpose greater than oneself can be a transformational experience of service, focus, and motivation that is life-changing while in uniform but which leaves a gap upon separation or retirement. Walking away from major responsibilities for mission achievement and the care and well-being of one's unit, even through an honorable separation or retirement, can create a void that has to be addressed transformationally.

Most military veterans have gone through this developmental phase (military experience) early enough in their lives and as volunteers that it has had a profound effect on their self-concept and self-worth. Some of this has been altered through trauma of various types, which has created painful challenges to their emotional and physical well-being, including their family life. So when we refer to transformational change, we have to adjust our anticipation and hope for the program to have a salutary consequence for the individual who has been wounded.

The Growth Challenges of a Military-Based Transition Program

> "I feel as though I have learned more about myself over the past year than I have in the rest of my thirty-three years of life. When you are caught up in the chaos of everyday life, focused on execution and the task at hand, you never take the time for self-reflection and personal development. Over the past year, I have come to realize the power of introspection and taking the time to honestly reflect on my behavior and feelings as an essential part of the journey to become a better leader. It starts with the openness for change and continues with being willing to accept new challenges that make you feel uncomfortable, stretching yourself, and expanding your capabilities into areas that are less developed. Over the past year through self-reflection, I have come to understand who I am as a leader and how I can maximize my influence potential by improving my emotional and social competencies. But most importantly, I've learned that this process of self-development is never over. Good leaders are not born overnight, and it is a journey, a continuous process of self-reflection and development."
> (Chris Eckman, Cohort II)

When addressing personal growth in a formal graduate degree program, students often struggle with the issue of change in general and then personal change. This personal change may have broader connotations than merely coming to grips with cognitive learning, and in some cases, skill acquisition. Transitioning into a graduate program is a process with its own demands, many of which students have not faced before. Or if they have, it was probably some time ago and very possibly in an online program, which is different from a face-to-face, high-engagement experience, such as the MBV. The following are a number of hurdles that may be specific to veterans, but which may also be generic for anyone beginning a higher-education experience later in life.

We often couch issues in positive, motivational ways when approaching graduate certification, but when discussing change of almost any type, we must address the barriers that may push against the positive forces making the equilibrium stable. Let's call them challenges to successful transition and growth. In Chapter 1, I discussed the challenges to leaving the military environment and moving toward a civilian environment. This following discussion puts into a change framework these and other challenges that may be barriers to the change process and personal growth.

1. The first and probably most difficult challenge is moving from the known to the unknown, from a heavily structured environment to a mostly unstructured one. The average length of military service in the MBV program is between ten and eleven years, with a number of twenty-plus years veterans for whom this change is very challenging. Some who do have financial retirement from the military are often ambivalent about starting a new career, but most do not want to be idle anywhere between the ages of thirty-eight and sixty plus in military retirement. While a challenging graduate program may be an adventure to some, it can be seen as a strange and unknowable place to others.

2. Along with moving from the known to the unknown, the issue of uncertainty and ambiguity presents many with a high hurdle to overcome. Where it may be difficult to even imagine new outcomes clearly, the probability of a successful outcome seems elusive. Having learned to be successful within a relatively stable and straightforward structured environment, veterans need to learn how to deal with ambiguity and sense-making within various environments.

3. When approaching any new learning experience, one may be hesitant to assert with confidence their ability to learn new skills and go into new areas of learning and work. By adopting a growth mindset with effort and direction, one can achieve new competencies and personal growth. And one needn't feel fixed in terms of basic abilities and potential. This requires optimism and a positive approach to new learning, and we all vary on these dimensions. It's difficult to be self-confident when facing a challenge one has not succeeded with earlier.

4. Not only is a transitioning veteran facing a less structured environment, learning how to operate in civilian hierarchies may be challenging compared to military hierarchies. Civilians don't wear their rank and identity on their clothes as in the military. Some civilian organizations downplay the nature of their hierarchy, but one exists at some level unless it's an equal partnership of some sort. It's often not clear to whom one reports, especially if there is more than one boss, which is common within matrix and project-based organizations and professional partnerships.

5. Individuals differ in their degree of openness to new experiences, ways of thinking, diverse values, and new environments. Being open and accepting of different ways of conducting work and relationships is often a major struggle. We tend to have habitual ways of viewing both behavior and protocol that resist adjustments to new environments.

6. Being open to other people, sharing, and helping is often new to students, but in a supportive learning environment, veterans often deal with this challenge fairly quickly. We see evidence of this in their personal stories. Many veterans enter the program fairly closed off from others, especially those with whom they have little history, but learn to positively adapt by being more open, even vulnerable at times, with the members of their new unit.

   "I feel that I have made significant progress in allowing people into my life. I know that I have all my fellow cohort members to help me wherever life takes me." (Kris Beaver, Cohort VI)

7. Learning a new language of business, if they have not studied in this area before, is a challenge, beginning with financial accounting. Growing their critical thinking skills and applying them to organizational and business issues and decision-making is often a challenge and again often runs into a habitual way of thinking and assessing.

"I've seen amazing growth in my own business skills: So many times I have said to myself, 'I wish I would have known that ten or fifteen years ago!'" (Kathy Takayama, Cohort VI)

8. Learning how to translate military experience and skills into civilian terms requires a fundamental translation of resumés and a rethinking of what values and skills from the military will be useful in a civilian context. Skills and values such as a strong work ethic, personal discipline, a strong service orientation, a focus on mission attainment, team skills, and leadership skills need to be translated and highlighted in this new approach to applying them within a civilian context.

9. Learning the new skills of reaching out to others and networking may be resisted, and most often *are* until one has some positive experiences with it.

"Personally, I have grown in various ways. The most influential lesson I learned while here was not in an academic setting, but in the art of networking." (Ray Altamirano, Cohort VI)

10. Learning new approaches to self-assessment, self-knowledge, and self-acceptance to provide the information that underlies appropriate developmental goals in this new environment is challenging.

"I found the overall MBV program can best be explained as an awakening. It is a professional and personal awakening that is only experienced as you complete this program and actively participate in the cohort." (Destiny Savage, Cohort III)

11. After adopting new ways to assess oneself, the next hurdle is gaining experience in setting personal developmental goals to achieve new competencies in leadership and influence and in career search and decision-making. Veterans come to the program with a strong foundation in leadership skills and values, so learning new competencies may be challenging, but the goal is to increase their effectiveness in their performance of leadership and

influence wherever they are in organizations or their own venture. Fortunately, on this dimension, there is very little resistance to setting goals for self-improvement and competence development. Most veterans, it seems, are quite familiar with this drive and challenge.

12. While it is often assumed that transitioning means going from point A to point B, often the biggest challenge is managing the transition itself, the process of transitioning, the complexities of their life and family as the veterans transition between careers. Veterans who have experienced multiple deployments internationally quite often face a challenge of reintegration with their own family, and this can be the most emotionally challenging of all. The process of transitioning often includes taking steps back before taking steps forward, so it may not be a straight line.

"The MBV experience is one of personal transformation. At USC Marshall, I found a community of teachers, administrators, alumni mentors, and fellow students who were deeply committed to my development. Through the MBV program, I learned how to position myself and tell my military story to civilian employers. . . . I leave this program with a much better understanding of myself and how my military leadership experience can bring value to any organization." (Michael Bottenberg, Cohort III)

It is probably too ambitious to think that a single program lasting only ten months focused on learning business skills, strategies, and language can achieve success in overcoming all these hurdles, but now we will discuss how we approach change in the program.

"I was very surprised by the collaborative nature of the program and the deep self-reflection that took place. I found the emotional intelligence and the entrepreneurial focus to be extremely beneficial to me personally. . . . I felt that this program provided that (camaraderie) to me, while encouraging me to think differently about what is possible in our own lives and the business worlds. . . . I am sad that the program

is over, but at the same time I am implementing the leadership principles from class into my daily work with great results." (Anthony Friel,
Cohort III)

Incremental versus Transformational Change

"The assumption that absolute truth exists, and our search for it, blinds
us to the subtlety and presence of the truth of our gifts and sense of
self. This latter is the truth with a small t. By serving as stewards to our
own innate potential, even if it is through increments both imperfect
and incomplete, we also shift the focus of attention from authority
to authenticity; in so doing, we learn to lead from our gifts and inner
wisdom rather than from external edits and what an expert said."
(Michael Jones in Barbour and Hickman 2011)

"MBV, in contrast, transforms its cohort members into something
greater than they were before." (Troy Baisch, Cohort VI)

In Cohort VI, whose members graduated in May 2019, we had twelve students quit their jobs mid-year who had no intention to when they entered
the program (later, you will find out that another five declared their intent
to leave their jobs at the final session). But they began seeing themselves in a
new way and imagining their options in an entirely new way.

This kind of change is more transformational than incremental.
Incremental would be more about getting promoted in place with a new set
of skills. Transformational is seeing entirely different options for your life
rather than as being "stuck." In some cases, they saw themselves as better than
where they were in their career. Most of this group walked away from security
rather than seek more of it. There are also a fairly large number of students
who never considered doing their own venture and business, but toward the
end of the program were committed to starting their own business.

"As individuals, we have become more than we ever thought we could
be. . . . Every week we hear about someone else quitting their job

because they discovered what they really wanted to do. More and more often we hear about the latest developments in a cohort member's new business ideas." (Ryan Long, Cohort VI)

Cleve Stevens described the demands of transformational change, in *The Best in Us*, as requiring courage, love, imagination, and commitment. Courage to do and be different from your past and others, loving yourself enough to foresee positive change and the value of making the effort to achieve it are key here.

The program addresses these requirements in various ways. Veterans understand courage but add to it a big component of humility. In the context of others like themselves, the social comparison, along with a lot of support from their brothers and sisters, assists in the expression of courage and some risk-taking to begin to make major moves. We begin the work of self-love through self-assessments, positive interpretations, and feedback. Imagination is stimulated through many possible options by way of guest speakers, industry panels, career-development events, and other special programs that are included within the university environment. Commitment is introduced through goal-setting of competence goals around intentionality, and the support of one's goals partner and the entire cohort for personal change and growth.

One of the keys to transforming ideas and goals is getting support to try out new behaviors and move away from your comfort zone. The concept of a growth mindset (Dweck 2006), where effort is more important than talent, provides the freedom to attempt new competencies and practice within a supportive context. To imagine possibilities, one has to both stretch and visualize what might be different that carries value for the individual. With multiple students quitting their jobs in Cohort VI, there seemed to be a contagion of awareness of dissatisfaction with one's current state, and a feeling of stagnancy or underemployment concomitant with a sense of possibility and of the greater challenge and satisfaction that comes with growing one's capabilities. In an environment where social support, trust, and collaboration are the norms, the ability to see greater possibilities for oneself becomes evident at the individual level as well as at the level of the cohort. In a secure unit of membership with a lot of demonstrated support for each individual, being part of and aware of others discovering unique possibilities for their future provided a positive atmosphere of exploration.

"I have never been part of an institution that has been so inclusive and supportive of my success and the success of my cohort brothers and sisters. That has made a lasting impression on me and the cohort. This MBV program is also a continuation of the leadership training I started twenty years ago when I stepped on the yellow footprints of Marine Corps Recruit Depot San Diego. The MBV program is far more than a degree. It's a journey and a newfound brotherhood." (James Galindo, Cohort III)

Transformational change then becomes almost an ideal outcome for many of the veterans. To reach this point of imagining a different life, career, and self, the individual has to initiate a number of actions:

1. **Become increasingly self-aware** while completing significant self-assessment, being honest about what is working and what is not, and one's own sense of what needs to change. This is the starting point for any self-imposed change effort.

2. **Learn to self-confront and identify areas and behaviors in one's life that need to change** in order to be both more successful and enjoy greater satisfaction in life. Take charge of one's impulse to deny or be defensive about one's behavior.

3. **Focus on key elements of your behavior and habits**, and imagine alternatives to these habits and areas of behavior. Understand why changing would make one more effective, so that this becomes a priority.

4. **By focusing on being more self-aware and mindful, choose those areas you wish to change.** Begin with a limited goal set, so change is more doable in a reasonable time.

5. **Seek stretch goals and move outside your comfort zone.** Make sure goals are challenging but realistic.

6. **Set some goals that are actionable for change.** Identify first steps. If you can't take action, you won't make progress.

7. **Set up a way to monitor or measure both actions and results**, reassess, and continually renew your efforts and focus. What gets measured gets done. Keep track and review frequently.

8. **Be able to take risks.** This is the stretching and the willingness to risk your comfort.

9. **Ask for help, or join others doing similar work.** Not feeling OK about asking for help is one of the most common sources of resistance to personal change.

10. **Develop a support system** that authenticates new possibilities and provides both feedback and actual assistance. Social support or social proof that others are challenging themselves as well provides affirmation for one's efforts.

11. **Develop values that support big moves** rather than values of safety and a fixed mindset. Become convinced that change is not only appropriate, but desirable.

12. **Understand that change in behavior, habits, and aspirations is real work.** It's not sufficient to memorize the ten best qualities of effective leaders. Reading about others' change is reassuring, but not the work that will have to happen to make changes for oneself.

13. **Ask someone you trust to both support you and hold you accountable**. Go public with your goals, and enroll someone to assist and check on your progress.

14. **Gradually develop a new sense of self-confidence** in your potential and ability to move forward more dramatically. Practice, small successes, and positive feedback will lead to greater self-confidence in the new behavior.

15. **Celebrate small wins and accept the fact that change is difficult**, so you always need to accept and embrace where you are and the challenges you have. Then focus forward, rather than continue

to dwell on your difficulties, barriers, or why you haven't made changes in the past.

16. **Choose optimism.** Don't wait to feel optimistic. Understand the benefits of being optimistic and the downside of pessimism.

"If I were to sum up the changes for me through this program, it would be that I feel like I am gaining control back of my life." (Carlos Amador, Cohort VI)

"One word comes to mind that defines the greatest noticeable aspect of change, and this goes for me as well: confidence." (Blake Harper, Cohort VI)

Being surrounded by supportive and empathic colleagues seems to make a big difference as individuals take bigger risks or make more dramatic changes in their perspectives and ambitions. Also, the constant dynamic of social comparison creates almost a norm for allowing oneself to step out and step up. With so many of the cohort considering major changes, it provides the social dynamic for others to consider it as well. Here are some comments and evaluations from students in Cohort VI about personal growth and the growth of the cohort as well.

"I think many of us walked into this thinking this program would help our professional lives, but I would argue that it has added to our personal and spiritual lives just as much. Once again, we all feel like we're part of something greater than ourselves and part of a mission." (Victor Ting)

"As for me, I have transformed, and feel that I am ready to work again and make a difference in what I am doing. . . ." (Eric Martincavage)

"I've noticed change in five areas: higher performance, strategic dialogue, greater courage and accountability, a higher level of trust, and authentic interactions." (Tony Lloyd)

"It's like a second calling within the cohort to seek out others that need help and go all in providing it." (Andrew Hodlin)

"The cohort has grown into an incredible support system that is invested in seeing its members succeed." (Ronald Byerley)

"I have recently decided on a career path and when I reached out, I had at least ten responses within an hour. . . . While I expected to experience change regarding my search for a career, I did not expect the change I would experience in my personal growth." (Annie Migle)

"This program has certainly been a transformative experience for me. I have grown most notably in my level and ability to engage the business world." (Darren Denyer)

"As far as personal growth, I'm glad I stuck it out. Being part of a business program was never something I thought I had any interest in or would be part of. . . . I have grown tremendously since then and find myself much more in tune with what's happening around me when it comes to business and entrepreneurship." (Keith Nelson)

"The overarching theme that this program has fostered is confidence. . . . 'How do I transition from being a professional pilot to businessman?' Responses have included: 'There is no bridge, no straight line. You just have to do it!' . . . Now the idea of transitioning into a businessman is within reach and very exciting." (Kevin Elardo)

Goal-Setting

Early in the fall semester, all students are asked to set goals for themselves to increase their leadership and influence competencies. This is done with the assumption that everyone has a solid foundation in leadership, so it falls on the individual, through self-assessment and choice, to select areas they would like to improve or to develop. One of the self-assessment strategies asked the students to assert what dimensions of a list of twenty-two competencies they would like to commit to develop. Some examples: "being more intentional about my goals," "enrolling others," "influencing others," "developing my network," "speaking more powerfully," "being more proactive," "being more politically aware," "improving being assertive," "developing greater self-confidence," and "managing up" more effectively.

Each student is asked to select three to five goals for competency development and at least one for their career search with as specific a target as possible, knowing that goals are dynamic and may change over time within the program. Then they pick a goals partner with whom they can discuss goals, competencies, efforts, and progress toward goal attainment. Goals partners are a support mechanism—someone with the same assignment, and with whom you feel you can work well, will track your progress, hold you accountable, check in with you, encourage and nudge you when necessary.

This partnership may last all year or only for the first semester. At the beginning of the new semester, each individual can stay with their current partner, choose a new one, or actually pair up with another partnership to have four people giving and receiving feedback. Some partnerships continue post-commencement as friendships or continued work on personal development.

Twice during the year, all goals partners are asked to report out their progress to the cohort. This is a fairly straightforward reporting session, but it gives the partners a chance to assess their progress, summarize, and share. They also report how effective the partnership is. Early in the process, each partnership completes a formal planning process together as to how they intend to work together. Learning how to track your progress may be fairly subjective, but they have to agree on how they will measure effort and success toward achieving their goals. This could be a journal, actual counting of episodes (e.g., meeting new people or businesses), or a discussion of those times people tried out new behaviors and received feedback.

We encourage students to identify stretch goals, those that are just beyond their reach but actually attainable, and those that move an individual outside their comfort zone, where they usually stay as a matter of habit and security. Among the frequently chosen goals: to "improve my understanding and expression of empathy," "listen more actively, or actually listen," "develop greater patience with others," "become more open to new ideas," "be a better team member or team leader," "manage relationships better," "network," "be able to speak up in a group or be more comfortable at public speaking," "lead a more balanced and healthy life," "learn to trust more easily," and many other specific dimensions of emotional intelligence.

It is reasonably apparent that members of the cohort feel safe and supported enough with their colleagues in the program to be able to discuss and experiment with new behavior. Understanding that you have a choice in what you take on as a challenge, and how you aspire to different and greater challenges seems to be contagious. In Cohort VI, over a dozen members left their current employment during the year. This major movement implies a sense of support by brothers and sisters, and faith in one's own abilities to grow, search, and change into a version of themselves they see as more desirable and in line with their potential and aspirations.

For some of this group, this newfound awareness and willingness to step away from basic security to reach higher is transformational. They see and experience themselves in a new way focused on growth, and a more satisfying way, a way that fits their own sense of what they're capable of, personally and professionally. One of the most dramatic expressions of taking charge of one's ability to contribute and use one's voice was at the final session in May 2017, when one of our quieter women veterans left the podium after her final statement, and said, "I'm going to have a seat at the table!" Then she paused and raised her voice to say: "No, I'm going to have a f—g seat at the table!!" She ended with: "even if I have to bring my own chair!"

I remember my emotional response to her publicly taking charge of her own voice and destiny right there in front of the seventy-seven other veterans in the room and program staff. We were all somewhat stunned, then broke into applause that recognized the change in her from the beginning of the year when she was not very assertive, to the end, that day, when she announced her emancipation from a posture that no longer served her and a personal transformation into a powerful person with a powerful voice.

Another story that is dramatic concerning a change in one's life, including the goal-setting process that assisted the change, is from a final discussion board topic of early April 2016. I will quote the entire post here. You met the author, Ty Smith, at the end of Chapter 3, and it was at his retirement ceremony, in May 2016, that I began to write this story of our time together.

"There is always room for growth. This is a statement that I have come to understand with my whole heart, mind, and spirit. The MBV program has helped me to grow in ways that were previously unimaginable. It has taught me more than analytics, strategy, and entrepreneurship. Although I have learned these subjects, as well as others, I have also learned more about leadership than I could have hoped for when I started this journey. At the beginning of the first semester, I knew I needed a lot of work, personally and professionally, if I expected to do well as a civilian. I knew I needed to regain my focus and put forth reasonable effort at developing multiple competencies in order to be successful in my professional life, as well as at home with my family.

My career has taken me to places both physically and mentally that have opened my eyes more than I would have hoped for had I known twenty years ago what I know now. My career has taught me that, although most people believe in the imaginable limits society and government place on us as human beings, these limits really do not exist. I have found what many veterans who have served during times of war have found: there are no limits. We really are limitless as to what we can achieve in life. Man is limitless when it comes to the lengths we will travel to in order to be successful, even if success means doing evil and inhumane things to other men. There is no limit as to what we are capable of doing in the name of love, love for ourselves, love for our comrades, love for our country, love for madness. With this being said, throughout this program, I have come to realize that I have been given a *rare* chance to realize just how limitless we really are, even though my country expects me to return home and live as though I am aware of imaginable limitations, when I am not.

This new view of the world caused me to lose my desire to want to understand the emotions of others. It also caused me to become a less empathetic person. One can imagine how this could impact my ability to be a good husband, father, brother, and son. It is also imaginable that I could start to travel backward, instead of forward, as a leader. When Professor Turrill asked us to aggressively take note of the leadership competencies we needed to improve upon in order to be successful, I did not realize how impactful this assignment would be for me personally. Taking note of these competencies forced me to have the discussion with myself about what is most important to me in this world. Over the course of the last year, I have become extremely aware of just how much I had begun to falter when it comes to competencies such as emotional awareness and empathy. When I realized just how poorly my behavior had become due to the fact that I had lost my ability to acknowledge my own emotions and those of others, as well as my ability to show empathy, I was ashamed.

One year later, I can proudly say that I notice a difference in myself. My wife notices a difference in me. My wife actually thanks me for listening to her when she is feeling emotional about something. I had not been aware of just how poor of a listener I had become after returning home from my last deployment. I am closer to my children as a result of this program. I am happier! Do not get me wrong. I have good days and bad days just like everyone else, especially after the passing of my little sister, but I can acknowledge that my good days now outnumber the bad. I have become more lenient with my seventeen-year-old son now that I have rediscovered empathy. I can now tell myself that I was once his age. Now more than ever, I can laugh with him, understanding that he is exactly like I was at this age (my poor mother). I have a very long way to go, but thanks to this program, I am on my way.

As we sadly leave behind the MBV program on May thirteenth, I also want to leave behind the sadness and anger that have plagued my heart over the last few years of my career. I have been so sad and angry at the loss of my comrades; my feelings toward man and how evil we can be; my family at times when I felt that no matter what, they just did not understand; and people who have not served, for how could they ever understand our sacrifice? I have been sad and angry for many other reasons as well, all related to my experiences at war. I WILL leave behind this sadness and anger that have created the turmoil that has plagued my heart over the last few years. For years, I have felt as though I have been living in a storm that is aware of only me. I did not realize that although this storm is very real, it is not around me, it is *within* me. I did not realize how powerful I could become if only I chose to acknowledge this storm and harness its power to do good! Instead,

I chose to develop an apathetic outlook on life and people. This is no longer the case for me. I have already begun to leave this sadness and anger behind. Already, I feel more free, a little lighter in step. I am no longer a victim of a storm that plagued me and only me. I understand now that it *is* me.

In closing, I will leave you with a quote that I discovered some time over the last year: Fate whispers to the warrior, 'This is a storm in which you cannot withstand.' The warrior whispers back to Fate, 'I AM THE STORM!'" (Anonymous, 2015; Ty Smith, Cohort III)

Jaime Hinojosa—Cohort IV

I was born in Carlsbad, New Mexico, a small town in the southeastern corner of the state where my family worked in the local mines and farms. However, my father was a career sailor and served in the United States Navy for twenty-three years. As I grew up, moving along the eastern seaboard of the United States to each base, I have always thought of New Mexico as home. The summer before my senior year of high school, while my father was in transition to a new duty station in San Diego, I moved home with my grandparents and graduated from Carlsbad High School, in 2001. I was always drawn to serving in the military, but my family pushed me to attend college. Upon high school graduation, I attended New Mexico State University, where I majored in mechanical engineering and minored in mathematics. It was during the fall of 2003 that I made the decision to join the United States Marine Corps. After an internship with a large automotive company, I knew there was something much bigger that I needed to do. I applied for the platoon leaders program and was accepted to attend officer candidate school in the summer of 2004. After September 11, I was drawn toward service, but wanted to finish school. With the war in Iraq starting, I felt it was my duty to serve my country in a time of war and did not want to look back and regret not serving. On the day of my graduation from college in 2005, I was commissioned a second lieutenant in the US Marine Corps. I would begin my journey as a marine officer at the Basic School in Quantico, Virginia, a few weeks later.

My career in the Marine Corps lasted eight and a half years. I served as a combat engineer officer with Marine Wing Support Squadron 374, where I was both a platoon commander and company commander of the engineer company. During this time, I deployed to Iraq twice, once as part of the squadron and once as an advisor/trainer embedded with the Iraqi army. My last duty station was as a small group instructor at the US Army Engineer School Captains Career course. As an instructor, I was responsible for teaching engineer tactics, mission planning, and leadership as a small group leader. While I was working at the US Army Engineer School, I was able to attend the Missouri University of Science & Technology during my free time. Over a three-year period, I was able to earn an MSc in engineering management with an emphasis in construction and an MSc in explosives engineering.

I left the Marine Corps for many of the same reasons I joined—because I wanted to experience something new, different, and much more than where I was at the time. I also met my future wife and knew that our career paths at the time would never align. So I decided to leave active duty and begin my transition in the summer of 2014. The transition from active duty to civilian life was an entirely new challenge for me, much more difficult than any education program I had experienced and certainly more difficult than getting into the Marine Corps. As I reflect on my path to becoming a marine officer, I realize that, as tough as it was, I always had a group of fellow marines experiencing the same transition and instructors to guide us along the way. As I left the Marine Corps, it felt as though I was alone in my path out. I had to find a new career, new home, and new way of life outside the military.

There were plenty of opportunities available to junior officers—the tough part was finding the right fit, and in a location I wanted to live. I chose Los Angeles because my wife was attending school at UCLA. After submitting hundreds of resumés, I finally landed an interview with a construction company for a project engineer position. I worked for two years as a project engineer for a general contractor, starting from a position that was similar to a new college graduate. It was tough to accept at the time, given the responsibility I had in the Marine Corps, but it was work, and I knew I had to prove myself the same way as when I first joined the marines. After two years of working as hard as I could, I was unsatisfied with where I was in the company. I felt l had the potential to work on larger projects but was afraid of leaving because of how tough it had been finding a job in the first place.

In the spring of 2016, an old Marine Corps friend introduced me to the MBV program at USC. I attended an info session and was hooked. The students who talked about the program and their experiences immediately grabbed my attention. I knew this program would be able to give me the bump I needed to move ahead. The program was great because once again it was like the transition into the Marine Corps—I was with a group of veterans who were in the same position in life as I was, and we were all working together to help each other through the program. The program was much more than business classes. I felt part of a greater community of friends and family. Upon completion of the program, I continued to work in the construction industry. It took me a few months, but I was able to seize an outstanding opportunity with Hathaway Dinwiddie.

Currently, I am a project manager with Hathaway Dinwiddie, a large construction company in Los Angeles. I am working on a design-build multidisciplinary laboratory building at UC Irvine. The team I work with is a multidisciplinary group of top professionals in a very dynamic environment. My life could not be happier at this time. I have a wonderful wife, an amazing job, and a new baby on the way.

James Galindo—Cohort III

I grew up in Ventura County, California, wrenching on my '66 Mustang, playing HS football, running HS track, and studying fine art. I enlisted in the Marine Corps as an infantry rifleman in 1994. I fathered my son in 1998, after returning from a deployment to South America with Marine Security Forces South. I was in the marine reserves, a single father and a student when 9/11 happened. I was willingly recalled into active duty, to the disappointment of my family. I was a marine scout sniper and served in a quick-reaction force for homeland defense at Camp Pendleton and later during the Iraq Invasion with First Regimental Combat Team, First Marine Expeditionary Force. When I returned home from the invasion, I found myself in a custody fight for my son. The California courts used my time away in service to our country against me and, coincidentally, I lost primary custody of my boy. I left a ten-year military career after my reenlistment contract expired to fight the courts to regain custody.

I was frustrated with the courts and the injustice. I took a job in banking for twelve dollars an hour as a processor to start building my private-sector career. After less than a year as a processor, I was able to convince management I could make the bank more money as an account executive. I knew I would never regain custody of my son making as little money as I was and having an unfinished college degree. I became rookie salesman of the year and quickly grew my business base, drawing from the leadership capabilities I learned as an enlisted combat veteran. I married my fiancée, who stood by my side during my combat deployment and custody fight. Within two years, I was the top producer for my region and was finally starting to make progress with the courts.

The recession of 2008 closed nearly all lending operations. At this time, I was newly married, had regained primary custody of my son, and had a daughter on the way. The recession was an opportunity to go back to school to finish my degree. I changed my major to a BS in business and used my severance package, GI Bill, and school loans to finance my education. I graduated from Cal State University Channel Islands in 2011.

I returned to banking and started back at the bottom. I was quickly promoted to management, drawing again from leadership and grit learned from my time as a non-commissioned officer in the marines. I built three teams for the bank, helping to streamline efficiencies while increasing effectiveness and impact. After five promotions in five years, I was now at a plateau in my career. A marine brother with whom I had served in Central America sixteen years prior sent me a link highlighting an MBV program at USC. I attended the information seminar in February and was so excited at this opportunity of a lifetime that I began filling out forms within the day. I was accepted into the program in June 2015, with classes starting a month later.

It was in this program that I grew in my leadership, networking, and academic abilities. I was now surrounded by fifty other veterans who had the same drive to better themselves. During the course of studies and in the inspiration from veteran classmates, I found an opportunity to get back to my fine art strengths. I built a modern armor memorabilia Trojan helmet that was embraced by the veterans of USC. I formed Seminole 4 Designs LLC, named after my scout sniper team's call sign of Seminole 4. I filed and obtained both a design patent and the "Tactical Trojan" trademark from the US Patent and Trademark Office. I began to fabricate period-correct memorabilia helmets for USC veterans, veteran alumni, and supporters of USC veteran initiatives. Each serialized helmet, helmet stand, and plaque is custom made of authentic period-correct military items. A helmet was gifted to Dean Ellis of USC Marshall School of Business, and the dean wore the helmet at our commencement ceremony. The helmets have begun to build a brand identity and community for USC veterans.

After completing my master's degree, I was promoted a sixth time and am now a senior relationship manager for Bank of America Merrill Lynch Global Commercial Banking. I volunteer on the USC board of counselors, alumni veteran network, and Marshall Partners, and have been working to promote the MBV program at my bank. To date, the bank has hired eight MBV graduates, equating to well over a million dollars in annual compensation. I continue to build custom helmets to reinforce the USC veteran community and am now working on my first fine art series that will provide a combat veteran's visual perspective on matters.

Tyler Hufstetler—Cohort IV

I joined the Marshall ranks in 2016 with my peers from Cohort IV MBV. USC is a unique university and Marshall even more. What attracted me to Marshall was its ongoing mission to develop the student to become a member of the Marshall team. Promotion of the team and not the individual is very important to me. This is a subtle but very important distinction from other top-tier business programs. Others might pitch themselves as developing leaders who will change the world. The reality, though, is that the schools are producing highly trained individual contributors who will inherently focus on self and not the team.

My childhood and upbringing directly impacted my view on leadership and where self was prioritized. I grew up outside of Dallas, where we raised horses and cows. While I was young, my parents instilled in me the work ethic required to care for large animals. At eight years old, I received my first horse. I would pack a lunch and go exploring thousands of acres of ranch land. The maturing and growing during this time helped shape my perspectives on leadership. My animals had to eat, and they needed to be groomed and cared for before I could think about my needs. I was learning selfless service.

While growing up, I was also heavily involved in football and Scouting. Both relied on the overall success of the team, not the individual. In many ways, football added to my foundational understanding of selfless service. Each member of the football team is to execute his assignment—whether that brings glory or not—in order to advance to the team's overall position. It is a vivid display of selfless service.

I was fortunate to be able to continue playing football while I attended the United States Military Academy at West Point. West Point, while developing its cadets as leaders of character, sharpens cadets' resolve with multiple iterations of failure. An individual who does not collaborate with his peers will fail. It is impossible to graduate from West Point by relying solely on self. This tested my mettle and put me in an environment where I had to constantly conduct comparative analysis.

The army provided me opportunities to learn from others who have different backgrounds and perceptions. It afforded me the opportunity to test certain assumptions of people based on socioeconomic backgrounds. I had soldiers who came from wealthy and poor families alike. They represented the inner cities and rural farms. Each brought with them some of their personal issues, but to be a member of the team they had to check their differences at the point of entry. This is what I loved about the army. There was no room for polarization based on politics, religion, or race. While serving as a combat advisor in Afghanistan, not once did I witness a soldier using personal politics as a litmus test for helping someone. In the end, it was and always is about the team. The mission always comes first, but we always prioritized the care of people.

Marshall and the MBV were a natural fit for me. It is a program that encourages collaboration and promotion of the team, and assists in the refinement of skills. Most people can attend any business school and become certified by that institution to conduct business analysis. But I wanted to be a part of a team where my peers would challenge me, like iron sharpening iron. The MBV could focus on preparing someone to be an individual contributor, but that's not who leaders are. Leaders are members of a team. The MBV program takes tested leaders, refines their skillets, and places them inside organizations where they will immediately contribute to the team's success.

I am passionate about helping teams and organizations. More specifically, I enjoy helping organizations bridge the gaps during organizational changes. When my wife and I decided to move back to my hometown outside Dallas, I was unsure where I would be working. I connected with a teammate from the MBV (Adam Cohen) who opened the door for me at his employer. The opportunity has been fantastic. I'm leading teams around the world that are helping organizations complete the last mile of digital transformation. I am not working as an individual contributor, but as a member of a team. My peers and customers are comfortable in my planning because they know my background and understand I represent a strong brand. Fight on!

Joseph Ntiamoah—Cohort V

I'm Joseph Appiah Ntiamoah, and I currently work as a senior consultant at Kaiser Permanente with Strategic Initiatives in Redwood City, California. Also, I work for the air force reserves as a Medical Service Corp (MSC) officer (the civilian equivalent of a health service administrator) at the 349th Medical Squadron, Travis Air Force Base (AFB). My journey began in Ghana, my country of birth, where I obtained my bachelor's degree in economics from the University of Ghana. Shortly after, I moved to the United States through the diversity visa lottery program with the ambition of obtaining a master's degree. Full of aspirations, I enlisted in the United States Air Force six months after I arrived. I served as an aerospace medical technician, which was eye-opening and helped spark my interest in the health-care industry. I was blessed with some amazing leaders and mentors who geared me into commissioning as an MSC officer. This decision was a great turn in my life.

As an MSC officer, I was constantly challenged and groomed to lead. I was entrusted with vast resources and responsibilities. I served as the group practice manager (GPM), where I guided the care of approximately 9,000 enrolled patients and 171,000 eligible enrollees. I supported 178 clinical personnel recording an average of 43,000 patient encounters per year. During my time as GPM, my clinical skills came in handy and helped gain the trust of clinicians, with which many administrators struggled. After a little over two years, I took over as the resource management office flight commander for the 61st Medical Squadron; Los Angeles AFB. I led a flight of thirteen staff members and administrative operations for 178 clinical staff members. In addition, I managed an annual budget of $9 million and a $1.2-million systems network budget. At some point during this journey, my skills and experiences, coupled with long boardroom discussions on managing patients/resources, brought into perspective how I could play a vital role and make a difference in health-care delivery in my own small way. I often got flashbacks from stories of how people died in hospital hallways and holding areas, waiting to see a doctor in my country of origin and other underprivileged countries. Not to even mention the issues of insufficient nurses, mental-health, and outpatient services. Being stationed at Los Angeles AFB, I took the opportunity to obtain a world-class education from USC. I applied and was accepted into the MBV program, Marshall School of Business.

The MBV experience was pivotal in my life. Working through the multiple self-assessments, ropes courses, presentations, negotiation exercises, trade shows, and business plan exercises enabled my self-confidence, and built an extensive network and solid personality. I gained different perspectives by interacting with other cohort members, professors, board members, and goals partners. I was able to fully develop a business plan to start a business in the tourism industry. The MBV program, being a business program dedicated to veterans, naturally exudes camaraderie, dedication, passion, and perseverance. My cohort was full of go-getters ready to leverage their skills and network to achieve great things—and it was contagious! This experience truly prepared me for my civilian career. When I came across the opportunity to interview with Kaiser Permanente, I was more than ready. When I graduated from MBV, I looked back and was amazed at how far I had come. In ten months, I had rebranded myself, started my own business, gotten into a new civilian job, graduated from USC with a master's degree from Marshall, and become a part of the Trojan network. My family couldn't be more grateful and proud. Looking back, I came into MBV trying to check the box for a master's degree, but I graduated with much more. Many of my cohort members attest to this fact, as well. I now consider myself a lifelong learner, constantly developing and preparing myself for my ultimate goal of helping underprivileged countries to adequately access health care.

Post-MBV, I'm pursuing an additional master's degree, in health administration at USC's Sol Price School of Public Policy, working for Kaiser Permanente, setting up my tourism business, raising my family, participating in the air force reserves, and building my network of professionals. To me, MBV brings things into perspective; it helps you find your niche. Keep in mind that it is different for everyone. Each day, I find myself getting closer to my goal of impacting lives through health-care policies and reforms across Africa and underprivileged countries around the world.

Fight on!

Kristine Stanley—Cohort IV

Where to begin? My name is Kristine Stanley. I served twenty-four amazing years in the air force. I joined at nineteen from a small town in Ohio in 1987, retired from London, UK, in 2011, and now live in Los Angeles. My journey is similar to most. I met my future ex-husband while we were stationed in Misawa, Japan, had my daughter there, moved to Hanscom AFB, Massachusetts, where my first son was born, and then to Edwards AFB, California, where my second son was born.

The kids and I transferred to our last assignment in London, where my daughter graduated from an international high school, my older son moved back to the States with his dad (which is how we ended up in LA), and the youngest spent five years in the British school system.

So, basically the typical military family, except I was the active-duty member for the entire time and having a dependent husband was not the norm back then.

I served as a personnel specialist, and retired at the rank of master sergeant. The two biggest lessons I have brought with me from the air force are: having been encouraged, and having had the opportunity, to find solutions to the obstacles I encountered; and learning how to be a leader through mentorship, education, and practice. Problem-solving was encouraged as well as volunteering, education (both military and personal), and maintaining one's composure. I've learned these qualities have directly impacted my life after service as well as the amazing friends I have met along the way.

So that was the easy part. This next volume of my life after service is so much more complex and confusing, filled with self-discovery, self-care, new environments, new people, less structure, and a lack of leaders and women mentors. It's a whole new world, and figuring out how to navigate it is a conscious decision I make daily.

The last seven years since retiring I have learned so much about who "Kristine" is and how she is influenced by "MSgt Stanley." I spent my first year finishing my intern hours for my degree in mental health. I was fortunate to find a placement within a transitional housing program run by a non-profit on the local Virginia campus. This was my introduction to the veteran community. I worked with homeless Vietnam veterans. We bonded over our shared time in service and, as they let their barriers down, they shared their stories with me, often for the first time to anyone. I struggled to discover how I could be a therapist and still have fun at work. What I discovered in our residential setting is that we knew when to be serious and when to be more ourselves. Every time one of the residents approached me in the hallway, they would always smile, because they never knew what I was going to say, as I love to tell jokes. What was so special about these brief moments is that I knew for thirty seconds that day they felt happy, that I had brought them happiness, and that is one of the greatest gifts I have received. When my time ended, they presented me with a plaque, and I wore my uniform for them one last time.

My next opportunity was with The Mission Continues, to which I owe all my success. I did a six-month fellowship at the National Veterans Foundation, which led to over three years of employment. I was fortunate to be given the freedom to discover what services are available to veterans and their families through outreach and engagement in the community. I discovered that women who have served were not being considered part of the discussion when it came to planning for transitional housing. In addition, approval for our service-connected disability claims and employment to mention a couple areas of our lives, were being overlooked by those in positions of influence. So began my unexpected journey as an advocate for women veterans. Meanwhile, I am still continuing to discover who I am and how I fit into this, what I felt like was a world of chaos.

My next opportunity came and went in a blink of an eye. I learned firsthand that, even with money, successful agencies, and a perfect mission, nothing is guaranteed.

My first weekend in the MBV program, I also started working for a very well-known veteran mental-health agency that had partnered with a well-known university to support veterans and their families. Needless to say, my life became very interesting overnight! This was a milestone in my journey, realizing that not everyone is the right fit for what they may think is their perfect job. I experienced great joy working with my teammates, yet found great frustration with the lack of leadership.

It was my first experience with this. The feelings were intensified based on working with other veterans and all of us sharing the same vision and expectations from our leadership, which was also composed of veterans. My lesson here is, although people may have served, it does not guarantee they are going to practice their leadership skills once they are out of uniform.

On a positive note, the delight I experienced being around seventy-seven other successful veterans was also another marker in my journey. Until this time, I had only worked with veterans in the most need, so it added to my confusion in my transition from service. It made me question: Are we all in need? Am I in need? Why is this so difficult for some of us? Then I saw the other side of the coin and realized that if I did support those in need that one day they may be in the MBV program. This experience was exactly what my soul needed.

If you've been keeping up, you may be wondering how my career is going at this point. Well, it isn't. The previously mentioned agency closed, and all of us were invited to find new employment—another marker in my journey. There I was, twenty-four years of experience in service, almost holding two master's degrees, and an extensive network, yet I could not find another job. So once again, I was like many veterans and feeling the struggle of life after service. It was only because I happened to be at the right place at the right time to see the right people that I was able to begin my third job in five years.

I had what seemed to be the dream job, building a website and program to support women veterans to connect to the mental-health support they sought.

Well, this leads to the point in my story where Kristine had to stop, sit down, and regroup! I felt I had found my home. I was in the largest non-profit supporting homeless veterans. I had an opportunity to use everything I had learned to create a program that would be the solution. I had hopes to stay with the agency for years, to grow and move up into more senior leadership roles and flourish. Spoiler alert—that did not happen. What *did* happen? I learned that if you make the right decisions (as hard as they may be) for the right reasons, the universe will let you drive the Karma Bus.

Very recently, I have learned and practiced self-care and spent a lot (and I mean a lot) of time reflecting on the importance of quality leadership and I have developed a great appreciation for how the military does not encourage personalities into the workplace. These growth opportunities and discussions of leadership "out of uniform" always bring me back to the day Professor Turrill opened the discussion of leadership in a room of military people. My first thought was: I have two-and-one-half decades of leadership experience—what do I have to learn about leadership? Well, he knew that we had a journey ahead of us, and we needed to revisit what we had been previously taught. Key points included that knife hands are not effective, not everyone appreciates colorful four-letter words, and yelling is not the solution.

As I write this, I am just reaching a point of closure and yet another turning point in my journey. This fantastic job did not match my expectations—quite the opposite. This being the largest company I had worked for, I made some very incorrect assumptions that I would like to share now. Just because someone holds a position of authority does not ensure they are leaders and have the ability to manage people. Unfortunately, these people are often able to coerce others into going along with them, and when they are stressed, the truth comes out.

I am very stubborn, and it often takes the universe several tries to get my attention. Well, it took a year this time, and my mental health paid a huge price. A quality I mentioned earlier, self-composure, has been both helpful and not to me in this civilian world. I must mention, it has only been brought to my attention over the last several months how it impacts my work environment. Let me explain. When we are in service, we are given tasks with which we do not agree, yet we maintain our composure and get the job done. Now add twenty-four years of practice to this and, well, I have a great poker face at work. Which can be good when needed, but when working for someone with no experience with the military and the people who serve, it can be very frustrating and present unique challenges.

Now, add these skills behind a composed person; quitting is not an option. Work until the job is done. Do it right the first time. Your work is a signature of your ethics and devotion to the mission. Do not partner with someone who only has their own needs and desires in mind, who lacks communication skills, has no leadership qualities, and has a malicious personality. If you are cringing, you should be. This was a much-needed learning opportunity for me. I learned what the human relations department does.

So my story leads us to today. I literally have written my letter of resignation, found a new job I will start soon, and, during my time off, completely re-evaluated my life and priorities. What I haven't mentioned throughout all of my journey is that I have become well-known as a women's veteran advocate, held several prestigious positions within the veteran community, and have a hard time saying no, so I have thousands of volunteer hours. This has helped me develop as a leader in the community and become a mentor to other women veterans—two achievements of which I am very proud and which bring me much joy.

As of today, my plan is to move to Ohio and reconnect with my family after thirty-two years of being away. To take time to enjoy life, raise bees and possibly chickens, and volunteer on my terms. This experience showed me that, no matter how hard I work and bring success to an organization, it will always be their dream, and they will take it back when they see fit. I want more from life and believe I have so much to offer to other veterans and the community, but I want to do it on *my* terms. I have had my ups and downs since leaving the service, but I have found my identity as Kristine, and I will use my time in the military as my foundation to continue to do great things. I know the best part of my future is out there.

If you have reached this point in my story, I would like to leave you with the following thoughts. Women have been defending our country since the beginning of conflict. Our journey is different, but our patriotism, desire to serve, leadership, and grit are as strong as or stronger than those of our male counterparts. We want to continue to be leaders in our communities when we come home. Leaders are human. Every decision we make is for the betterment of others, right or wrong, and we carry the weight of our decisions with us for life. Sometimes, you just need to take a time out, regroup, and prepare to kick some ass on your journey to happiness.

Nikkea Devida—Cohort VI

To say that I grew up in a dysfunctional environment is not an overstatement. I am a second-generation American citizen. Both sets of my grandparents immigrated through Ellis Island in NY from Italy and Ireland. I grew up very poor in a very wealthy neighborhood, Westchester County, New York. My parents had an abusive, violent marriage for twenty-one years before they finally divorced when I was nine. Police visits were not uncommon to defuse violent tempers and break up their nearly lethal fights, such as the ones that caught my father with his hands wrapped around my mother's throat. For as long as I can remember, my mother was severely hearing impaired, ranging from about 70 percent hearing loss while I was growing up to over 90 percent before she passed away from lung cancer at age seventy-seven, in 2007.

I went to the United States Air Force Academy (USAFA) and into the military to escape my family. I was considered a pioneer when I entered boot camp at USAFA in June 1982, as a female cadet. We were only the seventh class of women when I graduated with a bachelor of science in management in May 1986. Academics were extremely challenging. Most of our core curriculum included math, science, and engineering courses. My fondest memories were the backdrop of the Cadet Chapel shimmering against the Rocky Mountains and singing in the prestigious Cadet Chorale. We performed at the National Cathedral, at the presentation of Carol Burnett's Lifetime Achievement Award, and in other shows around the country. Unfortunately, there were also several incidents of sexual assault and harassment, which continued to a lesser extent when I was active-duty air force. One time, I was raped by a military officer when I was a cadet deployed on a summer program in the Philippines. I never reported it because, back then, reporting sexual assault had career-ending repercussions.

Immediately after graduating from USAFA, a female air officer commander of a neighboring squadron had the courage to approach me with an opportunity to attend a personal-development program with her. In hindsight, this may have saved my life because that program set me on a course of healing . . . a journey that has continued in earnest. The tools I learned from that workshop and the hundred others I've attended, developed, taught, and produced since have made me into who I am today. Investing in myself to pay for that first workshop took absolutely every ounce of courage I had, including admitting that I needed help to overcome a problem with a severe eating disorder, bulimia, which I developed at the academy.

As a contracting officer in the AF, I received high-level training in contract negotiations, project management, systems, operations, and logistics. I was stationed at Hanscom AFB, Massachusetts, where I negotiated and managed approximately $200 million dollars of defense contracts . . . at the age of twenty-two. I worked on contracts to support the Strategic Defense Initiative (SDI), also known as "Star Wars," and received the Secretary of Defense Superior Management Award as one of the best project managers in the military in Washington, DC, by Caspar Weinberger for my work on the TOSI (Technical Onsite Inspection) program in support of the INF (Intermediate Nuclear Forces) treaty with Russia.

On the outside, I had all the trappings of success. On the inside, my soul was dying. All the abuse and trauma were catching up with me. Despite my stellar job performance, I was crashing down on the inside. I had a lot of demons to overcome.

My battle with bulimia evolved into binging and purging two to six times per day, every day, ultimately ending my career. After being hospitalized for four months at Malcolm Grow Medical Center at Andrews AFB, I was medically discharged from the air force in 1990. No one, including me, knew back then (and even up to my VA disability claim being changed from 30 to 100 percent service-connected in September 2018, nearly thirty years later!) that my bulimia was actually a severe military sexual trauma (MST) and PTSD response I developed at the academy. In hindsight, just knowing that would've changed the entire trajectory of my life.

I served in the Cold War. Back then, there was no Transition Assistance Program (TAP) to inform separating service members of their benefits, and there was no public awareness about MST and PTSD for military women. Despite many interviews, I couldn't get a job after the air force when I got out in 1990 during a major recession. I could barely even get a minimum-wage job, so I taught aerobics for fifteen dollars per class, and worked as a restaurant hostess and at a music store.

After eighteen months, I finally got a job in corporate America as a senior buyer at Bindley Western Drug Company (a pharmaceutical company), then, as a purchasing and project manager for Macmillan Publishing (a division of Viacom), Walt Disney, and Nova Development (a software development company). I received great experience and training in project management, supply-chain management, contracts, negotiations, systems, operations, and logistics in the private sector and military.

Meanwhile, my healing journey into personal and spiritual development continued. I pursued and studied peak performance and human potential at every level: physical, emotional, mental, and spiritual. When I learned about neuroscience, cellular biology, psychoneuroimmunology, and how to change subconscious beliefs in 1995, I was able to see improvement with the eating disorder in about six weeks. That got my attention. I changed my subconscious belief around other areas in my life and saw changes and results quickly. That's how I became an accidental entrepreneur. I started working with other people informally, and they got results. Then I started training others how to do it for themselves. I created my own transformational breakthrough system called Accelerated Change Template (ACT)™ Belief Change System as a way to overcome my own anxiety and trauma (fastresultsformula.com).

In January 2015, I received IRS approval for my non-profit initiative, called Sisters Who Serve, in less than thirty days! Sisters Who Serve is dedicated to securing and providing education, resources, training, and mentoring to military women and women in military families to support their physical, emotional, spiritual, and financial well-being. Sisters Who Serve is a premier resource for military women and women in military families.

My vision has been to raise $1 million to bring awareness and solutions to the unique issues facing women veterans, military women, and their families to support those experiencing PTSD, MST, other traumas, and the everyday challenges of transitioning from military to civilian life, along with training those who choose to become entrepreneurs. I wrote, recorded, and performed a song called "Sisters Who Serve" as my personal tribute and theme song for the foundation. I debuted the song in November 2013, to honor veterans to an audience of 1,000 people and opened the California Women's Conference in May 2014, to honor women veterans to an audience of 4,000 people.

Getting a master's degree has always been on my bucket list, and I overcame many obstacles for VocRehab to approve my education benefit that expired years before I ever knew I was eligible for it. It's hard to believe that, prior to MBV, I'd technically been out of the academic environment since graduating from the Air Force Academy in May 1986! Part of what I achieved is proving to myself I'm never too old to pursue something new. Just getting accepted and approved for the MBV program was a huge victory, and I had a goal coming into it to get every ounce of value I could from it to make better and more strategic career and life decisions. The entire MBV experience was a life-changing and transformational year of personal and professional growth for me. The program was extraordinary. I know I am a different person and a better version of myself coming out of it.

I'm proud to say I exceeded my expectations by achieving a 4.0 GPA, which allowed me to be invited into both the Beta Gamma Sigma and Phi Kappa Phi Honor societies. I am much more competitive with myself than I am with others. Whatever I do, I always aspire to do and achieve MY best. It's not about being *the* best or better than.

As if the academic workload wasn't enough, I entered both the New Venture Seed Competition and the Social Venture Competitions at USC to compete and up-level the strategy to combine Sisters Who Serve for military women (sisterswhoserve.org) and ACT (Accelerated Change Template belief change system; actvirtualbootcamp.com), as well as my understanding of how to pitch to investors. I am proud that I made it to the finals.

I think the most impactful change I've made is in my view of leadership, power, and influence. The assessments we took at the beginning of the program were extremely insightful as benchmarks for my growth throughout it. As a result of the program, I believe I see the world much more clearly, and I'm leaving behind my resistance to making a bigger impact through networking, managing up, politicking, power, and influence. My biggest transformation revolves around strategically building relationships and connections to move my vision forward.

The most unexpected bonus of the MBV program has been meeting and developing meaningful friendships and connections with classmates, faculty, and staff. I didn't anticipate feeling such a sense of connection, belonging, and loyalty with USC and MBV. I feel grateful, blessed, and honored to have met and spent this time with MBV Cohort VI. I've made lifelong friends, colleagues, and connections.

I think, for the first time in my life, I truly feel as though I have strong support and that I'm not alone in whatever I choose to pursue going forward. It's been an honor to get to know everyone in and around the MBV program, and they can contact me any time if they need an introduction, sounding board, someone to party and go on an adventure with, a shoulder to lean on, or an honest reality check.

I'm forever grateful for the opportunity to have participated in the MBV program, and I'll do my best to positively represent and recruit for it. The support and guidance I've received from everyone—classmates and faculty alike—have been truly life-changing and transformational. To me, graduation wasn't the end, just the beginning for us to connect even more deeply, and collaborate to leverage and make our impact in the world even greater as Trojan veterans

CHAPTER 7

SUMMING UP, OWNING UP, AND LETTING GO

Our Last Day Together—May 5, 2018, Cohort V

I arrived early at the site between Hoffman Hall and Bridge Hall, a grassy area called the Marshall Lawn. The breakfast was already set up, and there were staff there to serve. The traffic on Exposition Boulevard was very loud. Philip Folsom and his team arrived early and ready to begin. The trainers who had arrived seemed mature and experienced, important with my group of ninety veterans, whose average age is thirty-six and whose average training experience includes significant outdoor challenge activities and many leadership training courses.

I began with my challenge to the cohort to focus on our last day, reach closure around issues and relationships that are important to them, reignite the sense of community, and prepare for separation. Acknowledging that something important is about to end that challenged us and brought us closer to each other is important, to celebrate the event and recognize that we will not regularly be seeing each other in this common quest in the near future. Also, acknowledging that we have achieved this common stated goal and that our striving was finished was important. Additionally, some debriefing, processing, and a final statement make the point that we are saying things that should be said in this intimate context, and (hopefully) not waking up in the future feeling we wished we had said that or acknowledged someone in the cohort.

I've watched students and other groups separate with no ending ceremony, and wondered how they deal with their awareness of closure. The more intense and intimate the relationships and joint efforts for success, the greater the need for recognizing the ending as cleanly as possible without carrying held-over feelings and concerns away from the arena in which we all have worked so hard and given so much. Commencements themselves are such rich rituals and ceremonies.

Programs with close interpersonal and team dynamics should address this issue of separation quite seriously. In the case of veterans, their bonds through their common military experience create a stronger dynamic than in an average degree program. Also, a strong sense of shared empathy for each other's struggles—whether they're wounds and disability from service, or struggles with transition or the usual course of events and aging—is meaningful. Another major, mostly implicit, commonality is the understanding that everyone in the room has volunteered to serve their country, to serve a purpose beyond self, which calls for a self-altering process that is physically and mentally challenging and the adoption of a point of view that places the mission first.

This common base of a challenging initiation process is a major factor in the bonding and respect the veterans have for one another. This respect is enhanced with the knowledge of special advanced training where not everyone succeeds—often only a fraction of those who begin the special training complete it successfully. This creates an implicit hierarchy of respect starting with a common intent to serve followed by a common initiation through basic training and special advanced training that is both challenging and rare, and ends with combat or similar assignments that involve personal risk and sacrifice. The hierarchy could continue with special recognition in combat for bravery, personal sacrifice, and contribution. Because we took away the hierarchy of rank, the hierarchy of service, contribution, achievement, sacrifice, bravery, and honor became the hierarchy of respect.

There was another hierarchy of respect I recognized, possibly because of my long experience with graduate students and their selection into advanced study. I admired overcoming adversity, persistence in the face of handicaps, and breaking new ground by accepting education and personal growth. Many of our students were first-generation college students. Many had attended multiple schools to put together an undergraduate degree. Many were from backgrounds that did not support academic learning or achievement, including those who had multiple siblings who took alternate routes to their lives that did not reflect higher aspirations.

Most of all, I encouraged them to view this final day as an opportunity for insights, reflection, and a final day of committing to their best to be able to move forward and out of this supportive, caring environment with high self-confidence and utmost optimism.

Philip introduced the day's activities and goals and his team. Everyone was given five small rocks on which they were instructed to inscribe their top five values in life. Over the course of the morning, they would deposit three of the rocks in reverse order of importance into a container, leaving them with their two most precious values to take with them to the afternoon session in our classroom. At the end of the day, they would still possess their most important life value to take with them. Their second most important value would be left behind at the end of their final personal statement.

Philip organized a total group rope-pull, with four equal groups holding an end of the rope at all four corners of the compass. His instructions were to score as many points as possible in a short time by moving the centerpiece of the rope across a fixed position in the ground. Once the signal was given to begin, all four teams began pulling in different directions. The groups were pretty equal, so no points were scored during the first period, and only one team won a point during the second period. Someone in one of the teams suggested partnering up with another team to score more points, so the third period was more lively and just as competitive. When time ran out, the total point scores were about four.

During the debriefing, Philip shared with the group that the highest score ever achieved was 300, and that was accomplished by middle-school children. You could see insight begin to creep in, and a number of students experienced actual embarrassment once it did. Philip had never said it was competitive. The goal, as announced, was to score as many goals as possible, and all four groups assumed it was competitive, so they gave it their all against the other teams. This was, of course, a natural assumption given the design of the four groups. It raised the issue of acting immediately on assumptions based on past experience and expectations within a culture, without focusing specifically on the stated goal, the lack of stated rules (constraints), and the special environment in which this activity was taking place. Each person dropped one of their values rocks in the container.

The rope pull

After the debrief, the cohort met as a whole and were asked to select a CEO of a fictitious organization in which they all would be members. They immediately called out one of the senior members of the class to play this position for the next activity. He immediately and forcefully demurred, saying that the cohort did not need a leader. Philip insisted they pick a leader, so their second choice was a Navy SEAL, who did step up to play the role of CEO of this fictitious organization. The organization was split into fifteen semi-autonomous production groups, and each was assigned a manager and about five workers. The workers were given blindfolds, but not the manager. Each team was to build something at the direction of the manager under timed conditions, not knowing what it was. So each manager had to develop a process to communicate and instruct without telling the team what they were building.

Philip and his team went to the truck and brought back fifteen large boxes that they distributed among the teams. On opening the box, the team managers discovered they were to build a Huffy bike for children, eight boys' and seven girls' bikes. Team managers now had to quickly read the instructions, meet with the CEO for further organizational direction, and give useful directions to the blindfolded team members on building this mystery product.

They took about thirty minutes to accomplish this task using tools provided through the larger organization. Originally, the teams were to be given forty-five minutes, but our experience the prior year led us to believe that for this group of veterans, this was too much time. Not only did the teams build the bikes, but their team leaders also had to make sure they did quality checks on the product to make it safe to ride.

A major debriefing took place, first led by the student CEO and then by Philip and his crew. It focused on what helped, what got in the way, and how the process and teamwork could have been improved. The bikes were all lined up in front of the total members of cohort, when the back door to Hoffman Hall opened, and fifteen fourth graders from the South Los Angeles community filed out and stood in front of the bikes. Their organizer, and a community partner of mine for over fifteen years, was Bennie Davenport, who hosted my undergraduate business students in doing team projects for Blazers, a youth educational and after-school house he founded almost fifty years ago as a basketball after-school site for community teenagers.

His mission had greatly expanded over the years, and the fourth graders he brought in to receive a gift of a bike were a special group chaperoned by some parents and a school principal. They had conducted a written competition among 110 children writing about what they would do with a new bike and why they should be a recipient.

Since time was getting short, Bennie asked three of the kids to read their essay, and all had written that they would give their bike away to less fortunate kids than themselves, one residing in Honduras. The photo-op was exploited by all three groups putting on the event: Philip and his team, Bennie and his team and parents, and myself and my partner, the program director, James Bogle, representing Marshall. The veterans were moved by how this experience had developed with the kids taking ownership of a new Huffy bike built by the veterans during their last day on campus together.

I think it fair to say the veterans had not anticipated that the very last day of the program, they would produce a product that would be accepted and enjoyed by a special community group. However, I found them not surprised that they would end up in service to others in the community, even if they were not members of it themselves, since many of them were either currently active in their own community or planning to get active once they completed their transition and settled into a different environment. The kids were very grateful, the parents in attendance were moved, and the principal expressed his amazement and gratitude at this engagement and sharing. The children were encouraged to interact with the veterans, and many of our veterans interacted with the kids and their families in attendance in Spanish.

Bikes built during the morning will be given to children from the community.

> "What we thought at first to be a simple (and on the face of it, even silly) exercise in teamwork turned out to be something much bigger. We did not know it at the time, but in engaging in this simple exercise, we'd actually become unwitting accomplices in an act of generosity and kindness on behalf of some children who desperately needed and deserved it. I think about that moment of denouement when we realized what we'd done, and it is still hard to keep myself together. . . . In that one moment, we all realized that we still have the ability to make a powerful and meaningful impact on the world and the people around us." (Troy Baisch, Cohort VI)

The morning was quickly ending as all participants, families, and group leaders said goodbye to each other and began drifting away. Some of the kids had not owned a bike before, and some of the veterans helped them learn to ride it on the cement outside of Hoffman Hall. It was a joyful scene and a positive intervention in the last day of the cohort's time together. The activity had created an optimistic and sharing mood and a new perspective for the veterans as they moved to wrap up their time together in the afternoon session.

While the community participants were collecting bikes and kids, the cohort congregated around Philip near the beginning space, dropped another rock, and Philip finished the story of the Hero's Journey he had begun during the ropes course day at Culver City, the first weekend in September. He had brought them full circle to the end of this journey, which would later culminate in a five-hour afternoon session inside one of the large classrooms. He encouraged the veterans to once again accept the challenge of the quest, overcome the difficulties and dangers, return with the gifts of service to others, and to use the framework of the myth to understand their journey together of the last ten months to prepare for closure and their next transition and personal quest.

The end of this special journey was discussed in terms of deep personal insight in seeking one's best self and character, and changing one's thinking to adopt a growth mindset and the opportunity to achieve a purpose beyond self, and readdress themselves to making a contribution to the wider community. This entire focus and orientation stands in comparison with some other orientations that focus solely on building one's personal wealth. This is not to say that the veterans are not interested in their market value or compensation. Most knew almost the exact dollar amount they needed or expected at the end of the program. But the overarching purpose tended to be focused on things greater than themselves, and many or most of them were committed to almost immediately give back to their community and the next group of veterans. They intended to pay it forward as quickly as possible.

Lunch, as usual, was informal and held out on the enclosed patio between Popovich Hall and Fertitta Hall. Overlaying this final meal together were feelings of optimism, gratitude, and sadness about separation. There was much to discuss, share, and say to one another, but there was an overarching sense of there being too little time left. One of the students in Cohort VI (Rose Simpson) used the day to write personal notes to the other eighty-four members of her cohort. One of her personal goals for the year had been to meet and get to know everyone in the cohort, and this was her final test of it. Since I was included in the reading of the post, I can attest to her success. While this act definitely fit the nature of the wrap-up weekend, I had never seen someone during the final day write a public note to every other student in the class, in any group I had worked with. This was just one of this kind of expression of caring about everyone in the cohort, both as a peer, but also as a family member. It was also a direct example of someone making a final statement, mostly of gratitude, to every other student in the cohort so that she could feel that she said everything she wanted to and reach some sense of closure with her brothers and sisters.

Many of the students used a few minutes of the lunch hour to develop their thoughts on what they might say to the cohort as their final personal statement. I had suggested about a month earlier to think about what they might want and what they would leave behind. This, at first, seemed to be a difficult assignment, and there were many who drew a blank on both the meaning of the assignment and how they might accomplish it. My suggestion was for them to look at their behavior and attitudes that were no longer useful to them, or that they'd grown out of during their journey of self-discovery. "What no longer serves you? What are you willing to leave behind as you exit this experience and transition to the next phase of not only your career, but your personal growth?" If leadership is the expression of their best self, this process continues to evolve as long as one is aware of and in charge of their own behavior, and is motivated to continue the process.

I invited Philip to share the meanings he attaches to working with military veterans, specifically with our MBV program at Marshall. Since Philip and I have worked together for about fourteen years, we share values and goals for this type of education and growth and always celebrate moments of personal insight. Also, watching veteran groups becoming closer over the course of a single day on the ropes courses is meaningful to us both and reinforces our commitment to individual growth and community development within the same educational strategy. The following are Philip Folsom's comments on the MBV program and his work with veterans:

> "As a cultural anthropologist who also consults extensively in both the corporate and non-profit worlds, I believe the veteran conversation to be one of the most important and impactful ones we are currently having in our society. As a veteran myself I see a wide range of opportunities for not only healing and reintegrating a large section of our population but also learning from our veterans how to heal and successfully integrate often-isolated portions of our society to the benefit of all. The USC MBV program is the tip of the spear in that vital conversation of where we are headed as a society.
>
> It might just save us.
>
> In many ways, veterans function like the canary in our country's mental health coal mine. How veterans are dealing with clinical anxiety, depression, and suicide is a strong indicator for other high-stress careers such as police, firefighters, incarcerated people both in prison and reintegrating back into society not to mention the inner-city youth growing up in chronic poverty, trauma, stress, and violence. Right now that trend is increasing at an alarming rate and typified by the male suicide rate in the United States increasing by almost 40 percent in the last ten years alone.
>
> One of the primary differentiators veteran communities share with other groups such as first responders, athletes, and even gang-affiliated youth and incarcerated populations is the fact that they are

all honor-based cultures. The rest of the civilian world is pride-based. These two cultures are fundamentally different and studying veterans gives us the ability to understand, utilize, and integrate the positive aspects of these vastly different operating systems to get the best of both worlds.

Pride (civilian) cultures give us innovation and growth while honor cultures give us meaning, resiliency and performance. In the history of mankind there has never been an example of heroism without honor; we will always do more for others in our tribe than we will do for ourselves. Society as a whole is desperate for honor as well as authentic meaning that only comes from service and connection to something beyond self-service.

Versatility and adaptability as a culture are the keys to not only survival but evolving into sustainable thriving.

In addition to bringing the resiliency and performance that sit at the heart of honor-based cultures back into our world, veterans also hold the raw ingredients for meaning and purpose that can only be found in the expression of service to something bigger than ourselves. When this is transformed into workplace meaning and purpose, it becomes a primary driver for both employee engagement and retention. Both engagement and retention are key profit drivers in every industry.

One of the other central challenges for veterans (or any of the other honor-based social groups) transitioning into the civilian world is the overwhelming pressure of having to redefine the foundational categories of life. These categories include values, mission, role models, and tribe. All honor-based cultures define and provide these central pillars of life for their participants and when veterans re-enter the civilian world, they are suddenly faced with a crippling barrage of life-defining questions. Without the answers to these questions, life can quickly become a meaningless journey of anxiety, depression, and, too often, suicide. Suicide is a terminal response to a life without meaning.

The USC MBV program is a dojo for the exploration and discovery of these core beliefs.

In addition, USC shares the hidden superpower of the US military, which is the united front of men and women from all over the country coming from vastly different cultures, backgrounds, education, and experiences, unified behind a common mission, vision, and values. This alignment forms a mighty tribe.

The USC Trojan family holds a uniquely similar dynamic to the military and is one of the reasons the MBV program has flourished here. In addition, the USC community carries many of the cultural unifiers that the military has. It even has a warrior as its mascot and "fight on!" as its slogan.

It's an honor to serve those that served and be part of the reintroduction of honor into our world.

It might just save us.

Fight on!"

Philip Folsom
Cultural anthropologist and corporate consultant at Wolf Tribe

US Army veteran
Co-founder of SPARTA Veteran Suicide Prevention Program

The Final Session

After lunch, we reconvened in the large classroom for our final session. We were getting very close to the end of the year—just one afternoon, the last Saturday afternoon of forty-two afternoons over a ten-month sprint. The students' final personal statement to the cohort was not an easy task to give instructions for, but most of them got it fairly quickly. The statements could be a moving expression of frustration, achievement, and, in some cases, long-held regret, sadness, and sometimes anger. We learn a lot during this session about individual childhoods, often the escape from poverty, gangs, immature behavior, etc. We also hear grand aspirations and optimism, often sadness at leaving the cohort, and many personal insights and stories of transformational growth. Over the six years, I've heard at least a half dozen attempted suicide stories followed by a resolute commitment to life. One of the other main themes is survivor's guilt. Those who were witness to the casualties of combat but survived themselves often experience what they describe as survivor's guilt. One of the best resolutions to this emotion was expressed by a marine in Cohort V (Michael Guadan, whom you will meet at the end of this chapter). He dealt with these feelings by telling himself that his friend or other lost unit member would want him and other survivors to live fully not just for themselves, but for the person whose opportunity to live fully had been taken from them. And so he felt an obligation to live the way the absent veteran would have wanted to live, and would want him to live as well. I noticed heads nodding and tears in response.

The stories of redemption, growth, sacrifice, humility, overcoming deep grief, dedication, striving, and maturity were many, and elicited strong emotional responses from all of us in the room.

I would usually select the first person to present based on what I thought was genuine emotional insight into their own condition, adversity, achievement, and growth. Then I never called on anyone after that. Individuals came forward as they felt ready or compelled. Some would hold out to the very end. Getting around to everyone in the room in the larger cohorts took more than the entire afternoon.

It was not unusual to be fairly emotionally drained at the end of the afternoon's session. For many of us, we felt we knew the individuals a little better having witnessed their final statements. Everyone left with their final stone on which was written their most important value instructing their lives, love, family, integrity, achievement, strength, courage, health, etc. The second year we conducted this ending, I felt the need to define my own foundational value, which ended up through a quick introspection to be commitment. I had always felt love and family were a given, but commitment took great effort, insight, and intentionality, much in service of the other values.

During Cohort VI's final session, the session developed into stating both sides of what was gained and what was to be left behind. Our program director, James Bogle, contributed to the following two lists that show the nature of the positive side of what was gained and the extent of what the individuals felt they could discard at the end of the program, those behaviors that no longer served them either personally or professionally.

Taking with them	Leaving behind
Confidence, self-worth (most frequent)	Self-doubt (most frequent)
Safety to take risks	Fear of being alone
Family and relationships	Distrust
Friends and trust	Fear of civilian life (and accounting!)
Connection to USC	Apprehension
Leap of faith and family	Lone wolf mentality
Sense of community	Selfishness
Essentialism	Regret
Courage	Insecurity
Humility	Fear of success
Integrity	The past
Intentionality – all in	Hesitation
Discernment	Reluctance to network
Loyalty	Safety
Loftier goals	Blind loyalty
Grace, strength, self-care, give to others	Blind ambition
Listening	Procrastination
Value of time	Excuses/complacency
Perspective	Survivor's guilt
Emotional intelligence	Indifference/passivity
Impact	Anger
Honesty and authenticity	Negativity
Self-evaluation taught me who I am	Fear of quitting job
Team within a business endeavor	
Passion for finance (!)	
Compassion (self and others)	
Self-awareness	
Direction	
Investment in self	
Creativity and self-expression	
Resilience	

"I left behind lack of confidence, fear of the unknown, and fear of failure. I graduated from the MBV program with the outlook that I had the opportunity to create the life I truly want, and I had nothing or no one to hold me back. I looked at my life as a blank canvas and I could paint the picture any way I wanted. What a blessing it was to be in this position!" (Natalya Turner, Cohort III)

While both lists were quite long and many of the behaviors were mentioned more than once, the two most frequently mentioned behaviors were similar: confidence versus self-doubt. We could generalize and state that this may be at least an implicit goal of most graduate programs when students focus on increasing their competencies in knowledge and performance and feel more capable in both functional areas of knowledge and in the ability to lead.

When thinking about transitions and transitioning, it becomes clearer to me that we move from uncertainty and self-doubt because we're moving into new territory, both contextual and personal competencies. If and when we can successfully transition, we end up with a greater sense of confidence and competence, both about where we have gone, but also about the process and journey that transitions demand of us. Add to that a greater sense of confidence that we can survive and thrive through the next transition that we will face.

Competence is skill-based, with knowledge and intent built in. Skill-based competence requires practice, and the military is adept at drill, practice, discipline, and focus. When thrust into an unknown and unstructured environment, you are unlikely to develop competence and confidence early in the process. That many of our graduating students could conclude that they were leaving behind their uncertainty and taking confidence with them into their transitioning provided a sense of accomplishment and satisfaction for our part, program management.

Never did we feel that this was 100 percent, and we always wanted a greater consensus of self-confidence in our graduates, but I had learned many years before that our process and satisfaction were based on one person at a time growing and succeeding in our eyes and in their own sense of personal growth. We celebrated small wins and recognized the successes of each individual who successfully completed the process, and encouraged an ongoing lifelong learning process to continue progressing toward their best self as they continue in the various transitions they will face.

One of the most interesting emotions to be left behind was "fear of leaving or quitting one's job." During the final session with Cohort VI, five individuals indicated they were going to leave their current job, much to the surprise of our program management, who keeps close track of these types of transitions. As these five new students declared their impending freedom from employment, both our program director and the director of career services almost audibly gasped! It was a program goal to assist with job and career transitions, but to hear about the potential of five new unemployed graduates during the last day was traumatic to those keeping track of the employment of each cohort, but I suspect freeing to those making that choice as well as to the others listening and sharing in that fairly dramatic outcome.

In Cohort VI, this meant seventeen of the students either did, or expressed their intention to, walk away from their current employment because it no longer served them, their needs for growth, contribution, and advancement. Apparently, the need for security was a driving force for many, so as they observed others take a chance to make a positive change, the more open all members of the cohort became. There was almost a contagion within Cohort VI to leave situations that were not providing opportunities for growth, and take the risk of seeking new avenues of employment success and satisfaction.

There was much respect accorded those who stated they were moving on, and this led to others feeling that they, too, could take the leap of faith into an unknown state of uncertainty with the confidence that they could do this! This is where replacing self-doubt with self-confidence was most powerful, and it wasn't just in the individual, but could be sensed within the entire Cohort VI. This leap of faith to leave one's unsatisfying job was an actual outcome that harked back to the leap of faith all had engaged in at the ropes course in the prior September when they had stated their major goal in life, climbed a thirty-foot pole, stood on a small wooden platform, controlled their body's tremors, focused on their goal, and with the support of their team on the ground, taken the absurdly risky leap toward the symbolic goal, grabbed it, and hung on.

At the end of the session, I felt compelled to make some comments either in summary, wrap-up, or affirmation of our time together. I typically would make notes prior to the session to give me some guidance extemporaneously, but also typically did not use the scripted notes. I needed to be congruent in expressing what was on my mind, and more importantly, what my immediate feelings and emotions were. As a result, I often don't remember what I said afterward, but during the 2018 final session (Cohort V), I remember sharing with them that "you have enriched my life, and for that I am both grateful and appreciative for having been given the opportunity to work with you for these quick ten months and sharing the journey of transition."

I have found throughout my experience during these six cohorts that paying attention to my intense engagement with both the individuals and the total cohort left me feeling satisfied that we were doing the right thing. I felt we were fairly successful in our intent and design, and somewhat transcended from my everyday awareness and prior classroom and program experience to a higher level of awareness, respect, and satisfaction. The final session had become the culmination of my journey of embedded engagement and changed my lived experience in ways that can only be discussed from this personal point of view.

If leadership is the expression of our best self, and our best self is expressed within intense engagement interpersonally and with a total group, then leadership needs to be discussed in terms of one's lived experience. To be the external critic or to objectify it will miss the point. I'm reminded of what one of my early colleagues would say to refer to this phenomenon: "How do you describe or explain to another what corn on the cob tastes like?" How do you describe and explain the power of the sense of achievement for completing a marathon event? It is useful to share one's experience in case there are dangers involved (including legal restrictions), but many experiences must be lived to be fully understood. And Teddy Roosevelt's quotation about the man in the arena, where he indicates that being either a critic or an observer won't provide the essence of the action or outcome supports this approach. One must be in the arena, on the field of play, cross the finish line of the marathon, even if they're alone.

For Cohort II, here are my final comments that I shared with them at the end of the afternoon to summarize both my intent and my experience with them.

These comments guided my classes throughout the six years I was fortunate to have worked with the veterans.

> "I did not come here to impress, but to engage.
> I did not come here to inspire, but to activate.
> I did not come here to persuade, but to share, to influence, to challenge!
> I don't want you to come over to my side, but to develop your side.
> We can get there together!"

My intent at the close was the same as at the opening: Keep the focus on the people in the room, not on the instructor, not on those leaders who have gone before and paved the way, but on the veterans who were currently in the arena and about to transition out to experience the results of their personal growth efforts during the ten months together.

At the end of the afternoon, some leave the room quickly, but others hang around for a while, allowing the mood to linger. One of my sailors came up to me in tears, expressing his appreciation for being allowed to be part of Cohort V and this experience.

I will hear other stories later that night at the banquet, most of which will be beautiful, appreciative, and focused on their personal growth during the program. There is more than a hint of sadness at the awareness of having to separate from a unit to which they had grown attached, and with whom they had learned about possibilities for a future they had not imagined. One of the comments I remember from a member of Cohort IV's final leadership paper:

> "...and you were right. It was one of the most moving things I have ever been a part of. To see all of us get up there and speak in front of each other about our darkest secrets with no fear...was magical!" (Joshua Moffie, Cohort IV)

And, Troy added this comment:

> "Saying goodbye to the brothers and sisters you've spent so much time with and shared so many amazing experiences with is a hard thing to do. The staff and instructors have invested so much of themselves

and their time and wisdom and mentorship to help us succeed. It's extremely impactful emotionally." (Troy Baisch, Cohort VI)

I am typically exhausted, however elated, by the time to go home. Fortunately, my wife drove us home.

Now meet another six alums. Also, you will read a graduation address by Antonio Randolph of Cohort IV, whose personal story is also included here.

Commencement for the women of Cohort IV

Michael Guadan—Cohort IV

I served eight years in the USMC and started my career in law enforcement. Prior to MBV, I worked for a small IT and telecommunications firm. Today, I work for Mark43, a software startup that provides software solutions for police departments and public safety agencies. My wife and I have two children under age three and reside in south Orange County.

Reflection from individual statements: Survivor's guilt. In our final session, a lot of fellow MBVs brought up survivor's guilt and sought an answer as to why they were here while others were not. Truthfully, I don't know if anyone can answer that. Far too many veterans are narrowly focused on the *why* instead of the *how*. A part of transition is adapting your framework and moving the lateral limits of thought and expression. Veterans are simply asking the wrong question. Instead, collectively, we need to undergo a mind shift that instead asks: How? How do I best honor and preserve the memory of heroes who sacrificed everything?

In my opinion, we do it by living extraordinary lives. Extraordinary is a subjective term and is not directly correlated to finances. Extraordinary is about living life as if we had a second chance. If any of the heroes were able to live again, can you imagine what kind of life they would live? I think about that often, when I need perspective, or I get angry. I think they would spend the precious time with their families. They wouldn't fight with their partners; they wouldn't freak out over the small stuff. Seriously, think about how many more hugs, "I love you," and "I can, and I will" they would deliver. Most importantly, I believe they would extend their hands and help those less fortunate. That hand out is what transition and the veteran community is all about. It is what separates us from those who seek individual fame and glory. As veterans, we must seek collaborative success and share our knowledge and opportunities. What is done is done. None of us can change the past. What we can do, however, is change our outlook on the future. When you do, you will see a life filled with purpose, optimism, and perspective. A life that is eerily similar to our time in the service.

Darren Denyer—Cohort VI

I grew up with two grandfathers I idolized—one I knew, the other lost his life serving our country in 1961. Both served in the enlisted ranks of the United States Navy during WWII and beyond, both had stories and experiences that left me in awe of what they lived through. Their lives sparked my interest in serving my country in my own way, leading me to NROTC at the University of Colorado, Boulder, and a commission as a naval officer and subsequently as a surface warfare officer. As is the case of everyone who puts on a uniform, the stories, experiences, and actions we are led to take often combine luck, timing, and opportunity. Those three elements led me into a career I will never forget, down a path into incredible experiences during our War on Terrorism, and eventually on to the University of Southern California.

I awoke on the morning of September 11, 2001, to an email from a naval online forum in my apartment in Boulder, Colorado. "I think we've just been attacked," the email read, and I ventured groggily over to our TV to see if there was merit to the email. The first tower had been struck, but even then, it didn't seem real, until we watched in horror as the second plane met its mark. A third aircraft was bravely sent to an early demise while a fourth met its mark at the Pentagon. As we know, these events changed our nation's course and career where I have only known us at war. It was about a week after the attacks that I learned that a high school classmate of mine, returning to school in California, had lost her life on Flight 93. This knowledge gave me purpose. As the conflicts built up, I continued my schooling and eventually received my degree and commission, in December 2004.

My first taste of the navy as a newly commissioned ensign was to the pre-commissioning unit of USS *Halsey* (DDG 97) in Pascagoula, Mississippi. It was here I cut my teeth as a leader, eventually learning I didn't know much and needed to learn all that I could from those around me. We eventually commissioned the ship into service in San Diego, and prepared for our maiden deployment with the ship's newly minted navigator, LTJG Darren Denyer. I learned a great deal the previous two years, about the ship, about leading, and about being a good follower (this took some work). We deployed to the Western Pacific in support of Joint Special Operations Task Force—Philippines and battle group operations outside of Japan. We supported special operations ashore, dealt with disaster, and experienced the surprise of a Chinese submarine. I ultimately learned my passions were not onboard a ship.

My search for a place led to me back to the Philippines, in 2006/2007, as a battle captain in Zamboanga, Mindanao. I volunteered to support this Joint Special Operations Task Force in a corner of the world that didn't receive much press, but which remained a critical access and training point for those aligned against the US and our allies. I knew from this experience that leading folks "in the mix" was where I wanted to be. I got my wish when I returned home and found a new outfit being set up called Maritime Civil Affairs. I knew this was where I wanted to be: a new unit, a new capability, small teams, massive responsibility, and adventure all rolled into a job that few could effectively conceptualize. I built a team and a capability, did many things for the first time, blazed a new trail for navy expeditionary combat command and for myself as a person. This job, this passion, took me to the Caribbean, South America, Europe, and throughout Africa. While the wars in Iraq and Afghanistan raged on, my team was a warden on the edge looking for hot spots and helping those who didn't want to succumb to the cancer spreading in our world. We were responsible for access, influence, and information operations that allowed us to work with governments, militaries, international organizations, local municipalities, and the everyday citizens of the locations we worked in.

I found my place, I found my niche, and then the navy changed the rules. As the war dragged on, the navy began to shift its focus back to the gray hulls and away from expeditionary forces. My civil affairs capability was to be transferred to the reserves. For me, I knew where I wanted to be. It was a gamble to leave active duty and support this capability. I made that move in 2010 and never looked back. I stood up the first detachment in San Diego, and prepared to deploy them to the Middle East and Africa. We mobilized, trained up for six months, and then the navy changed the rules again and divested from our capability, sent us home, and me into a spiral.

I have held subsequent reserve commanding officer jobs and remained stuck in a civilian career that has never been fulfilling or provided much in the way of upward mobility. I continued to search for a meaningful place, eventually working with Naval Special Warfare Command in San Diego and subsequently deploying with Joint Special Operations Command to support operations overseas. It was there I saw combat for the first time, saw the trauma of war, and even lost a friend. I deployed with a purpose, had a mission, worked at the apex of military operations overseas, and then had to go back home and be sliced away from that world yet again. I spiraled into a low point of my life, devoid of purpose, a team, a tribe, a growth trajectory in a selfish world outside of uniform. It took its toll on my wife and kids. I knew I needed a drastic change, but where to find this?

Fortunately for me, my life and story changed when I was told about the MBV program at the USC's Marshall School of Business. It was a colleague from my first ship, now reconnected at a reserve command in Seal Beach, who was at the time in the program. I visited the campus, spoke with staff, and did some soul searching. It took me no time at all to recognize this was what I needed, where I needed to be, who I needed to be with in order to relocate my purpose, find new paths, and have the tools to traverse them.

From day one to graduation, the MBV program was everything I needed and more. Our cohort took two weeks to come together as a family and support one another through our demanding academic schedule. It gave me the tools to confidently go into the world to seek out a place, or build one of my own, and do so with a network and family built to support me and my classmates. This program, and its world-class faculty, provided more than business knowledge. It provided emotional and intellectual growth that gave us the confidence to engage the business world through our own lenses and experience. The program showed us how we add value to the business realm, why we're an asset, and how to show those in the civilian world why they need and want us in their business. I am beyond grateful for a program that took a risk to be the first of its kind and placed a massive bet on the veteran community in a way that gives us the opportunity to grow, build, hire, and ultimately be value-added to our families and communities in ways we didn't think possible. Many of us have newly minted strength to continue our fight on!

Antonio Randolph—Cohort IV

I am the product of a middle-class family system that has been physically rooted in a Midwestern environment for decades, but with significant southern influence. My dad was from Augusta, Georgia, and my mom grew up in Memphis, after spending some of her early years in her birthplace of Greenwood, Mississippi. My three older sisters were southern-born, and my parents migrated to Michigan shortly after my youngest sister was born. It was there that my younger brother and I were born and my siblings and I were raised.

In our home, courtesy, etiquette, and proper grammar were mandatory. Hard work was the standard while education was preceded in importance only by God and family (in that order). As far as effort and dedication—the key ingredients of hard work—went, my father was the standard of the standard. He worked fifty years for one company, Chrysler Automotive, and he never missed a day, religiously worked overtime, yet still found time to catch one of our games or attend a science fair here and there. He and my mother purchased books of all kinds and stacked them on the shelves—not in our den or living room, but in our bedrooms. The disappointment and inconvenience of rainy days, banishments to our rooms for punishment, and the associated TV restrictions were bearable and manageable because of books. I read, we read, and it became fun from early on. The idea of connecting to the past, escaping from reality to walk in someone else's shoes, and the discovery of techniques and processes that could explain the happenings of the world while adding utility and making me skillful was mind-blowing. This is what books and learning offered and freely gave me. There was also a tremendous support system in place for us all. For me, this was coupled with the efforts of my oldest sister, a nurse who is still the smartest person in my family. She quizzed me, pushed me, and challenged me academically. By age five, I was doing multiplication, writing cursive, and reading far above my grade level. At the time, success was considered a foregone conclusion. I was set up for it, leaving only the exact nature of it up to chance.

With limited opportunities growing up in the Jim Crow south, the options for my parents were virtually non-existent to pursue education beyond grade or high school. My siblings and I heard the stories of the struggles, injustices, and my family's resistance to the status quo. We were most astonished when my uncle told us about my maternal grandfather and why he and my grandmother had moved the family from Mississippi to Tennessee and changed their surname. He did so to avoid being captured by white supremacists and publicly hanged. This was far from an idle threat in 1940s Mississippi. What did he do to create such an uproar? He had beaten a white man to the edge of death after being spit on and called a nigger. My parents would use experiences such as these to mold and develop a unique type of child, five times over, with a unique focus, unique agenda, and unique methodology for dealing with such people, problems, and events.

Growing up in Detroit, a town where at least 70 percent of the white population lives outside its borders and very few whites are willing to sell their suburban homes to people of color, it was evident that segregation was there, by design, with racial tensions always on high. Through it all, my mom preached tolerance, emphasized her belief in equality, and forced us into scenarios with kids who didn't look like us or even have the same belief and value systems. Some tried to intimidate us. Some tried to demean us. Many tried to one-up us. But through it all, my mom pushed us back into the ring, and with a twist. She forced us to fight without throwing a punch and tasked us to use the power of influence to achieve cooperation and win battles: force of mind is far more powerful than force of hand. We learned to use our intellect to manage our conflicts, to shut down detractors without pushing them to their breaking point, and to keep our eyes on the real prize: progress, development, and improvement.

As time moved on, the years passed, and the grades were completed at some of the best public and private schools in the state of Michigan, but life as a young adult, without my father, who passed away when I was seventeen, was harder than I had presumed. Eventually, a series of poor choices were made that delayed my growth and advancement; the nudge I needed came from Uncle Sam. First, boot camp at Great Lakes, Illinois, then eight years as a sailor. Next, officer candidate school at the Alabama Military Academy, now nine years a soldier. I haven't been perfect, and I have fallen many times, but I am seasoned enough to know that one failure doesn't define me, so it shouldn't define my perception of others either. We all have our share of them, and it is irrational to think that mine are worse than anyone's else or even more relevant than anyone else's. Learning to let go means learning to overcome fear, reservation, judgment, and all the barriers that stand fast to render one's personal progress, development, and improvement immaterial.

So here I am, two score and four years later, the product of a deliberate strategy of two loving and supportive parents and great siblings who had the first and a lasting impact on my joy of learning, my resolve to overcome obstacles, my empathy for others, and my desire to excel. In the process, I have become a capable leader and manager, a USC MBV alum, and a proud citizen-soldier.

What led me to the MBV program?

How did I figure out that USC was the best grad school option for me? My enrollment in the MBV program was largely because the program met each of my top-six preferred criteria: 1. It was a top-twenty-five business school. 2. I live and work in Ohio. If possible, I didn't want another degree from an institution in the Midwest (most of my peer group had degrees from institutions in the Midwest). 3. I had a short window of opportunity (i.e., twelve to eighteen months) where there was a slight decline in the intensity of my civilian workload and military commitments. 4. The total cost had to be on the lower end in comparison to other graduate schools, with the likelihood that my GI Bill and scholarships would assume virtually all of the costs. 5. A good athletic program was ideal and would give me a sound reason to plan returns back to the school/area after I graduated. 6. It had to be a veteran-friendly school.

With these six preferences in mind, and with extensive legwork and careful analysis, I had five other opportunities that I was considering: Cornell, Indiana University, Notre Dame, Michigan, and Carnegie-Mellon. I had established communication with each of these schools, and their business school admissions staff had virtually assured me that I had a place at their institutions, pending a passing GRE and application submission. At best, these schools could satisfy four of my top six. And then there was USC.

I discovered the MBV program after a late-night Google search that led me to the website. For the most part, all six boxes were checked; I knew I had found a winner. So why was I compelled to pursue a business degree in the first place? I had two major motivations: 1. Originally, I wanted to complete my master's to make my mom proud, but she passed shortly after I applied and just after I was informally accepted after my Skype interview with James Bogle. I decided to make my efforts a tribute to my mom and her emphasis on education, self-improvement, and getting better. 2. I am on the cusp of making it to the executive level, and I needed a master's as a credential to keep me competitive with my peer group and in hopes that it would also serve as a differentiator on the military side.

Has the degree added tangible value to my professional life? Yes. I was offered an executive position at another reputable company shortly after graduation, and I had a couple more options that were comparable to my current position, but because of my wife's career and the fact that they were located far from Ohio, I opted to pass on them, at least for now. I am still in my current civilian position, which has afforded me the chance to continue to build depth and strengthen relationships, and I was also given a significant battalion staff role to start the new fiscal year after temporarily serving as executive officer, S2, S3, AS3 simultaneously during a three-week annual training. I am waiting for time and opportunity to intersect; in the meantime, I am learning, developing, and getting better personally and professionally.

(The following is a commencement speech written and delivered by Antonio Randolph for Cohort IV's final banquet.)

Class of 2017 USC MBV Cohort IV dinner message (Inspired by Takiesha Waites-Thierry, written by Antonio Randolph, edited by Adam Robertson)

> "The increasing time and shrinking value of money has found its antithesis: an education from the University of Southern California's Gordon S. Marshall School of Business. This is a timeless gift that we have earned, our families have commendably supported, and USC has impeccably packaged to set in motion perpetual prosperity, now and henceforth, thus adding tremendous value to struggling firms within corporate America, ingenious start-ups on the move, and optimistic non-profits striving to burgeon beyond the break-even point.

We all came to USC with some measure of concern about the difficulty of the MBV program's curriculum and some degree of doubt about our capabilities, but we leave here prepared to handle Thor's hammer, catch Captain America's shield, and endure Wolverine's sheers with regards to both life and business. With hopefully no blood, probably minimal sweat, but very likely many tears later, we leave USC as superheroes in our own right. Our families are proud of us, our kids are now Trojans-in-waiting, our bosses will now respect us more for our ties to the cardinal red-and-gold brand, our communities will want us to lead them . . . somewhere, and we can borrow Traveler, our famous galloping mascot, anytime we want for our company picnics—all of this thanks to our affiliation with USC, the Marshall School of Business, and the MBV program.

For some of us, we have fulfilled requirements that our foremothers and forefathers could have only dreamed of; and for others, we are adding another link to the strong chain of success that has been the mark of generation after generation; but for all of us, May twelfth will be a special day that bonds us to the USC fold and makes us the pride and joy of the Marshall family.

As each of us walks across this stage next week and accepts our degree, we know that our left hand will accept, in it, the promise to build upon the legacy of USC and Marshall both ethically and morally and with unwavering wherewithal and grit while our right hand will shake in agreement to give back, even if a dime at a time or a penny on the dollar, to keep OUR facilities modernized, OUR faculty top-notch, and OUR school and the MBV Program the biggest and best draw for future, high quality students like ourselves. (This paragraph has been placed on the wall in Popovich Hall on campus.)

Class of 2017 and MBV Cohort IV, greatness awaits us, so I command us all in the name of Tommy Trojan: Don't keep it waiting, go get it, make the best with it, stay bonded to our MBV family, remember that assets minus liabilities equal shareholders' equity, and, as always. FIGHT ON!!"

Josh Lagana—Cohort IV

My name is Josh Lagana and I'm a southern California native who served ten years in the army's military police corps. Growing up, I always had a strong interest in serving in the army, but I didn't think I would act on that interest until certain events occurred in my life, driving me to ultimately raise my right hand and make that commitment to serve my country.

I grew up with my time divided between divorced parents, but I spent the majority of my time with my mom. I was highly active as a kid and explored multiple sports, skateboarding, and snowboarding, and my mom did everything within her power to support and fund my expensive interests. Aside from playing sports, I was active academically as well. At the age of fifteen, during summer break after my freshman year in high school, I took the city bus to attend college courses at the local community college and continued to attend night classes during my sophomore year. I was motivated to graduate high school early and earn an academic scholarship. By my junior year in high school, I had already completed twenty-one college credits, and my dream seemed within my reach. But unfortunately my plan was hindered by an unpredicted and uncontrollable circumstance.

During my junior year of high school, I became severely ill and was bed-rested for almost two months. It put my education and active lifestyle to a complete halt. Doctors struggled to identify the problem and diagnose my illness, and expressed much concern for my health. After being put through a variety of tests, I began to get better without a definitive diagnosis. By this time, I had fallen too far behind in school to return with my classmates and was required to attend an alternative studies program in order to catch up. I was no longer able to pursue my goal of graduating high school early and the recovery period prevented me from getting back into sports and continuing my active lifestyle. When my graduating class was preparing for graduation, I was still playing catch-up, feeling a sense of disconnection from my peers. I knew earning any type of scholarship at this point was out of the question and that I wouldn't be able to afford college myself, which influenced my decision to act on my interest in joining the army.

On August 22, 2005, when I was seventeen, I boarded a plane to attend the US Army's Military Police Corps basic training and Advanced Fort Leonard Wood, Missouri, Individual Training (AIT). Having joined during the surge, I found myself deploying to Iraq immediately after graduating AIT at the age of eighteen, then with a one-year break between my next deployment to Iraq at the age of twenty, turning twenty-one overseas. While most of my friends were celebrating their graduation from college, I was celebrating my return from my second tour in Iraq.

During my time in service, I continuously strived to be the best and was determined to set myself apart from my peers. This drive led me to participate in the 2007 Army's Military Police Warfighter Challenge: an intense three-day competition between thirty-eight teams consisting of the army's best military police soldiers. My team placed third. Post competition, I attended Special Forces Assessment and Selection, Airborne School, Air Assault, Pathfinder, and, more importantly, college. Aside from my dedication to progressing in my army career, I placed education as a top priority, especially being that part of my reason for joining the service was to gain education benefits. During the entirety of my time in the army, I was always enrolled in college courses, even if it was only one course at a time to work toward a bachelor's degree in business administration. By the time I left the service, I had only a few courses remaining and graduated within a few months.

After graduating, I knew I wanted to continue pushing forward and sought out opportunities to develop professionally. I spent two years managing a small business startup, but didn't feel accomplished and felt lost, so I began researching master's programs in hopes that working toward higher education would not only help me grow professionally, but would give me guidance and direction. I found the MBV program and, without hesitation, applied, because I knew without a doubt it was what I needed.

The MBV program is far more than a master's degree program. It is a family of service members who share a common desire to develop, grow, explore, and accomplish greatness post their military service. It taught me valuable lessons, not only from the curriculum taught during sessions, but from the students themselves. The program brought together a very diverse group of veterans from different branches of service, with various backgrounds, and at different transition stages from their service. This mix of service members created an environment that allowed for classmates to learn from each other, which, to me, was invaluable.

Entering the program as a recently transitioned veteran, I was filled with uncertainty and doubt, but during the program, I built confidence in my ability to perform in the business world, gained a sense of direction that allowed me to regain focus, and discovered who I wanted to be. By no means did this come easily, but the MBV program put us into a supportive environment where we could be open and honest with one another without concern of being humiliated or judged. The confidence and focus I gained during the program led me to pursue a career as a consultant within a big-four consulting firm, where I apply the knowledge from the MBV program and the valuable skill sets from my military service.

Destiny Savage—Cohort III

I have always felt a call to service. Since a young age, I have been active in my community, either doing outreach for the homeless in Carlsbad, California, or representing my high school at Girls State. Service to others has always been at the forefront and the heart of what motivates me.

I have always been grateful to call the United States home, and had a strong desire to serve my country. When it came to college planning, I found that the ROTC scholarship would not only help me financially go to school but also help with my desire to be part of something bigger than myself. I ultimately chose USC because of their commitment to graduate leaders who aspire to assume the highest level of citizenship responsibilities.

As a public policy major, I had an amazing opportunity to serve as an intern to Senator Boxer. I worked with her policy team on many issues to include helping improve girls' education as well as the impact of this education on alleviating poverty within communities.

Upon graduation, I became a commissioned officer to the United States Navy and reported to USS *Paul Hamilton* (DDG 60). We were tasked with presence operations in the South China Sea, East China Sea, and Yellow Sea, as well as theater security cooperation exercises during Cooperation Afloat Readiness and Training (CARAT) Malaysia and CARAT Indonesia. As the public affairs officer and community relations project coordinator, I met a variety of people, including senior international officers participating in CARAT, young girls in primary school in Lumut, Malaysia, Japanese elders in a nursing home in Sasebo, Japan, and students at the Genesis School for Special Education in Singapore. Again, these events strengthened my resolve to pursue a career in an organization that seeks to improve the lives of so many remarkable people.

The navy afforded me an amazing opportunity to become a personnel exchange officer to the Royal Australian Navy. I directly represented the United States Navy as I was stationed abroad in Sydney, serving as a liaison between our two countries as we continued to develop our naval training and relationship. This experience allowed myself and my family to represent the US Navy on a global level, and living abroad was an opportunity that I will forever cherish.

In addition to the incredible people I met overseas during my deployments, I also had the distinct privilege to serve as a department head. Onboard USS *Pinckney* (DDG 91), I served as the engineering officer, in charge of sixty-six people responsible for the entire engineering systems of the ship. The five divisions with whom I was in charge became a family during extended periods of deployment and the division officers I worked to develop were responsible for the physical and mental safety of their sailors. On my final tour, I had an amazing opportunity to serve as the executive officer aboard USS *Cowpens* (CG 63). With a larger ship and various departments came different challenges, including sailors struggling with mental health, challenging domestic situations, family members living across country borders, and children with special needs. I was continually humbled by the resiliency of my sailors to take care of the persistent tasks associated with weapons equipment maintenance while dealing with their own issues. Learning through my sailors' experiences, I grew in my leadership abilities while gaining a greater understanding of the complexities of the human experience and what I could do to lessen the burden.

I recently completed my twelve years of service to the United States Navy. Upon getting out, I looked to the USC Marshall School of Business for continuing my education and developing my skills for the private sector. When I discovered the USC MBV program, I was delighted. I saw this as an incredible opportunity to harvest the opportunities USC brings (from the challenging curriculum to their strong business network) and to strengthen my opportunities as I transition to the private sector. As I have learned through my cumulative years of travel and education, immersive learning is the most effective. The MBV program widened the aperture of my experiences and equipped me with the tools necessary to fortify the relationships and interactions to move to the private sector. Upon graduation, I was able to use my USC network, specifically the board of counselors, to land an amazing and rewarding job with KPMG as a senior associate with their people and change practice, focusing on behavioral change management and talent management.

As I continue to build my brand and reputation in the private sector, I am able to draw on my experiences with the navy and MBV program, where I had the opportunity to interact with community leaders, military liaisons, and business leaders. The reflection on these experiences assists me in developing my own unique point of view, allowing me to bring invaluable and unique insight back to KPMG, augmenting best practices in leadership and positively affecting change.

Kathy Takayama—Cohort VI

I grew up as a navy brat. My dad was a pilot who retired as a captain. He taught me to be an eternal optimist, which is interesting coming from a man who experienced two stints behind bars—once as a child, a prisoner of the United States in the Japanese internment camps, and once as a Vietnam POW as guest at the Hanoi Hilton. He always said that we can't change our situation (like being behind bars), but we have control over the way we look at it. We can look at the good or look at the bad—we choose.

I attended college at the University of California at Davis. I earned my bachelor of science degree in applied mathematics with an emphasis in computer science and statistics, often tutoring along the way. While earning my way through school as a part-time bank teller, I fell for a navy recruiter's line: "Have I got a deal for you!" Since his deal included paying for my last two years of college and teaching, which I loved, I jumped at it. I served four and a half years as an officer at the Naval Nuclear Power School, eventually taking on a leadership role as the mathematics department division director.

Transitioning out of the military was pretty easy for me. I returned to the bank to re-open my account, and one thing led to another. Eventually, I was hired as a statistician for the executive officers at that hometown bank. My desk was in the same room as the operations team, whose members frequently needed help getting their computers to do what they needed them to. I truly love helping others. Within a few months, the IT manager recruited me, saying, "Since you're already doing our work in this office, why not join us?" In my new IT role, I was responsible for getting all of the software and hardware working throughout the bank, including learning about computer networks for the first time. Eventually, this grew into a program-management position managing the launch of new bank branches throughout northern California. I was responsible for getting the telephones, computers, networks, and data lines up and running.

While attending classes on how to install, configure, and maintain our networks, I impressed one of the instructors who recruited me to become a Novell-certified instructor teaching networking classes half-time and working half-time as a consultant for small companies in the Sacramento area. This allowed our instructors to bring real-life experiences into the classroom, differentiating our courses over other Novell- and Microsoft-certified courses offered by competitors. I was thrilled to be back in the classroom.

One of the students taking a Novell networking course thought I would be a great addition to a growing team at Hewlett Packard (HP), so after spending about six years as an IT program manager and two as an IT instructor, I joined HP as a research & development program manager. And it is there that I spent the majority of my career (twenty years). Each year I led more and more complex and visible programs, contributing to the success of HP, eventually leading enterprise security solutions programs that combined hardware, software, and firmware.

My most recent role at Hewlett Packard Enterprise (HPE) was as a senior program manager leading worldwide teams who delivered cutting-edge technology solutions to telecommunications companies. Our solutions combined many of the assets from HPE, including servers, storage, networking, cloud, and services into an easy to implement kit.

Everything was ticking on smoothly when, all of a sudden, there was a major shift in my life. On June 26, 2016, at 2 a.m., my husband (who seemed perfectly fine the day before) passed away from a massive heart attack at the age of fifty-six. We had been college sweethearts from UC Davis, married over twenty years. He was a financial advisor with a significant client base in northern California, so I assumed we would grow old together there. Nearly 2,000 people attended his celebration of life and I was amazed to hear the number whose lives he significantly impacted. He truly made a difference.

When Mike passed away, I took a couple of months off work. I contemplated the impact he had made on others. I was very well respected, successful, and a hard charger at work, but this made me think that if I were to die that day, I would only have coworkers at my funeral saying what a great worker I was and the impact I made at work. I had already started some volunteer activities, but after Mike passed away, my focus was more on volunteering than on working.

> HPE VERN: I am most proud that I founded the Employee Resource Group (ERG) at HPE in Roseville, Veterans Employee Resource Network (VERN), where I served as chairman of our board. VERN is a group of employees (both veterans and veteran supporters) who support veterans and veteran causes inside and outside of HPE. We grew from four members in November 2015 to over sixty today. Last year, we volunteered over 600 hours, donated $10,000 to the veteran community, and made a significant impact in recruiting, hiring, and retaining veterans.

> WVA/WVG: I am a lifetime and Plank member of Women Veterans Alliance (WVA), which started in January 2015. Today, over 4,000 lady vets receive our weekly newsletter. I was on the board of directors of the associated non-profit Women Veterans Giving (WVG) and led the conferences scholarship committee, which helps to empower women veterans to grow professionally by sending them to conferences.

Wreaths Across America: My family raises money to fund annual scholarships in my father's name by selling wreaths for Wreaths Across America. A portion of the wreath proceeds goes to his scholarship. I am one of the primary fundraisers for our cause.

Takayama Scholarship: Every year since Mike passed away, I have handed out $10K in scholarships in his name. This past year, with the assistance of half a dozen friends and family and through six months of planning, I led our first golf tournament fundraiser and silent auction with over 200 participants and raised $50,000. It's a lot of work, but it helps keep the memory of Mike alive for me, our family, friends, and in the local community.

Miscellaneous: I just like to help where I can. Last year, the HPE Roseville site had a couple of opportunities where I had the privilege of giving a helping hand alongside other HPE employees. We packaged up 20,000 meals for starving children, and assisted the Red Cross who was sorting through a warehouse of donations for the Paradise/Camp Fire victims. I am also always willing to donate to fundraisers—I consider sharing with those less fortunate among the privileges of being a full-time employee.

Recognition: my many volunteer activities have been recognized over the past few years. In 2018 and 2019, I was nominated for HPE's Women's Excellence Award for my leadership and contributions to not only HPE but the community. In 2018, the Sacramento Kings honored me as a Hometown Hero, and California assemblyman Kevin Kiley recognized me for my impact in the community. In 2019, the USC MBV program honored me as a veteran who served her country and continues to serve her community. I am most proud of being selected by the USC for the Order of the Arête, the highest honor bestowed on a USC graduate student.

Coincidentally, around the same time I was away from the office after Mike's passing, our business started shifting from the kits, and the program-management role wasn't as vital as it had been. Our business was also going through a reorganization, so I was assigned a new manager. This was a perfect time to shift careers. When my new boss asked what I wanted to do, I said I wanted to learn more about the rest of what goes on to make a business successful: finance, marketing, operations, etc.

So my manager worked me into a chief of staff role, and as our business unit grew, I also became our operations officer. In this new role, I constantly found ways to improve business processes to help make our group more efficient and successful, and worked closely with finance to plan and track our operational expenses.

As I was broadening my general business knowledge, I thought it was the time to start working on my MBA. My lifelong retirement goal was to get back into teaching by becoming a professor at a university (which requires a master's degree, for starters), where I could teach part-time (to hopefully cover medical insurance) and invest the rest of my time following my other passions of helping veterans and women, particularly young girls in technology. I imagined bringing my lifetime of experiences from the business world combined with my teaching experience (after being professionally trained by the US Navy and Novell on how to present in the classroom) to a business school where I could inspire future business leaders to spread what they learned from me, worldwide.

So I decided to start working on my MBA. Through one of the WVA events I attended, I heard about a special master's degree opportunity at USC that was specifically for veterans. You had to be a veteran to apply, and they only took the top 100 candidates per year. My initial response to James Bogle, the program director, was that I knew the cost of a two-year MBA from my nearby University of California at Davis, and was convinced an MBA from USC would be far more expensive. He convinced me that, with it being a one-year program and with the support of USC alumni and supporters, the cost could be reasonable. The game changer for me was the way he described the Trojan network and how graduates committed to the "Trojan to Trojan Promise" of responding to the reach of another alumni. This increased network that provides far more value than just an MBA on its own was what convinced me to invest the time, effort, and money into the USC MBV program.

I was thrilled to get the acceptance letter in the mail from the USC Marshall MBV program. In July 2018, I started my every-other-week trek from northern California on Thursdays, flying into LA for twelve hours of class/discussions on Friday and nearly as long on Saturday, followed by a trip home Sunday morning, ready to continue my full-time job with HPE each Monday. Some people (who don't have an MBA) say job experience is good enough and it's not worth getting an MBA, particularly for someone my age (fifty-six years young when I started). But to those naysayers I have to say, "You don't know what you don't know." And I've discovered you're never too old to create new opportunities.

The MBV program provides a solid and broad exposure to foundational concepts—accounting, finance, marketing, data analytics, and operations. And then there's the finesse where you learn from other's experiences around leadership, communication, and negotiation. And the course—by far my favorite—"Leadership: Power and Influence" was like icing on the cake. So many times during this program I said to myself and others: "I wish I would have known *that* ten or fifteen years ago!"

Throughout the program, our mentors encouraged us to find our passion and take steps toward a lifelong career, or at least a first step to our next career. I admit that I procrastinated, always convinced that getting through my case studies, papers, accounting, and finance homework plus keeping up with my full-time job (and sleep) was higher priority. After all, I already had a full-time, well-paying job at a large company, so I didn't *have* to find work. It wasn't until the last few weeks of school that I actively focused on figuring out what was next. One of my mentors asked what I wanted to do. I said that when I retired from HPE, I wanted to teach business classes at a university, thinking of our local Sacramento State University or a community college a few miles from my home. He said that while I was still on campus, I should look into the different departments at USC Marshall and talk to the department chairs to learn about what it's like to teach at a university.

It turned out there was one department that was right up my alley: data sciences and operations (DSO), which teaches:

Operations—my current role at HPE, so I have some experience.

Statistics—my degree from UC Davis is applied math with an emphasis in statistics and computer science, so I'm familiar with statistics.

Program management—I have been a program manager at HPE and other companies for over twenty years.

Supply chain—in my R&D program management role, I was very engaged with the supply-chain program manager.

So the DSO department teaches everything I've worked on in my career—as if it was designed specifically for me!

Then I started getting lucky.

The chairman of the DSO department happened to be married to our MBV managerial accounting professor, Smirty Randhawa (what are the chances of that?), who provided a very warm introduction. Even before I met Professor Randhawa, it seemed like he liked me! Later that day, Dr. Randhawa happened to be having lunch with our program director, James Bogle, who also provided him with insights about me. This truly was the Trojan network in action, helping a soon-to-be Trojan graduate. Additionally, I'm sure there were other Trojan contacts mentioning me to Dr. Randhawa whom I didn't even know about, like other professors and Dr. Turrill.

In a one-hour informational interview with Dr. Randhawa, I learned about his department and he found out more about me. I provided a resumé, but wasn't looking for an immediate position. He saw me as a jack-of-all-trades for his department, so was interested in me as a potential professor. He said all fall positions were staffed the spring before, so he didn't think they had a position for me. I said I wasn't looking for a position that fall—the following spring would be plenty early enough. Just in case, he referred me to his scheduling professor.

The scheduling instructor said he did have all classes staffed with professors for the fall, but at the last minute, one of the adjunct professors who was teaching undergrads happened to drop out, and they needed an operations professor. What are the odds of that—a position opening up that I was actually qualified to teach (as an adjunct, only a master's degree is required, not a PhD)?

It turned out this particular class was beginning operations for undergraduate students, which has many sections and several instructors. They want it to be consistent across all sections, so the majority of the quizzes, exams, homework, and slide decks have already been worked out or would be created by the team of professors. What a great way for a beginning instructor like me!

To top it off, back at HPE, our CEO announced at the beginning of May (the month I walked for my MBV graduation) that HPE would start offering retirement transition, where I could work part-time. Who would have imagined that?

So after a lot of incredibly lucky circumstances, amazing timing, plus assists from the Trojan network, I am getting ready to teach my first classes as a university professor at one to the top business schools in the nation, and continue to work half-time for HPE!

Within two months of graduating from the MBV program, I had sold my house, packed up, and moved from my hometown of thirty years, where I thought I would spend the rest of my life. The passing of my husband was a tragedy, but had that not happened, my life would have never turned in this direction. My son just completed his MBA six months before I finished mine, and is now 100 percent independent of me financially, which also gave me the freedom to do whatever I wanted.

Even with my volunteering, in order to free up time to work on my MBV, I had to significantly decrease my volunteer time in the past year. That meant less time leading the WVG scholarship committee—someone else stepped up to take the lead. At HPE, since of our four-person board I was the one that led most volunteer events and veteran partnership engagements, we expanded our board to ten members and raised new leaders in the past year, with me just providing consulting from the sideline. Now, when I leave northern California to start a new career in southern California, both veteran groups can stand on their own—last year, that would have been a huge challenge.

So since starting the MBV program just one year ago, many pieces of my life have fallen neatly into place: my personal circumstances after my husband's passing and my son graduating, my work with the early retirement, and the advancement of my volunteer groups all just in time for me to take advantage of the incredible opportunity to pivot my life and start my accelerated retirement plan of becoming a university professor. I attribute this pivot of a lifetime to the USC MBV program. Not only from the incredible learning from the top-notch professors, but—more importantly—the many Trojan connections. Without USC's MBV program, my life would have continued in the same hometown at the same job doing the same thing for at least the next half-dozen years until I was ready to retire from HPE.

I am incredibly lucky and thankful to be where I am today, and am forever grateful to the Trojan network. Fight on!

CHAPTER 8

ON THE HIGH WIRE

Throughout my experience with the veterans, the words of Warren Bennis kept reminding me that "managers do it right," but "leaders do the right thing." Before Bennis, Peter Drucker said that "efficiency is doing things right; effectiveness is doing the right thing." With a constant stress on efficiency and cost control, I came to the conclusion that we were doing the right thing. We were being effective in designing and delivering a first-class education experience to a relatively small market that, from what we knew, needed this type of program to enable their transition from military to civilian life and careers. We were meeting a critical need of an underserved group—one percent of the public who volunteered to serve for the benefit of the other 99 percent of American citizens.

My generation, the Silent Generation, were mostly conscripted into service in our early twenties or when we graduated from college. I taught for one semester and then responded to my draft notice. It wasn't so much the concept of service that drove us, but duty, responsibility, and obligation. Fully understanding this difference between service and duty was probably my biggest insight into the differences with this group of volunteers, who stepped up and stepped forward to uphold the Constitution of the United States, and thus committed to protecting other residents and citizens of our country. Their service mentality permeated most of what we did together. I'll share a small example of this orientation. If I was perceived to need assistance, there would be four students on their feet, not asking if they could help, but taking action to help immediately.

The program was designed to be efficient, however, with only one year of residency required, and meeting on every other weekend for two days throughout the year. This cut the cost of a two-year business degree in half, and required only half of the time. Like other executive formatted programs, the alternate Friday/Saturday format allowed students to be fully employed *and* be full-time students. This strategy, however, didn't include a second year of specialization in a particular subject that a full two-year business degree would provide. However, several of our graduates took a second year (or more) to obtain a second master's degree in a specialized field, or changed their focus entirely. For example, one student, who had been an accountant when we met him, took a two-year program in health administration after finishing his MBV so he could change his professional focus entirely. Several have enrolled in doctoral programs as well. In each cohort, there have been ten to twelve students who want to continue their education to give back through higher education.

For the first six years, the faculty taught in the program on overload, so our program didn't take faculty away from other courses that they were teaching. Outside of my partner, James Bogle, and other management staff, there were no additional faculty hired to teach in the program, so we were more efficient in the use of faculty as well.

In reference to the university, USC has had a consistent positive involvement with the military since World War I, when an ROTC unit was established on campus, and the campus became very involved with the war effort. So, for over 100 years, we have committed university resources and our involvement in support of the military, and most recently we have become one of the highest-ranked universities seen as favorable to veteran education and being welcoming to veterans. We were the first West Coast school to welcome the Warrior-Scholar project to campus in the summer, and to add a week of business education to the program.

Since 1880, the university has been committed to its urban location in Los Angeles, as well as to its involvement in the surrounding community. There were opportunities to move the campus out of our urban context, and each time, the university recommitted itself to both its urban beginnings and also to engaging the local community as an employer of choice and a community partner. All its recent strategic plans include a commitment to the public good and efforts to positively address local and larger issues that are in need of solutions. With an approach to blend both basic and applied research and to encourage community involvement both on and off campus, the university has consistently supported a community outreach effort and programs.

The MBV is one of these community service and outreach programs. A major research effort in 2013 by the School of Social Work's Center for Innovation and Research on Veterans and their families found that there were multiple needs of veterans transitioning out of the military that needed to be addressed. Up to 80 percent didn't have jobs, 40 percent weren't secure with housing, and many left with physical and mental-health issues, according to the lead author of the study, Carl Castro. Education assistance was one of the top three expressed needs of transitioning veterans.

Also, the way the idea and the program began at Marshall was our response to an original enquiry of the California Department of Veterans Affairs, through retired marine colonel, Rocky Chavez. Our response by designing and delivering a program was specifically to an expressed community need. Appropriately, the 2018 USC Strategic Plans subtitle was "Answering the Call." I was also impressed with a values statement expressed in more than one strategic plan for the university that outlined this set of values: ". . . the values of the Trojan family, including caring and respect for one another as individuals, appreciation of diversity, team spirit, strong alumni networks, and a commitment to service," is closely aligned to the expressed values and culture of the MBV program, its students, and alums.

In terms of the student body, USC is typically first or second in the number of international students in attendance. In a time when embracing diversity and inclusiveness is desired, the MBV is performing quite well. Sixteen percent of our students are naturalized citizens, which could be seen as a proxy measure of our international population plus one actual international alum from Britain. Compared with 40 percent of the military on active duty being ethnic minority groups, about 60 percent of the MBV cohorts are in those groups, the largest difference being Hispanic. Only about 12 percent of the active military are Hispanic, while about 30 percent are represented in MBV, and 16 percent of MBV students are Asian/Pacific Islanders. So, diversity, as typically defined, is greater in the MBV than in other programs. As I mentioned in Chapter 1, this diversity most likely reflects our location in southern California.

The design of the program fosters inclusiveness, at least in terms of the veterans. Only veterans can apply and be selected. This homogeneous characteristic does not stifle the other dimensions of diversity and inclusion, since we find much diversity within the individuals in the program in terms of their background, work experience, style, preference, personal values, and decision-making, as well as issues like risk-taking ability or tolerance for ambiguity and uncertainty.

The cohort structure and lock-step curriculum create greater equity among students, as do our community values of collaboration, sharing, and helping. Those students with a special background in a specific subject area, or who were business majors as undergraduates, are encouraged to help others without that background rather than compete with them. These values plus a commitment to everyone's success in a rank-agnostic policy also increases the likelihood of greater equity among students. We've been fairly successful in keeping external status concerns from tilting the playing field in someone's favor.

> "I had always thought my educational endeavors were mine alone to pursue and accomplish. I quickly learned that any other program would have been exactly that, but not the MBV program. My experience is compared to an overseas tour where you and your unit are closer and tighter than any unit stateside. If one person struggles, we all struggle. If one person succeeds, we all celebrate and are proud to say they are on our team!" (Richard Herrera, Cohort III)

Recruiting

We would use our recruiting informational sessions to bring our current students in to talk with the recruits about their own experience in the program. I observed and processed their comments and mannerisms carefully, from off to the side, to understand their perceptions of their experience. These brief appearances and presentations by various students were insightful for me and uplifting. We would consciously pick different personalities, some extroverted and some more introverted, to speak. To my amazement and positive surprise, their presentation and personal stories were always positive, and real. Real, meaning they shared the challenges and pitfalls they faced and endured, but always ending on a positive note. They appeared to be well integrated into our community and program, and congruent with their own aspirations.

No one ever let us down or left the recruits with negativity about the program or unanswered questions. They never avoided a question, even when an accurate response might reflect poorly on the management team in attendance, the three or four of us. One of our strongest recruiting techniques was simply to invite the potential applicant to sit in on a class, to actually experience the dynamic of the live classroom.

These recruiting meetings left me with a sense of meaningfulness, that we were doing the right thing. Speaking to recruits after each information session, I always talked with someone who had decided to apply. And the most passionate recruits, interestingly, would typically be older, and say such things like "I feel like I've come home again" and "This is what I've been looking for."

And it was our current students as well as recent alums who would be most powerful in their statements about their experience in the program. We would hurry through our introduction to get the students in front of the recruits more quickly. We were never disappointed. On the contrary, it was inspiring for us, the management team, to hear how passionately and eloquently the students would present the program, their experience, and their responses to questions.

Cohort Culture

While the group as a whole didn't monitor others' deviant behavior very much, there were norms that grew, based upon our interactions, our conscious discussion of appropriate and expected behavior during the first month, and of course, the ethics and ethos of their own military background. The common background in the military created a firm, stable, platform on which grew a strong dynamic of focus, support, and high performance.

No one preached positive behavior or positive leadership, but the dominant, expressed presentation of oneself was typically positive, and optimism became a habit, often by choice. This wasn't 100 percent, as there were some unhappy moments and complaints about issues like a heavy workload, going too fast, not being clear enough in some of the classes, and being overscheduled. But the good-natured ribbing of the various branches never seemed to go too far or to get out of control, and often broke the tension.

They had their own interventions, when at times, something needed to be done, such as recognizing important events like birthdays, weddings, childbirth, family or friends' deaths, or serious illness. I think, given their background of injury to self or other loss of friends and comrades, they knew how to be sensitive and caring in the face of these critical life events.

Two of those events were apparent in Cohort V. One was our first child born to an active student. The baby was born six weeks prematurely, the night before our first class session in August, causing our student-mother to miss two weekends of class time. The cohort, even though we had not had any class sessions together except for orientation, initiated a gift and card for the new mother, and then stepped up to help her academically in what she had missed.

The second event was when Jamie, a member of the management team, left for two weeks to visit her ailing father in the Philippines. The second weekend, the class initiated a card across both sections of the cohort of concern to welcome her back. To the best of my knowledge, everyone in Cohort V signed it.

The veterans in the MBV tended to be very family-oriented, and family was consistently a top value expressed in a number of ways—sometimes formally in our values activity we used to wrap up our time together in May, but at many other times as well, including on our biweekly discussion board.

When asked about the future, whether it was career or money-focused, or the present, family was always a dominant theme. I suspect being absent from their families for extended periods on deployment would, by itself, create a strong focus. Whether the focus on families is unique to veterans is not clear, but the amount of conscious attention and discussion paid to families in the veterans' space makes very apparent the primacy of family.

A Culture of Caring

The above examples represent a culture of caring that extended to all members of the cohort and their families. The motto: "thirty-eight in, thirty-eight out" was established early in Cohort I and carried forward. There was a community commitment to the success of all members of the cohort. It wasn't a competition for achievement or rank within the class academically. This norm extended to the academic assistance of cohort members by those who had either special training or experience in a particular field of study. For example, in Cohort I, there was a CPA who voluntarily gave tutorials to those who needed help in accounting. In accounting, this was a fairly frequent occurrence across all the cohorts. In each cohort, there were volunteers who helped organize the assignments weekly so as to help everyone keep up to date and prepare for what was required each weekend we were in session. This type of academic volunteerism was in addition to regular study groups that met weekly to share the workload and discuss problems and cases. Obviously, a caution that needed to be made was one of academic integrity, where if an assignment was to be done individually without consultation or discussion with others, these helping arrangements stopped at that boundary. This had to be discussed so that students did not violate the rules, thinking that they were helping each other collaboratively.

On Saturday night at the total team meeting, the first agenda item was to celebrate someone's major event, a promotion, a new job, an award, etc. They cared about each other's progress, both inside as well as outside the program. The norm of caring, including giving and receiving help, was carefully nurtured within the program intentionally, rather than hoping it would happen, or crafting a culture of independence. While we teach and value an internal locus of control, we couch that orientation within a context of collaboration, openness, and ultimately, trust among members of the learning community. However, we often have experiential games and activities that are competitive, and the students always enjoy these structured competitive team games.

This common background of service and training made each cohort easy to deal with and compelling to be with. It was always the same, my leaving home at 7 a.m. to be on campus at 7:30, and not feeling very energetic or enthusiastic about the morning until I entered the classroom. At that moment, everything changed, and my outlook became, and felt, congruent and energized. This was the right thing to be doing, and my life, professionally, was meaningful at that moment and throughout the entire experience. It was not an awareness created by my thinking or by decision, but by being present within an arena of volunteers with a common background, a common mission, and a commitment to brothers and sisters with whom they probably did not serve, but with whom they now feel are committed to a common goal.

In the brief time we were together in this learning environment, we set aside rank, branch of service, and other differences that would not be meaningful in this competency quest or in the next act professionally. But, this was also a key issue in our relationships, that while military rank was set aside, our rank (program management) was accepted, making the classes and program work (mostly) smoothly. We, as the management group, were rarely challenged in our positional authority, but it was quite clear to me that we also were the subjects of great expectations for both our performance and presence. Similar to my challenge to them, the question to us was always there: do we show up, and how do we show up? As we watched and observed them regularly and consistently, so did they of us. It was a powerful integration of role and function, but everyone knew their part, and expected others to do their part, as well. It seemed clear to me that our role wasn't merely administrative, but one of leading, being able to walk the talk representing the concepts, values, and skills of the very topic of leadership we discussed within our sessions and the broader program. I'll share a comment on graduation and separation that represents the experience of (trying) to let go:

> "It's Saturday night and for some strange reason I check my USC email. I didn't check it because of a routine that I developed over the last ten months as I would check emails on Monday after a class weekend. I checked it because I already missed being part of the cohort. We graduated yesterday, and it was bittersweet. I am happy to not have homework or a school project roaming through my thoughts. It has only been twenty-four hours, and I am a bit saddened that I won't be spending time with the cohort on a regular basis. I don't think I was ready for this to be over. . . ." (James Galindo, Cohort III)

Program Outcomes

A quick snapshot of outcomes is that we have graduated about 97 percent of the students, and our career employment numbers have about 91 percent of our graduates employed within ninety days of commencement. This includes those who are staying in current employment or on active duty. We are working on a more rigorous outcome measure that will assess whether students not only are employed at or just after graduation, but if they achieved the goal they set when they entered the program. This is the personal goal and personal growth measure, and so far we are running about seven out of ten graduates saying they did achieve their personal career-growth goal. It is in this gap that our career service program is working hardest in matching needs and wishes with opportunities. Education programs are not placement programs as such, and make it clear that they don't guarantee placement (since this is an individual effort issue), but MBA programs are constantly judged on this outcome, and this discussion within the broader national culture is putting pressure on institutions to pay more attention to it so that graduates come out prepared for the future economy in which they will spend their adult lives.

Personal Learning and Insights

I've talked a lot about what we did, the level and quality of the outcomes, problems, and individual challenges we faced, and the level of engagement we experienced. So, trying to summarize what I learned in these past six years will necessarily have some major redundancies in the summary of the insights.

The first idea that comes to mind is a general observation and conclusion. Our expectations may drive our perceptions, but by being aware, paying attention, listening, and observing, our perceptions gradually—no, actually, rapidly—begin to change. Did I expect stern, tough, grim veterans focused on being tough and invulnerable while being distanced from relationships because of the challenges and threats they endured? Was I expecting wounded warriors who needed special treatment because of their injuries, both physical and emotional? Was I expecting heroes showing up with uniforms ablaze with medals and ribbons? Was I expecting resistance to ideas of emotional intelligence and empathy? Was I expecting strict hierarchical behavior, rank-conscious behavior, and status differences?

Suggesting those types of expectations would probably be telling as to some of my thoughts as I entered into my work with the program, the faculty, and the individuals who were admitted.

First, we expected and planned for a small group the first year—twenty, to be exact, as some form of break-even point financially, actually on the lean side. We admitted twice that number in Cohort I, lost a couple early, and finished with thirty-eight. At the end of Cohort VI in May of 2019, we had 392 alums successfully graduated. Our MBV family is still growing, with ninety-two new students enrolled in Cohort VII.

Second, they were very responsive, open, and focused. As I grew to know them both as individuals and a group, and over all six cohorts, I found them to be personable, friendly, respectful, and in touch with their competencies regarding what they needed to improve and where they needed to grow. They were committed to their mission of completing their transition work, graduating with a master's degree, and moving on in their lives and careers, either where they currently were or onto some new challenge, and in some cases, beginning their own businesses.

Often this new or continued engagement involved a non-profit effort of some sort, one they were doing when they entered the program, or one they started either in the program or subsequently. (See Kathy Takayama's personal story in Chapter 7 as an excellent example. There are many such examples within the other 43 alums profiled throughout.) We recently surveyed our alums and found that just over 60 percent of them were actively engaged in community volunteering or non-profit work, often in organizations that serve veterans. The following visual demonstrates the amount of involvement the veterans have in various organizations that have a charitable or non-profit focus. The visual includes the names and logos of the various groups and activities.

Health

Education

Children

Community

Veterans

We found the same dynamic when we needed volunteers to show up at recruiting events, alumni panels, or any other community or ceremonial event. We always had plenty of volunteers. In fact, we often have to deal with the disappointment of those who wanted to help, but either weren't asked or didn't know about the opportunity. I had never faced that willingness and active stepping-up to assist without any prompt or encouragement. This was unique in my experience and incredibly useful, helpful, collaborative, and caring. This behavior and willingness to help significantly affected my emotional modality. It changed my experience and how I experienced the students. As much as I see myself as a constant, I responded uniquely and consistently to this behavior, and it gradually changed my own sense of congruence as I experienced the program and my role in it. It created a sense of well-being while changing my own sense of membership. I became closer to the students as individuals and as a group. I experienced a greater sense of trust and openness with them. I valued my time with them, and I increasingly felt comfortable in our relationship, meaning open and congruent, as well as interested in their well-being. With so many within the cohort, it was difficult to engage with all very deeply, but with those who sought me out, we could establish ongoing communication and a useful relationship. That, to me, was where I could help them grow.

These core values of volunteerism, service, caring, and a sense of community with those with a common background were consistent and shaped the way I began viewing the world and opportunities. Any sense of cynicism about other generations of students or our current condition disappeared with my sense of this entire group as positive, contributing, and committed citizens, who, rather than exhibit characteristics of heroes or broken people, stood out as the best of us collectively. Their capabilities, competencies, and values create hope for our collective future when they become employed and deployed in civilian roles in which they can contribute to our collective welfare and growth and take on leadership roles and achieve impact in their service.

Leadership and service were often discussed together, and students often brought up the concept of servant leader. While the concept is sound, I don't use the term "servant," because of the implications of the word. As mentioned earlier, I don't use concepts of subordinate or follower when working with students on developing their leadership competencies. When expecting everyone in the class to develop their influence capabilities to achieve impact, I want all on the same level and not focused on learning hierarchical nomenclature and subordinate, or even servant values.

"Mission first, people always," is a strong military motto, used across branches of service. While it's relatively simple in concept, it's powerful in meaning, always focused on performance and goal achievement, while constantly taking care of and empowering your people.

One of our marine officers from Cohort II accepted a position with Amazon in a fulfillment center in Tennessee in the summer of 2015. In 2015, *The New York Times* ran a couple of investigative reports about the reported abuse of employees in Amazon in terms of the work pressure on production and productivity, and I used the articles as a case in the summer of 2015 with Cohort III, and asked our marine to comment on the article as he would a case. He wrote back the following reply, sharing his discussion of his approach to leadership with the eighty-eight employees under his supervision.

My leadership philosophy: "Mission first, people always!"

Mission: The pack team takes pride in consistently meeting objectives while maintaining the highest standards of safety, quality, and area readiness.

People: As the area manager, my mission is YOU. I care about the success and well-being of every associate in our team. As a member of the pack team, it is my desire to see every person thrive professionally and personally. The majority of my energy and time will be spent taking care of you and maintaining the integrity of our team.

As we continue to obsess over our customers and make history every day, we must commit two things to ourselves and each other. First, that we will treat each other with respect and dignity. Second, we will win with integrity. Thank you for your hard work and commitment. I

> look forward to working alongside you and promise to live these words through my personal example every day. Hold me to it!"

> "Overall, this was VERY well received by my associates. Many came up to me afterward and said thank you and that no manager had ever invested so much in them before." (Alex Urankar, Cohort II)

The message was strong, "I'm here to serve you and make sure you have everything you need to be successful, and you need to hold me accountable for this!" The response was unexpected, but probably not unusual in that type of working context: "No one has ever said anything like that to us before!" While the motto, "Mission first, people always" is a well-known military statement, the second part of the statement is rarely communicated to the employees who are doing the work in other segments of the economy. I would change the concept of servant leader to leadership as (or is) service.

In addition to the concept of service, humility was often closely aligned. In the first six years of the program, the expression of arrogance was mostly absent. One could stretch occasionally to find arrogant behavior, but it was not noticeable to me. And in my earlier expectations, I might have expected to experience a display of arrogance within and outside of the classroom, but at least from my observation and perception, there was extremely little of this type of behavior. Actually, I think it was more a display of humility that was constantly apparent, so if there was arrogant behavior, it paled in comparison to the expression of humility. Over all the six years, this was a significant difference between these veteran groups and other groups I have known and worked with.

Transition and Transformation

The purpose and goal of the program was to successfully assist veterans in their transition from the military to a civilian life and career. The Transitions Assistance Program (TAP) offered by all the branches was not sufficient in depth, scope, or content to assist senior leaders, NCOs, and officers to make this complex transition successful. We were invited to provide a graduate-level experience to prepare veterans for a business career either in an established organization or in their own entrepreneurial endeavors. We answered that call.

By engaging in a cohort model with lock-step requirements, we created a common experience on top of a common background for membership that has led to a more transformational experience and outcome. While camaraderie was achieved to replace that lost upon separation, a purpose beyond self and a new personal identity were more distant aspirations.

"The term cohort invokes a collective, communal, and cooperative feeling. It baselines a common objective through a holistic, comprehensive lens. And, this is the unique identifier, competitive advantage between our MBV program and all other MBA programs. The emphasis on real world, applicable entrepreneurship infused with effective leadership and combined with strategic vision separates 'doers' from 'talkers'. . . . While other MBA programs invite direct competition, resulting in rivalries and oppositions, this MBV program cultivates teamwork and promotes solidarity. This is a product of our shared experiences in uniform, coupled with the command climate set by our leaders. The tone of open and honest dialogue, sincere, authentic, and genuine concern for our teammates (not classmates) was the collaborative result of mutually defined factors of success (created and agreed upon by all fifty-one members of Cohort III). This collective agreement to ensure cohort-level success stemmed from the ideology that the program and team were bigger than any one individual." (Raymond Kim, Cohort III)

As the students opened themselves up to greater possibilities for themselves and witnessed others in the cohort engaging similarly, members of each cohort saw the potential for playing bigger or playing in a bigger game than they had thought possible before the program. Thus, for many, transition became transformation.

This grew and was nurtured in the context of a new family whose values are supportive, collaborative, and helping stemming from program policy and cohort designed expectations. By reducing the competitive nature of the program as well as leveling the playing field through reducing impact of rank, branch of service, and any other external factor that might interfere in the collective commitment to all members' success, the members focused not only on themselves, but also on the community or cohort level of everyone's success.

This elevation of focus, unusual in an academic context, changed not only the culture but the awareness of each individual that they were not alone. In a culture focused on "no one left behind," the main orientation for the members was how to help other members, their brothers and sisters. And the help they provided could come in many forms, from housing to homework to tutorials to transportation to invitations to social hours to make sure everyone felt included. Several times I heard the comment that the MBV was the Trojan family on steroids! They were proud of this closeness and more and more throughout the six years, this sense of common membership was shared across cohorts to include all 392 alums and the current cohort of students.

This collective consciousness was the beginning of a new purpose beyond self. Included in that purpose was the awareness of new possibilities for oneself because of the example being set by others in the cohort. More and more students gained an awareness that they didn't need to settle for a job or career or life that did not challenge them or provide personal satisfaction. This collective awareness became contagious, and in Cohort VI, five more students opted out of their current jobs on the last day of the semester.

Transformation starts with greater awareness, leading to greater openness to possibilities that were not seen previously, followed by a greater sense of self-acceptance and well-being. This higher level of awareness leads to greater positive self-regard as well as regard for others in their similar quest, and ultimately to greater optimism and growth. And this awareness of greater capability, as well as an increase in aspirations, was apparent as we continued through the year.

I would also describe this observation as a collective intervention into all of our lives, mine as well as theirs. We not only provided caring and collaboration, we affirmed each person in their capabilities and observed growth, and nurtured each other's optimism.

I've selected some quotes from the discussion board responses to a question I posted about observed changes in each individual and in Cohort VI as a whole.

> "The things we have learned will be useful, but the people we have become will change the world." (Ryan Long)

> "The most notable change that I've seen in our cohort as a whole is our exponential increase in confidence." (David Firouzi)

> "The feeling of the person next to you would do anything in their power to help the other succeed is evident in the program." (Irv Dingle)

> "The most profound change I recognize in myself is knowing that help is just a question or person away." (Eric McWright)

I would also encourage you to reread Mike Guadan's personal story attached to Chapter 7, a portion of which I will quote here, where he responds to the question of how to deal with survivor's guilt, a common question of combat veterans.

> "In my opinion, we do it by living extraordinary lives. . . . Extraordinary is about living life as if we had a second chance. If any of the heroes were able to live again, can you imagine what kind of life they would live? I think about that often, when I need perspective or get angry. . . . Most importantly, I believe they would extend their hands and help those less fortunate. (Extending) that hand is what transition and veteran community is all about. It is what separates us from those who seek individual fame and glory. As veterans, we must seek collaborative success and share our knowledge and opportunities." (Michael Guadan, Cohort IV)

And another comment from Nikkea Devida in Cohort VI represents the struggle to achieve personal transformation, and why it's so important and necessary.

> "I contend it takes much more courage to know ourselves, to love ourselves, to be at peace with ourselves, and be comfortable in our own skin . . . so that we can then be courageous enough to simply be present enough to connect with another human being authentically . . . so that they know they are not alone." (Nikkea Devida, Cohort VI)

These responses represent a small sample of comments and assessments that represent transformational thinking and aspiration. I've included a number of additional comments from Cohort VI in Chapter 6, which looks at personal growth and change.

The final concept I learned to respect and look forward to regularly was the high degree of engagement I experienced working with the veterans as students. It was this face-to-face engagement that I experienced each day as I greeted each class that led to my sense of congruence and meaning. Being fully engaged for brief, intensive moments, focused on both common and individual goals and aspirations put me into a state I can only describe as flow between myself and my students. So the question for me will be: Did my embedded engagement change anything for me? Did it enrich my life and add value to this year-long transition graduate degree program and the almost 400 veteran students who committed to it? I think the answer is an emphatic, "Yes!"

A Discussion of Lived Experience

I knew at the time I began writing this story that I was no longer an objective observer in the typical academic sense of the role. I had become emotionally captured by the phenomenon I was observing and to which I had serious responsibilities as academic director. I settled on the embedded condition after being introduced to the embedded journalists in the wars in Iraq and Afghanistan through newspapers and journals. For the journalists, being embedded in a military unit led to criticism that they could not be objective in their reporting. In my case, I added the concept of engagement, as I was drawn into my relationships with my students as I spent almost every contact hour of their program with them, as well as quite a few outside hours in other activities. And as I got to know them as people, my sense of engagement in my work and the students was greater than most any other engagement I had in my career dealing with topics of leadership, personal growth, and organizational and management concepts and skills.

The intensity and challenge of this deep engagement created a meaningful capstone to a long career in education. I became very grateful for this opportunity, and instinctively knew there would be no easy exit strategy from my involvement.

I accepted that as my positive fate freely chosen.

The Classroom As My High Wire

In my living room in Los Angeles, there is a piece of folk art (artist: Chris Roberts-Antieau). It is unusual in that it is made of fabric, and since mine is a copy of the original, it is behind glass. It shows seven cartoonish people in a pyramid on each other's shoulders on a high wire; beneath them are four people looking up in astonishment at their daring and risk-taking. The seven high-wire performers are smiling, and under the wire is a banner stating, "Life is the wire. Everything else is just waiting!" The original artwork I saw in a gallery in New Orleans in 2015 when we visited our son, who is making movies in that city. I was instantly struck with its meaning, and felt it spoke to me, but it was too expensive for me to consider purchasing it. My wife surprised me on our anniversary with my copy two years later.

The art and saying refer to the Flying Wallendas, a high-wire troop that has been active for over fifty years. The grandchildren and great-grandchildren are carrying on for the grandfather, Kurt Wallenda, who fell to his death in his final walk across a wire stretched between two hotels in Puerto Rico with no safety net in 1978. He was seventy-three. His wife, also a high-wire professional, said that during his preparation for the act, he focused on not falling, rather than on walking the wire successfully. He'd never focused on "not falling," and it determined his entire preparation routine of checking and rechecking all the safety procedures that he'd previously assumed were secure.

Later, Warren Bennis would call this the Wallenda Factor: not focusing on success but on *not failing*. When focused on success, one is fully engaged,

367

persistent, self-confident, and in possession of an almost selfless awareness. "Life is the wire," Karl Wallenda allegedly said. "Everything else is just waiting."

While I was initially puzzled why this saying was so impactful for me, it gradually became clear. My wire was the classroom, where my sense of being fully engaged with the veterans and operating at my best professionally was extraordinary. There was a lot of waiting in between my sessions, on the wire, in preparation.

There are times when we operate at our best, when we are challenged and required to step up and perform, where we feel totally congruent at that moment, and almost selfless—totally engaged. These moments may be fewer than we would like, and there is a lot of waiting in between. One of my Navy SEALs, Ty Smith (whom you met at the end of Chapter 3), shared a story with us that his highest point in his navy career was bringing all twenty-two men in his unit home safely from Afghanistan. He said there would never be another experience or achievement in his life that would top this, and he understood that. It struck me that he had walked his high wire successfully without a safety net and understood the personal impact of his effectiveness in achieving his mission.

Here is his story as he has written it.

Homecoming
(Ty Smith, Cohort III)

"My final deployment as a SEAL Operator in the summer of 2014 was by far the climax to a long and accomplished career in the SEAL Teams. It was literally the definition of 'going out with a bang.' During the nearly five months that we spent operating at the mouth of the Tangi Valley of Baraki Barak District, Logar Province, Afghanistan, we found ourselves in eight-to-eighteen-hour gunfights with the enemy twice a week, religiously, and for the entirety of the 2014 'fighting season.' During this deployment, I checked just about every metaphorical box that a special operator would dream of checking throughout a career in the special operations community. It was the deployment that dreams and legends are made of. But I knew in my heart there would be a severe price to pay once we got home. I've been around the community long enough to know that the injuries unseen are sometimes most fatal.

But before I get ahead of myself, I think it's important for me to paint a full picture of the weight I felt as the senior enlisted leader of SEAL Team One, Echo Platoon in the summer of 2014. Leadership is sometimes defined by the ultimate goal of the group being led. In my case, the summer of 2014 was a test of my capabilities as a leader because of what I had deemed to be my ultimate goal of the summer. While the Special Operations Task Force (SOTF) believed that our goal was to pacify the Tangi Valley of Taliban fighters in order to ensure a safe retrograde of American forces from the Tangi Valley, I believed my goal was much more important. I knew that accomplishing the goal of the SOTF would potentially come at the price of my losing one or several of my men considering the fact that the current rules of engagement (ROEs) were not in our favor, forcing us to work during daylight hours instead of at night like we would prefer. Also, we were vastly outnumbered as one of only three active special operations forces in the area that were still operating in highly contested enemy territory. I knew that my ultimate goal was to return to the US in the late fall of 2014 with all of my men and gear intact.

The burden of leadership I carried that summer, leading my men into combat at the most intense level, multiple times a week for nearly five months straight was beginning to really take its toll on me by the end of the deployment. By the end of the deployment, we had already been in more than fifty gunfights with the enemy that would later be confirmed to have resulted in the elimination of more than 500 enemy fighters in the Tangi Valley; we were numbered at fewer than thirty operators, and when engaged by the enemy, we were absolutely unforgiving. During that summer we had endured more rocket attacks than I've ever encountered in my career; several 'green on blue' incidents, this means that our friendly Afghan forces had actually turned their weapons on us and tried to attack us; we had also witnessed several of our friendly Afghan forces and army special operations forces wounded during the summer. For me, it was a daily feeling of, 'It's only a matter of time before one of my men falls. The odds are against us; if we keep operating at this pace and at this level, someone is eventually going to get hurt, and possibly fatally.' I can't begin to tell you how that feeling affected me on a daily basis as I prepared to take my team into harm's way and purposely kick the hornets' nest on a weekly basis.

By the end of the tour, I think I had pretty much reached my peak as an operator. Nothing tests you like actual combat. We train relentlessly and our training is as realistic as it comes. That's the reason we perform so well overseas and under fire. But when it comes down to it, nothing tests the operator like actual combat. During that tour, I had been repeatedly tested, and fortunately found worthy of leadership. But by the end of that tour, I was also a changed man forever. By the end of that tour, I had gained the most intimate understanding of the word fear. I learned that the most powerful form of fear is fear for the ones you love, not fear for your own self. My platoon mates had become the most important people in my life; they depended on me to keep them alive on a daily basis. Their families depended on me and I knew it. In fact, several of their parents delivered that message to me in person prior to us leaving the US for Afghanistan. Talk about pressure. Some nights, I would sit awake on my bed, nearly frozen with anxiety knowing that in several hours, I would be purposely taking the most important people in my world into a mission that would more than likely result in us being in a fight for our lives.

By the time we had arrived at the end of the tour and were headed home, I was emotionally exhausted. I was also baffled by the fact that I had maintained the integrity of my men during a summer that came with plenty of excuses for men to behave like savages. I was amazed by the fact that we had maintained millions of dollars of weapons and equipment without losing a single piece considering how disorienting war can be at times. I was baffled by the fact that I was still alive after some of the situations I found myself in that summer. But more than anything, I was amazed that I was bringing every one of my boys home. I wasn't impressed with myself—I was simply grateful. I'll never forget the feeling of relief when we landed in Germany the day we left

Afghanistan. I didn't sleep at all that night. Instead, I drank, I danced (and Ty doesn't really dance), I celebrated life with my boys, and at the end of the night, I cried.

I think it's impossible for me to explain to you what those men meant to me; I was more than responsible for their lives. They meant everything to me. They still do, because they are my tribe. Although what we accomplished during that summer in the Tangi Valley was nothing short of legendary according to our peers, those accomplishments meant nothing to me compared to the fact that I brought my boys home. I had seen the effect that losing an operator took on several of my friends who'd been in combat leadership roles before me. I feared ending up like them because I know they will never recover from that loss. I feel for my brothers and sisters that will forever carry the weight of losing members under their command. But I'm grateful that I'll never know that feeling. What I felt at the end of that tour was what I believe to this day is the manifestation of the greatest accomplishment of my life. I proved worthy of leading my men. They accepted me and elevated me as their leader, knowing what I was asking of them on a daily basis during combat. By bringing them home, I had proven that I was worthy of being with them, and that I loved them and would sacrifice all of myself in order to never abandon them. And although over time we will age and these stories will become memories, that's something that will never change. I will never abandon them.

For a couple of years, I attempted to weave this metaphor into my classes, but ultimately concluded that it was more personal than useful or clear to anyone else. But it continued to describe much of my experience with the veterans over these six years of the program.

The earnestness, trust, and openness with which we addressed each other and worked collaboratively on their needs and aspirations satisfied my needs for meaningful work. In a civilian workforce environment, where over half of employees are disengaged and disaffected, being fully engaged interpersonally and within the context of a growth-oriented program was an amazing experience, regardless of when it happens in one's life, and in this case, in my life. Not only did I encourage and celebrate their growth and achievements, but they encouraged mine by their presence, openness, focus, and intensity, and by their acceptance of my role and expression of my professionalism.

I would be forever grateful for this opportunity to engage fully with this special group of students with my background, training, values, and intentionality. Working with those whose humility, courage, integrity, and the most precious gift of serving others in a higher purpose and mission was transformational for me.

Also, there are moments, even in higher education that is so often absorbed in status, prestige, and individual egos, where the mission may be a higher calling, and we have the opportunity to do our best, be selfless and effective, and challenge others to pursue their wire and learn to walk it successfully, and understand that leadership is a call to service within the context of community. And we, like the military veterans we serve, must answer that call.

EPILOGUE

In the third week of April of 2020, we're all self-quarantined at home, and have been since March 13. The campus is closed, and all classes are being delivered online because of the Covid-19 crisis. As I'm reviewing a set of proofs for this book, a note about the activities of one of our alums comes across my screen. I will share it with you.

"A graduate of USC Marshall's Masters of Business for Veterans (MBV) flew to Guam on Wednesday, April 15, to deliver a donation of masks to the beleaguered aircraft carrier Theodore Roosevelt, which has been hit hard by an outbreak of Covid-19.

Lt. Col. Jengi Martinez MBV '15 happened to be on orders that week at March Air Force Base in Riverside (California) when she got a text from James Bogle, program director of the MBV program.

A pilot for United Airlines, Martinez is on active reserve with the 729 Airlift Squadron. Bogle asked her if there was a way to do a donation of 5,000 face masks, donated by a medical supply manufacturer.

'It was pure serendipity all the way,' she said. 'I happened to be there, and when I checked the squadron schedule, I saw that there was, in fact, a flight going out to Guam that week.'

The mission is the result of some fast Trojan family action, said Bogle. 'It was a lot of connections coming together in a short period of time to deliver these much-needed supplies to our sailors,' he said. 'Knowing the people involved, I am not surprised it came together so cleanly.'

Robert Harmon, a surgical technologist and medical device manufacturing entrepreneur, had a cache of 5,000 face masks to donate, sewn by a southern California group called the Healthcare Masks Collaboration OC.

He had heard from the head nurse on the TR that masks were in critically low supply. The question was how to get them to Guam quickly.

'I knew getting those sailors protective gear would have a huge psychological boost,' said Harmon, who himself is a veteran. 'I clearly remember getting care packages from strangers during Desert Storm. It meant everything to know people cared and made the effort back home.'

He reached out to John Semcken, a member of the MBV Board of Counselors who was himself a navy vet (and the advisor for the movie *Top Gun*) who quickly got in touch with Bogle. Did he by any chance know of anyone at March Air Force Base in Riverside?

'The fact that he thought to reach out to me was pure luck,' said Semcken. 'I knew Jengi was an Air Force pilot, but I could not find her contacts. Fortunately, we had MBV in common. All I had to do was contact James (Bogle).'

Bogle knew just who to call. Once Martinez saw there was a flight, she signed on to pilot the C-17 on its mission, along with other supplies and a crew.

'This is just another incredible Trojan Family connection,' said Bogle. 'I'm not at all surprised that it was Jengi Martinez who took this on and made it happen.'

'I love my Trojan Family,' said Martinez. 'I was honored to be of service.'" (*News at USC Marshall,* April 2020)

SELECTED REFERENCES

Baldoni, John. 2010. *Lead Your Boss*. New York, NY: American Management Association.

Barbour, JoAnn Danelo, and Gill Roberson Hickman, eds. 2011. *Leadership for Transformation*. International Leadership Association. Hoboken, NJ: Jossey-Bass/Wiley.

Batka, Caroline and Kimberly Curry Hall. 2016. "What's Good for Business and for Veterans," *Perspective*. Santa Monica, CA: Rand Corporation. https://doi.org/10.7249/PE196

Bennis, Warren. 1989. *On Becoming A Leader*. Boston, MA: Addison-Wesley Publishing Company.

———. 1989. *Why Leaders Can't Lead*. San Francisco: Jossey-Bass Publishers.

———. with Patricia Ward Biederman. 2010. *Still Surprised*. Hoboken, NJ: Jossey-Bass/Wiley.

———. 1993. *An Invented Life*. Boston, MA: Addison-Wesley Publishing Company.

———. with Patricia Ward Biederman. 1997. *Organizing Genius*. Boston, MA: Addison-Wesley Publishing Company.

———. with Joan Goldsmith. 1994. *Learning to Lead: A Workbook On Becoming A Leader*. Boston, MA: Addison-Wesley Publishing Company.

———. and Robert Thomas. 2007. *Leading for a Lifetime*. Boston, MA: Harvard Business Press.

———. 2000. *Managing the Dream*. New York, NY: Perseus Publishing.

Bialik, Kristen. November 10, 2017. "The Changing Face of America's Veteran Population." Fact Tank. https://www.pewresearch.org/fact-tank/2017/11/10/the-changing-face-of-americas-veteran-population/

Blanchard, Ken. 2007. *Leading at a Higher Level.* Pearson Prentice Hall.

Brooks, David. 2019. *The Second Mountain.* New York, NY: Random House.

Cameron, Kim. 2002. *Positive Leadership,* 2nd ed. San Francisco, CA: Berrett-Koehler Publishers, Inc.

Campbell, Joseph. 1990. *The Hero's Journey, Collected Works.* Novato, CA: New World Library.

Chatterjee, Anjit, and Donald Hambrick. September 2007. "It's All About Me: Narcissistic Chief Executive Officers and Their Effects on Company Strategy and Performance." *ASQ* 52, no. 3: 351–386. https://doi.org/10.2189/asqu.52.3.351

Cialdini, Robert B. 1993. *Influence: The Psychology of Persuasion,* Rev. ed. New York, NY: William Morrow.

Cohen, Allan R., and David L. Bradford. 1989. *Influence Without Authority.* Hoboken, NJ: John Wiley & Sons, Inc.

———. 1998. *Power Up.* Hoboken, NJ: John Wiley & Sons, Inc.

———. 2012. *Influencing Up.* Hoboken, NJ: John Wiley & Sons, Inc.

Conger, Jay A., Gretchen M. Spreitzer, and Edward E. Lawler III, Eds. 1999. *The Leader's Change Handbook.* San Francisco, CA: Jossey-Bass Publishers.

Department of Defense Bulletin. 2017. "The Demographics Report"

Dweck, Carol S. 2006. *Mindset.* New York, NY: Ballantine Books.

Etzioni, Amitai. 1961. *A Comparative Analysis of Complex Organization.* Glencoe, Ill. New York, NY: The Free Press.

Gardner, Howard. 2006. *Changing Minds.* Boston, MA: Harvard Business School Press.

Gardner, John W. 1986. *The Tasks of Leadership.* Washington, DC: Leadership Studies Program, Independent Sector.

Gentile, Mary C. 2010. *Giving Voice to Values.* New Haven, CT: Yale University Press.

George, Bill. 2003. *Authentic Leadership.* Hoboken, NJ: Jossey-Bass/Wiley.

Goleman, Daniel. 1998. *Working with Emotional Intelligence.* New York, NY: Bantam Books.

————. 1995. *Emotional Intelligence.* New York, NY: Bantam Books.

————. Richard Boyatzis, and Annie McKee. 2002. *Primal Leadership.* Boston, MA: Harvard Business School Press.

Hackman, J. Richard. 2002. *Leading Teams.* Boston, MA: Harvard Business School Publishing.

Heifetz, Ronald, Alexander Grashow, and Marty Linsky. 2009. *The Practice of Adaptive Leadership.* Boston, MA: Harvard Business Press.

————. 1994. *Leadership Without Easy Answers.* Boston, MA: The Belknap Press of Harvard University Press.

————. and Marty Linsky. 2002. *Leadership on the Line.* Boston, MA: Harvard Busines School Publishing.

Katzenbach, Jon R. and Douglas K. Smith. 2001. *The Discipline of Teams.* Hoboken, NJ: John Wiley & Sons.

Keeling, Mary, Sara M. Ozuna, and Chase Millsap. 2019. "Employment After the Military." In *American Military Life in the 21st Century, Vol 2,* edited by Eugenia Weiss and Carl Castro, 497–509. Santa Barbara, CA: ABC-CLIO, LLC.

Kellerman, Barbara. 2012. *The End of Leadership.* New York, NY: HarperCollins Publishers.

————. 2018. *Professionalizing Leadership.* Oxford, UK: Oxford University Press.

Kouzes, James M. and Barry Z. Posner. 2007. *The Leadership Challenge,* 4th ed. Hoboken, NJ: John Wiley & Sons.

Kranke, Derrick, Heather DeShone, and June Gin. 2019. "Societal Support for Veterans." In *American Military Life in the 21st Century, Vol 2,* edited by Eugenia Weiss and Carl Castro, 656–666. Santa Barbara, CA: ABC-CLIO, LLC.

Krieger, Diane. Spring 2017. "USC and the U.S. Military: 100 Years of Fighting On." *USC News.* https://news.usc.edu/trojan-family/usc-and-the-u-s-military-100-years-of-fighting-on/

Lawler, Edward E. III. 2003. *Treat People Right.* Hoboken, NJ: John Wiley & Sons.

LoPresti, Anthony A. and Donald Johnston. 2019. "The Portrayal of Veterans in the News Media." In *American Military Life in the 21st Century, Vol 2,* edited by Eugenia Weiss and Carl Castro, 627–641. Santa Barbara, CA: ABC-CLIO, LLC.

Maslow, Abraham H. 1962. *Toward A Psychology of Being.* Princeton, NJ: D. Van Nostrand Company. Inc.

———. 1971. *The Farther Reaches of Human Nature.* New York, NY: The Viking Press.

———. 1965. *Eupsychian Management.* Homewood, IL: Richard D. Irwin, Inc. and The Dorsey Press.

McCall, Morgan W. Jr. 1998. *High Flyers.* Boston, MA: Harvard Business School Press.

McCoy, Bowen H. 2007. "Buzz." *Living Into Leadership.* Redwood City, CA: Stanford University Press.

Mechanic, David. December 1963. "Sources of Power in Lower Participants in Complex Organizations." *ASQ* 7, No. 3: 349–364.

Merton, Robert K., with Allice Kitt. 1950. "Contributions to the Theory of Reference Group Behavior." In *Continuities in Social Research: Studies in the Scope and Method of "The American Soldier"* edited by Paul Lazarsfeld. New York, NY: The Free Press.

Ming, Vivenne. April 17, 2019. "How to Robot Proof Your Kids." Personal blog.

Moore, Harold G. (Lt. Gen. Ret.) and Joseph Galloway. 1992. *We Were Soldiers Once . . . And Young."* Random House Publishing Group.

Nanus, Burt. 1992. *Visionary Leadership.* San Francisco, CA: Jossey-Bass Publishers.

News at USC Marshall. 2020. "Direct Flight." April 21, 2020. https://prod. marshall.usc.edu/news/direct-flight

O'Toole, James. 1995. *Leading Change.* San Francisco, CA: Jossey-Bass Publishers.

Parker, Kim, Anthony Cilluffo, and Renee Stepler. April 13, 2017. "6 Facts About the US Military and Its Changing Demographics." Fact Tank: News in the Numbers. https://www.pewresearch.org/fact-tank/2017/04/13/6-facts-about-the-u-s-military-and-its-changing-demographics/

Pfeffer, Jeffrey. 2015. *Leadership BS.* New York: HarperCollins Publishers.

———. 2010. *Power: Why Some People Have It—And Others Don't.* New York, NY: HarperCollins Publishers.

———. 2002. *Managing With Power.* Boston, MA: Harvard Business School Press.

Quick, Michael W. 2018. "The 2018 USC Strategic Plan: Answering the Call, University of Southern California." USC Provost's Blog. https://www.provost.usc.edu/2018-usc-strategic-plan-answering-the-call/ [Plus Strategic Plans for 1994, 2004, and 2011.]

Redmond, S.A., S. Wilcox, A. Campbell, A. Kim, K. Finney, K. Barr, and A.M. Hassen. 2015. "A Brief Introduction to the Military Workplace Culture." *Work* 50, no. 1: 9–20, http://dx.doi.org/10.3233/WOR-141987

Reimer, David, Adam Grant, and Harry Feuerstein. September 11, 2018. "The Four X Factors of Exceptional Leaders." *Leadership* 93: https://www.strategy-business.com/article/The-Four-X-Factors-of-Exceptional-Leaders

Riggio, Ronald E., ed. 2019. *What's Wrong With Leadership?* Milton Park, UK: Taylor & Francis Group.

Robbins, Stephen P. and Phillip L. Hunsaker. 2012. *Training in Interpersonal Skills*, 6th ed. Upper Saddle River, NJ: Prentice-Hall.

Theodore Roosevelt. May 23, 1910. "The Man in the Arena" (speech, Paris).

Small Business Administration. November 2018. "Overview of Veteran-Owned Businesses." https://smallbusiness.com/resources/military-owned-businesses/

Smith-Osborne, Alexa. 2019. "Educational and Vocational Benefits," In *American Military Life in the 21st Century, Vol 2,* edited by Eugenia Weiss and Carl Castro, 522–531. Santa Barbara, CA: ABC-CLIO, LLC.

Sevens, Cleve W. 2012. *The Best in Us.* New York, NY: Beaufort Books.

Stoll, John D. September 20, 2019. "Mastering the Art of Impatience," *The Wall Street Journal* https://www.wsj.com/articles/mastering-the-art-of-impatience-11568977203

Tan, Chade-Meng. 2012. *Search Inside Yourself.* New York, NY: HarperCollins Publishers.

Tilsner, Julie. October 22, 2018. "V is for Victory." News at USC Marshall. https://www.marshall.usc.edu/news/v-victory

US Army. 2004. *Be, Know, Do.* Adapted from the official army manual, and presented by the Leader to Leader Institute. Hoboken, NJ: Jossey-Bass/Wiley Publishers.

Weber, Brandon. November 10, 2017. "How African American WWII Veterans Were Scorned by the GI Bill." *The Progressive.* https://progressive.org/dispatches/how-african-american-wwii-veterans-were-scorned-by-the-g-i-b/

Weiss, Eugenia L. and Carl Castro, eds. 2019. *American Military Life in the 21st Century.* Vol. 1 and Vol. 2. Santa Barbara: ABC-CLIO, LLC.

Zogas, Anna. February 2017. "US Military Veterans' Difficult Transitions Back to Civilian Life and the VA's response." Costs of War. Providence, RI: Watson Institute, Brown University. https://watson.brown.edu/costsofwar/papers/2017/us-military-veterans-difficult-transitions-back-civilian-life-and-va-s-response

ABOUT THE AUTHOR

Rich Schmitt Photography

During the first six years of the program, Robert B. Turrill was both the academic director of the University of Southern California's MBV program and its leadership instructor. He has been involved in program design, development, and direction and leadership instruction for fifty years at the university level, forty-seven at the Marshall School of Business at USC. He was the associate dean responsible for all of the master's-level programs at Marshall for almost twenty years. He was responsible for initiating and implementing multiple professional programs, both degree and non-degree, including the EMBA, and national programs for MBA program leaders. He created smaller service-learning programs and courses within the local Los Angeles community. He is the past director of the Presidential Fellows Program at USC, a leadership development program for university graduate students. His MBA and Ph.D. education was at the Anderson School of Management at UCLA in the 1960s in applied behavioral science for management. A recipient of multiple awards for teaching and program innovation, he has developed and taught courses in leadership, organization design, team design and leadership, interpersonal relationships, human resource management, and power and influence. He is currently professor emeritus of clinical management and organization at Marshall, and continues to serve on the MBV board of counselors. He served in the United States Army from 1957–1963, including two years active duty.

Bob lives in Los Angeles with his wife and has four grown children.

CPSIA information can be obtained
at www.ICGtesting.com
Printed in the USA
LVHW022105090821
694896LV00003B/6/J